WARMONGERS

WARMONGERS

HOW LEADERS AND THEIR UNNECESSARY WARS
HAVE WRECKED THE MODERN WORLD

R. T. HOWARD

AMBERLEY

First published 2017

Amberley Publishing
The Hill, Stroud
Gloucestershire, GL5 4EP

www.amberley-books.com

Copyright © R. T. Howard, 2017

The right of R. T. Howard to be identified as
the Author of this work has been asserted in
accordance with the Copyrights, Designs and
Patents Act 1988.

ISBN 978 1 4456 4852 1 (hardback)
ISBN 978 1 4456 4853 8 (ebook)

British Library Cataloguing in Publication Data.
A catalogue record for this book is available
from the British Library.

Typesetting and Origination by Amberley
Publishing.
Printed in the UK.

CONTENTS

INTRODUCTION

THE 'UNNECESSARY' WAR

A 'warmonger' is usually thought of as someone who enjoys unleashing war, perhaps even relishing the spillage of blood, or who is quicker than most of his or her contemporaries to reach for the trigger. Figures such as the Prussian statesman Otto von Bismarck, the Italian leader Benito Mussolini and Adolf Hitler, for example, all viewed war in these terms, and they are likely to spring to mind when we hear this term. This book, however, takes a slightly different meaning of the word. It looks instead at individuals who were responsible for starting, conducting or extending an *unnecessary* war or show of force.

Defining an 'unnecessary' war is not, however, an easy task. It is even arguable that no war of recent centuries is likely to have been 'unnecessary' because the costs of fighting it, and therefore the political risks attached, are so enormous. What, then, does the term really mean?

First of all, war may well be very necessary indeed to realise some ends. Territorial gain is the most obvious example: Hitler's invasion of the Soviet Union in 1941 or Saddam Hussein's attack on Iran in 1980 are obvious incidents of this type of 'aggressive war'; to seize the lands they wanted, both probably had no option except the use of force. Another aim might be to spread 'freedom and democracy': the American 'neoconservatives' of the early 2000s argued – as it happens, quite unconvincingly – that war was the only means of 'liberating' the people of Iraq and the wider Middle East. If indeed there were no alternatives then these episodes would fall outside the scope of this book.

Instead, in each and every case in this book, the warmonger could have realised his or her ends in different, less bloody ways. They could have realistically avoided using military force in favour of peaceful, or much less violent, alternatives that were conceivable at the time rather than with just the advantages of hindsight. This is true in two quite different scenarios.

The first is the decision to use military force rather than diplomacy and negotiations. Much of this book is focused upon individuals who could probably have avoided war altogether by astute diplomacy that they could, quite realistically, have pursued in the circumstances of the time. Louis XIV, Sir Anthony Eden, Nicolas Sarkozy – the list of this type of 'warmonger' is a long one.

But the text also provides examples of 'warmongers' who have used grossly excessive and disproportionate amounts of force – using a 'sledgehammer to crack a nut' – in those circumstances when war was perhaps unavoidable. Some examples include the wars for the Falklands in 1982, in Crimea in 1854–6 and against Japan in 1945. However, this book avoids more specific questions of military tactics, which is an issue for the specialist, and instead looks at the bigger picture of strategy and policy.

This book also considers two other types of 'unnecessary wars'. One is a war that is undertaken for no obvious reason. Some wars have been initiated, or escalated, without any clear motive and therefore appear to have served some other purpose, such as acting as a form of catharsis, in the mind of the perpetrator. Some examples include Richard Nixon's bombing of North Vietnam in 1972 or Woodrow Wilson's intervention in Mexico in 1914. However, this book does not focus much attention on this type of 'unnecessary war' for the simple reason that, years, decades or centuries on, it is often very hard to judge how events appeared, in the circumstances of the time, to those who made a particular decision. Putting much emphasis on this type of 'unnecessary war' therefore risks unfairly castigating decision makers with all the advantages of hindsight.

Equally, this book considers, but downplays, wars that were 'unnecessary' because they were 'futile'. Some wars can be criticised on the grounds that they never realistically had any chance of success at all: this was probably true of Russia's war against Japan in 1905, for example, or Napoleon III's intervention in Mexico, two enterprises that were undertaken over such vast distances that they presented insurmountable obstacles. Again, Napoleon's attack on Russia in 1812 and Nixon's bombing of North Vietnam fall into this category, as does MacArthur's planned invasion of North Korea and his planned assault on China. However, this type of 'unnecessary war' also faces an obvious difficulty: sometimes such futility is only evident in retrospect, and in the circumstances of the moment it seemed that determination in the face of adversity would win the day. If any call to arms is too easily deemed to be futile, then many important battles that were later won, notably the fight against Hitler's Germany in 1940, would never have been fought at all.

Of course, no single individual can ever take all the blame for any specific decision to go to war, just as no war can ever be blamed on any specific decision. The First World War, for example, represented the culmination of several key decisions made by several leading figures of the day, who in turn were advised and influenced by numerous other individuals, such as Austria's warmongering chief of staff Conrad von Hötzendorff, the belligerent Russian minister to Belgrade Nikolai Hartwig, and a number of highly aggressive French advisers who pushed Russia into a confrontation with Germany and Austro-Hungary while manipulating British opinion to ensure that London entered the conflict on their side.

The choice of people and episodes in this book does not seek to assign responsibility but to reflect the multiplicity of individuals who were responsible for what happened. The Suez War, for example, was instigated by Israel – whose role does not feature in this book – but encouraged by France and made possible by Britain. And figures like Sergei Sazonov and Charlie Wilson were not decision makers but individuals who played an important, and in the first case a central, role in influencing those who did make the ultimate decision. But all were, at the time, 'leaders'.

Warmongers also looks at some of the underlying causes of these disproportionate actions, for the individuals who have waged these unnecessary wars share a number of underlying characteristics, which might be termed 'The Five Sins of Warmongery'.

One such characteristic is hubris. Napoleon and Eugénie, General MacArthur, Ayatollah Khomeini are just some examples of individuals who have suffered from a grossly distorted view of their own selves and abilities, fatally distorting their own judgment about whether, and how, they should wage war. Hubris, for example, easily leads to complacency: Sir William Macnaghten and Czar Nicholas II, for example, were far too complacent about the strength of the enemies they faced as well as about the vulnerabilities of their own forces.

Another characteristic is obsession. Many perpetrators of unnecessary wars have become so obsessed with a particular issue or individual that they are unable to think clearly about it. This was true, for example, of Anthony Eden and Nasser, MacArthur and China, and, it appears, President George W. Bush and Iraq. Since 1945, some leaders have also been curiously obsessed with refighting the Second World War, whether it is emulating the deeds of Winston Churchill (Margaret Thatcher and the Falklands, and Charlie Wilson and Afghanistan) or with the story of appeasement in the late 1930s, a state of mind that one sociologist has referred to as '*reductio ad Hitlerum*'.

Such obsessions are also likely to develop into a more general irrationality, in other words a state of mind in which raw emotions, such as anger, spite, revenge and fear, loom large. Some examples of individuals who fall into this category are John Hancock, Jimmy Carter, Woodrow Wilson and Ronald Reagan. More generally, warmongers are likely to make very questionable assumptions about what they are undertaking: terms like 'inevitability' saturate their writings and rhetoric, as the case of Field Marshal von Moltke illustrates.

None of these four 'deadly sins' (hubris; obsession; raw emotion; the holding of assumptions) would be so important if a decision maker had the right advisers at his or her side to temper them. Many warmongers, however, have lacked good advisers to play this vital role. This may be because the same type of personality who quickly reaches for the trigger is also likely to be the same sort of person who is intolerant of criticism. They therefore choose advisers who tell them what they want to hear, not what they should be told. Louis XIV, President Nixon and Kim Il-sung all fell into this category.

These are just some of the traits of the many unnecessary wars that have been fought over the centuries, not least since 1648, when the Treaty of Westphalia ended long decades of war in Europe and, in the eyes of some historians, heralded a turning point in international relations by enshrining a new respect for sovereign borders. This view may well be unfounded but it does nonetheless make a convenient starting point of this text.[1]

Note: Names of individuals and conflicts appear in italics when they are referred to elsewhere in their own section of the book.

I

THE POST-WESTPHALIAN ERA

Louis XIV's 'Vain Conquests' across the Rhine (1688)
On 24 September 1688, the king of France, Louis XIV 'the Great', ordered his army to cross France's eastern borders and invade neighbouring principalities and kingdoms. He expected a brief war and thought that, within the space of just a few weeks, his soldiers could seize their objectives – a number of key towns and fortresses along the Rhine – and then withdraw.

It proved to be the beginning of the bitter, savage and protracted 'Nine Years War' that ravaged and ruined vast areas of central Europe, lands that today form part of Germany, Luxembourg and Belgium. What made the whole episode even more tragic was that it was a completely unnecessary war.

On such matters, Louis did not always make the right judgements. More than twenty years before, in 1665, he had demanded territorial concessions over vast areas of the Spanish Netherlands that he had no right to claim as his own and which he didn't have the resources to fight for. In making such grandiose demands he inadvertently frightened off his traditional friends among the Dutch and hardening the resistance of his existing enemies. If he had made more modest claims, then he would probably have won valuable concessions without a firing a shot. Instead he provoked his enemies – the Spanish, English and Dutch – into forming a joint alliance and then sparked a war that he went on to lose.[2]

A few years later, in 1672, he started another wholly unnecessary war, launching an attack on the Netherlands that was probably inspired by a group of hawkish advisers at court who overrode the more sensible, cautionary views of several key ministers. After six years of hard fighting, Louis seized new territories but inflicted huge damage on his own country, as well as others, by doing so. Years later, a leading churchman of the day, Bishop François Fénelon, famously penned an anonymous letter to the king in which he vociferously condemned the Dutch War, whose 'only cause was a desire for personal glory and vengeance' and which led to 'unjust acquisitions'. It was the key moment, he continued, when 'your name has become hateful and the entire French nation intolerable to all your neighbours' as well as 'the source of all the other wars' that followed.[3]

More than a decade on, Louis' armies did win a hugely impressive victory against Spain. In August 1684, after a nine-month fight, they had taken control of two disputed places – the city of Strasbourg and the vast fortress of Luxembourg – as well as some other territories, known as the 'Reunions', that lay along the border of present-day France, Germany, Belgium and the Netherlands. This was the high mark of his long rule (1643–1715) and the 'Sun King', as he became known throughout France and beyond, basked in the adulation he received. The king seemed to have ushered in a new era of French *grandeur*, and writers like Jean Racine celebrated his success. Louis was not just a fashionable figure but an individual worthy of true veneration.

But during the conflict of 1683–4, Louis had sometimes revealed a troubling and troubled state of mind. Just as he was drawing the war against Spain to a very successful conclusion, he had ordered his naval commanders to carry out a very heavy-handed attack on the city of Genoa, whose bankers and wealthy families had subsidised his enemies in the conflict: on 17 May, a French fleet had bombarded the city for twelve successive days and nights with more than 13,000 explosive cannonballs, destroying most of its buildings and killing many civilians in the process. This was retribution at its worst. Such an attack was completely unnecessary, partly because he had by this stage won the war in any event, and partly too because there was no need to pummel innocent civilians if he wanted to end Genoese support to his enemies. Success, in other words, seems to have gone to his head and impaired his judgment even more.

Nearly eighteen months later, he lashed out again, this time against imaginary enemies at home. On 22 October 1685, he cracked down on the freedoms that France's 850,000 Protestants had enjoyed for more than a century, and by doing so drove many of them to flee abroad. Louis doubtlessly congratulated himself that his political rule was now sovereign, or 'absolute', within his own borders but France had lost hugely valuable skills, talent and wealth as a result. This, like the assault on Genoa, was a sign of deep anger and aggression – the powerful, raw emotion of a true warmonger – rather than level-headedness.

In fact, signs of the same *excès de zèle* were evident throughout his court and in the French capital. An equestrian statue on Place Louis-le-Grand was 'so huge', gasped one writer, 'that twenty men could sit down to lunch inside the horse – and in fact did so while the statue was being installed'. It was a treasonable offence to turn your back not just on the king but even on his portrait. And there is also the story of the court poet who managed to cram fifty-eight favourable adjectives for the king into one single sonnet. This was, after all, a fitting tribute to the monarch at a time when the leading theologian of the day, Jacques-Bénigne Bossuet, described the French king as 'the living image' of God. The king's narcissistic traits also revealed themselves in other ways, notably by the construction of a vast palace at Versailles, outside Paris, that he planned to use to display all the trappings of opulence: work began in 1669 on the palace, a marble chapel, fountains, statues and orangeries, while the best tapestries, ornaments and canvasses were purchased and commissioned.

Perhaps by this time the Sun King also suffered from a surfeit of adrenalin which had hooked him on war and violence. From the moment of his coronation he had always like to see himself, and to be seen as, a soldier. In his younger days, he had even written that he preferred 'to conquer states rather than to acquire them'. Maybe this was because he had been born and raised during one of the most calamitous conflicts that has ever raged in Europe – the Thirty Years War. Stories of its battles, heroes and heroisms would have been constantly aired during his formative years and surely stirred his imagination. And he was probably old enough, aged just five, to have shared and experienced a great outburst of French national pride when news broke of the Prince of Condé's magnificent victory at Rocroi. But other traumas had still followed the Peace of Westphalia in 1648, which brought a generation of war to an end. In particular, France had then been gripped by civil war, forcing the young Louis to go into exile.

The result was that, by the time of his accession to the throne, the Sun King was not only determined to ensure the security of his homeland against foreign attack and domestic unrest but may also have become addicted to the thrill of war. Perhaps this was why, in his younger days, he was always keen to play his part in the conflicts he began. War, for Louis, was a way of winning *gloire* for himself and his country. On occasion he led his soldiers into battle or slept rough alongside them, even in the most uncomfortable surroundings. He had plenty of opportunity to do so because by 1688 France had as often been at war as it had been at peace.

Unfortunately, Louis lacked clear-headed advisers who were willing to counsel restraint. Contemporaries noted that 'there is a kind of subordination, for the people appear to worship their prince while he in turn worships God', adding that he was surrounded by 'deferential courtiers'. Not many people, in other words, were willing to speak out against one of the world's most revered and powerful leaders.[4]

Intoxicated by victory and addicted to war, Louis managed to overlook some clear warning signs that by crossing the Rhine he would be going a bridge too far. In July 1686, Spain, Sweden and a number of the German-speaking princes along the Rhine formed a loose alliance, the 'League of Augsburg', that gave Louis an obvious signal: if his armies overstepped the mark and posed a clear threat then they would unite against him. But Louis should in any case have known that the odds were stacked against him: he often referred to France's 'natural frontiers' stretching as far as east as the Rhine but overlooked the fact that much of the population of this region was German-speaking and, in some cases, Protestant. Attacking these regions was bound to provoke a very powerful reaction and confront huge opposition.

Louis must also have known that his country was not prepared for a long fight, which his attack might turn into, even if he hoped and expected otherwise. If other countries did pile in, then his small force would be hugely outnumbered. Reinforcing it would take some time and would mean levying a lot more taxes, perhaps stirring up the very unrest within France's own borders that Louis was anxious to avoid.

But Louis was undeterred and his army duly crossed the Rhine at Strasbourg and headed north towards the fortress at Philippsburg, near present-day Karlsruhe. If his men captured the citadel, then his army would have a bridgehead that would guard France against future attacks. At the same time, he hoped to intimidate some of the German-speaking states into becoming French allies while forcing his remaining enemies to formally recognise the gains he had made in 1684 as permanent.

What the Sun King failed to either see or acknowledge was that there were simpler and easier ways of realising these ends than by launching a full-scale invasion across France's eastern borders. If he wanted to protect his country from foreign attack, then he could have constructed a chain of fortresses on his own side of the Rhine that would have allowed his own men to maul an invading army. His chief military adviser, a genius called Sébastien Le Prestre de Vauban, noted how close Paris was to France's eastern frontiers and urged Louis to build adequate defences around the capital. Later, he would always add that the cost of maintaining the various fortresses that Louis captured during the Nine Years War – Freiburg, Breisach and Philippsburg – was out of all proportion to their strategic value. Louis could also have pressed some of the German principalities to declare their neutrality in return for a guarantee that he would respect their existing borders.[5]

Finally, he could have struck up an alliance with the Ottoman Empire, whose rulers shared his own enmity with the Holy Roman Emperor, Louis' chief adversary in central Europe. If the emperor ever attacked France from the east, then the Ottomans were in a position to launch a diversionary attack. Louis would have needed to keep such an alliance secret – doing deals with Europe's great Islamic foe would not help him to win him much admiration within Christendom's borders – but it would have reprieved him from launching any pre-emptive and highly risky wars across the Rhine. During the conflict that began in 1688, Louis ended up relying on the Ottomans' help in any event – they attacked Nissa and Belgrade in 1690 and took a lot of pressure off France by doing so – but an early alliance would have made the entire war unnecessary.

Nor could Louis force his enemies to acknowledge the permanent nature of French rule over Strasbourg and Luxembourg. Such 'guarantees' were really no more than meaningless pieces of paper, and he himself had taken little notice of Spain's supposedly 'permanent' right to rule over large swathes of the Netherlands (present-day Belgium) when he ordered his own invasions in 1667 and 1672. He would have done better to have simply reinforced his defensive grip over those territories so that his 'temporary' rule over them became too difficult to challenge.

Instead, by sending the Catholic French army across the Rhine and into German-speaking Protestant territories, he simply united his otherwise fragmented enemies. They now formed a 'Magdeburg Concert' of states and principalities whose leaders viewed him, with every justification, as an untrustworthy aggressor and who were determined to resist him. Seeing that Louis threatened the whole balance of power in Europe, other countries also piled in, including the Dutch Republic, Spain, Sweden and then England. The Nine Years War, a major European conflict which is also known as the War of the League of Augsburg, had begun.

In the early weeks of the war, Louis' soldiers seized several key fortresses and garrisons, including Philippsburg, Mannheim, Frankenthal and Mainz, followed by a succession of towns, such as Speyer, Heidelberg, Neustadt and Worms. But, as his enemies mobilized and the combatants carried out a succession of sieges and counter-sieges, the conflict quickly became a war of attrition. Over time, Louis became increasingly desperate, quadrupling the size of his armed forces at vast expense to his country, and inflicting ever more brutal and ruthless measures against not just his enemies but innocent people: most notoriously, he ordered his men to implement a 'scorched earth' policy in whole areas of the Rhineland to prevent enemy troops from living off the land. Eventually, as the exhausted warriors sued for peace in 1697, Louis was forced to renounce nearly all of the gains he had made not just since 1688 but since the peace of 1685. Although he kept Strasbourg, he lost Luxembourg and forfeited all of France's Italian territory, which it had held since 1628. But at the same time, he had nearly bankrupted his own country and provoked a strong sense of bitterness and anger towards France that was to prove both powerful and enduring.

But in 1688 Louis was not just interested in enhancing France's national security. Many of his letters or writings suggest that he was just as concerned about his own personal reputation and France's national *grandeur* and standing.

However, Louis could have established his own reputation, and that of France, in much cheaper and easier ways by taking the advice of his financial expert, Jean-Baptiste Colbert. Far-sighted and visionary – in 1670 he had even planted hundreds of oaks in the forests of Tronçais (Allier) in order to provide high-quality masts for the French navy of the nineteenth century – Colbert argued for commercial expansion and the development of a navy that would help France win new colonies abroad, as well as fend off the Royal Navy if the British attacked. This same approach won Britain easy victories and colonies abroad as far afield as India and the Americas, but Louis prioritised not this far-sighted vision but the pursuit of an unnecessary war on the continent.

He could also have bolstered both French national security and his personal *grandeur* by focusing his attention more strongly on events in England, where his ally, the Catholic James II, had become king in 1685. But by showing such aggression on the continent he provoked anti-French, and anti-Catholic, sentiment in both of these Protestant countries, driving them closer together into a formal alliance that hadn't existed in 1688. Distracted by events in the Rhineland, he also lacked the resources to stop William of Orange, James' challenger for the throne, sailing from the Netherlands to make his bid for the English throne. But had he kept his ally in power in London, then Louis would not only have hugely enhanced French security but also would have been championed as the great saviour of Catholicism.

Finally, Louis could have pursued both ends – *grandeur* and national security – simply by bringing peace to his country and allowing it to enjoy economic prosperity. Instead, in the words of Fénelon, France suffered badly. 'Children are starving to death,' he wrote in or around 1694, 'agriculture is all but abandoned, the towns and the countryside are being depopulated, all trades languish and no longer feed the workers. All trade is at an end. You have thus destroyed half of the real strengths within your state in order to make and to defend vain conquests outside it.'[6]

2

THE AGE OF REVOLUTIONS

John Hancock, 'The Military Art' and the American Revolution (1774)

On 5 March 1774, hundreds of people gathered in the centre of Boston, Massachusetts, to hear a speech about the growing political crisis that confronted them.

Thirty-seven-year-old John Hancock, a wealthy merchant who 'looked every inch an aristocrat', was a powerful orator. In the words of one contemporary, he was capable of working his audience to 'the highest pitch of frenzy'. And now he called for the people of Boston to prepare to 'fight for (your) houses, lands, wives, children ... liberty and God' so that 'those noxious vermin will be swept forever from the streets of Boston'. Towns throughout the colony of Massachusetts, he continued, had to organise local militias and 'be ready to take the field whenever danger calls'.[1]

The 'noxious vermin' in question were the British, who were the rulers of Massachusetts and twelve other colonies that comprise the present-day United States. Tension between Boston and London had risen sharply over the preceding few years. In 1770, British soldiers had shot and killed several colonists in a bloodbath that became known as the 'Boston Massacre' – Hancock was speaking on the fourth anniversary of the tragedy – and in December 1773 there had been a major incident in the city harbour that had sparked a furious exchange of acrimonious words. This was the 'Boston Tea Party', when several protestors seized and dumped vast quantities of British tea imports, worth huge sums of money, into the town harbour. As soon as news of the incident reached London, the British government prepared to retaliate with a series of repressive, hard-hitting measures. These 'Coercive' or 'Intolerable' Acts were being drafted and debated in parliament when Hancock spoke. Just days later, they became law.

In the history of the American Revolution against British rule, much attention has rightly been focussed on some of the other big names, notably the hugely charismatic Samuel Adams, who orchestrated and led resistance. But although his importance was played down by some contemporaries – including rivals like John Adams, who wrote a good deal of what we know about him – John Hancock was the first leader in the colonies to adopt a militaristic position from which it was very difficult to back down without loss of face. In other words, from the moment he mobilised these militias, in March 1774, it was probably too late to avert war with the British.

Up until this time, war was not inevitable, even if the British had begun to lose control over Boston and the surrounding area and started to rely more heavily on the use of force. The senior British commander on the ground, General Thomas Gage, made increasingly desperate calls for troop reinforcements but could still not maintain his control over the region. And when, in April 1775, a British force raided a colonial stronghold in the town of Concord, suffering heavy losses in the process, full-scale war effectively broke out. The other twelve colonies openly sided with their compatriots in Massachusetts, and the American War of Independence began.

Of course responsibility for the outbreak of the war cannot be solely assigned just to one side, the colonists or the British, let alone to one specific individual. The obstinacy of British leaders, notably King George III, bears a good portion of the blame. They failed to recognise the depth of local anger and indignation at aspects of British rule, most notably the colonists' insistence that, because they were unrepresented in the British parliament, London had no right to directly tax the colonies. Using force in a bid to quell such powerful feelings, and such legitimate grievances, was only going to aggravate a situation that sometimes seemed to have its own momentum.[2]

However, John Hancock must bear some of the responsibility for creating a war that never needed to be fought. In the history of the British Empire, other colonies went on to win their independence without using force, India being the most obvious single example. So too, in the same way, could the American colonists have won their own in the same peaceful manner or, at the very least, by using much less violence.

Hancock had not risen to power in Boston as a war hawk or even wanting to radically change the way of life in his home town. On the contrary, like most of his fellow colonists, he badly wanted to maintain the political cord with the mother country, even if he too had become increasingly exasperated with its policies. He also had much to lose from the anarchy and disorder that a state of war would inevitably bring. As the head of one of the biggest trading businesses on the continent, he owed his success to the peace, stability and economic freedoms that British rule had brought. Hancock also loved to live well – he had a taste for expensive clothes such as fashionable wigs, velvet breeches, silk jackets and shoes with gold buckles – and had a lot to lose if he was given years of harsh imprisonment.

But it was Hancock who made a key decision that considerably escalated the growing crisis. For along with other warmongers such as Joseph Warren, Hancock ordered his fellow Bostonians to organise and expand local militias that would be capable of fighting the British. He also urged other towns throughout Massachusetts 'to acquaint themselves with the art of war as soon as possible' and 'appear under arms at least once every week'. Six months after he had spoken in Boston, Hancock's call echoed in the Suffolk Resolves that were laid down by local leaders in the county, and by the end of 1774, as John Adams noted, 'our people are everywhere learning the military art'. Samuel Adams later ordered all the colonies to organise their own militias, but he was actually following Hancock's lead.

Hancock's actions may have been a natural response to the growing threat of British military action. But by arming local militias he was also escalating tension and provoking the very response he feared. At the same time, the colonists were now more likely to use force rather than look around for more peaceful alternatives; this is why in September 1774 Bostonians nearly attacked the British when completely unfounded rumours swirled that General Gage's men had killed several colonists. 'A civil war is unavoidable,' sighed one of the moderate figures, John Dickinson. The entire colony now became a tinderbox of tension as fears of an armed British response grew: the British 'have drawn their sword', noted Eliphalet Dyer of Connecticut, 'in order to execute their plan of subduing America'.[3]

But Hancock never needed to escalate the crisis with Great Britain by arming local militias. At the very least, he could have done this in a covert, surreptitious way that would have avoided alarming the British. By publicly announcing such a measure, he helped to push Massachusetts, and soon the other twelve colonies, along a path towards outright conflict. There were other, more peaceful strategies that he could have pushed for instead, all of which would have probably achieved the result that he was aiming for – the colonies' right to tax themselves. These peaceful strategies would have achieved the same result at a much lower cost than eight years of war.

One was a campaign of civil disobedience against British rule. The American settlers had already used this passive approach before, in the Stamp Act crisis of 1765–6, during the Townshend Duties in 1768–70, and then against the Tea Tax in 1773. And in each case they had done so with great success. Until 1774, the British government had relatively few administrators and soldiers in the American colonies, and it was therefore heavily dependent on the goodwill and cooperation of local people to enforce its laws and rules. This dependency, and vulnerability, became increasingly clear as tension started to mount. An example is the 'Continental Congress' in Philadelphia, where representatives of each colony began to meet from September 1774: although British officials had declared it to be illegal, they did not have the resources to stop its members from attending. Other colonists openly defied British orders by holding illegal local committees and brazenly risking arrest.

In October 1774, General Gage wrote a letter to London that revealed the power of civil disobedience to rattle the British. His own 'moderation and forebearance' (*sic*), and that of his men, he reported, were being very sorely tested by the civil disobedience of the local population. His army was desperate for better accommodation as winter approached but he was unable to find local carpenters and builders to carry out the work: any colonists who acted for the British faced retribution from local people. The resistance he faced was somewhat greater than mere disobedience, although it did not quite amount to a campaign of insurgency; local people were burning supplies of straw that were intended for the army, boats were being sunk with bricks, and wood carts overturned. There was a very real risk that supplies would run out, and 'large quantities' were urgently needed as a result.[4]

Hancock and the other ringleaders of revolution could instead have made life difficult enough for the British to moderate their position but not so difficult as to justify sending massive troop reinforcements. This is what did happen when, in February 1774, General Gage informed King George that he could not control Boston without several more regiments behind him: the number of British soldiers now surged from 48,000 in 1775 to 120,000 six years on.

Hancock and his counterparts could also have taken a more conciliatory line over the single most important issue – the right of the British parliament to rule the colonies. This was not something the British government would compromise over. 'Such ministers as would concede it,' prime minister Lord North allegedly said, 'would bring their heads to the Block.'

From the onset Hancock could have recognised the strength of British resolve over this matter and challenged it in a less abrasive and more indirect way. King George saw the issue of parliamentary sovereignty in black-and-white terms, claiming that 'the colonies must either submit or triumph'. But there was a shade of grey lying between these two extremes.

A starting point would have been to accept British sovereignty in principle but to have then demanded the colonies' right to choose how and when local taxes were raised. In early 1775, as he was forced to recognise the seriousness of the American revolt, Lord North conceded this subtle but important difference: on 20 February he introduced his Conciliatory Proposal in the House of Lords, agreeing 'to the suspension of the exercise of our right' to tax the colonies provided the Americans still contributed their share. But Hancock and the other colonial leaders could have sweetened the constitutional pill by quickly offering a medicine that was easier for London to swallow than the slogan of 'No Taxation without Representation'. Thomas Jefferson and Benjamin Franklin, for example, had argued that North's offer failed to address the real issue, which was not just how to raise taxes but how much to raise. However, they could have tackled this by requesting a certain amount of flexibility over this wider issue – perhaps a margin of a few percentage points over or above what London wanted. Once the British had conceded some ground, the colonies could then gradually have pushed them back even further, seizing their chance when London was confronted by moments of political crisis at home, or by the threat or advent of war. The sovereignty of the British parliament over the colonies would then gradually have become increasingly hollow.[5]

Even if war had broken out, the other colonies could have given only covert military assistance to the rebels in Massachusetts, allowing them to wage a low-level, protracted guerrilla war against General Gage's forces. Such a campaign would have imposed a financial drain on the British government that would have been impossible to sustain in the long term.

America went on to win its independence and Hancock played a minor role in the years that followed. But the United States paid a heavy price for its unnecessary war against the British. Thousands of colonists had been killed during eight years of conflict – this represented a very high proportion of the colonies' 2.5 million population – and the conflict had also bequeathed vast debts that continued to strangle its economy long after the war.[6]

Hancock's decision to militarise Massachusetts unnecessarily was probably motivated not by any level-headed assessment but by raw emotion on his part and on the part of the local population: anti-British feelings were running high in the years that followed the Boston Massacre, and by taking up arms Hancock and his fellow Massachusettsians were venting their anger.

Pierre Beaumarchais' 'Secret Mischief' in the American War of Independence (1776)

On 4 July 1776, the leaders of the thirteen American colonies dramatically announced their independence from Great Britain. Henceforth, they announced, the colonies would become sovereign states in their own right and would no longer have any ties of allegiance with London. In Paris, news of the announcement seized the imagination of a maverick and supremely gifted Frenchman called Pierre-Augustin Caron de Beaumarchais.[7]

A true polymath, Beaumarchais had by this time established a reputation in several different walks of life. Having started his career as a humble watch-maker, he had first made his name by pioneering new mechanisms that made clocks and watches accurate to within a second, and smaller than they had ever been. But he was also a brilliant musician and playwright, and in 1775 had written a very well-received comedy, *The Barber of Seville*. Then, as a journalist, he went to court against a notoriously corrupt Parisian magistrate called Goezman and stunned contemporaries by single-handedly destroying his adversary's reputation. He also undertook covert missions on behalf of the French nobility and managed to dissuade a would-be blackmailer from publishing scandalous material about some of the biggest names in the country.

Such obvious talents brought him to the attention of the royal court, firstly of Louis XV and then of the king's son, who came to power in 1774. He gave music lessons to members of the royal family and then made a watch for Queen Marie Antoinette that was small enough to fit into a ring. Recognising his cleverness and charm, the king, or someone at court, had offered Beaumarchais a chance to join the French secret service, and in early 1775 he was tasked with visiting London to gauge the relationship between Britain and her American colonies, and to make some suggestions about how any such ties could be ruptured. Beaumarchais now spent a very happy time in London, ingratiating himself with

British leaders and politicians and making regular visits to the houses of radical and influential figures in British political life, notably John Wilkes.

But he seems to have lived his life largely in his imagination, as if writing a play about contemporary events and enacting his own starring part. Anyone with an overactive imagination is at dire risk of losing touch with reality, and Beaumarchais now started to urge his paymasters in Paris to undertake a course of action that had the makings of a great play but which was also unnecessary and potentially disastrous. Within six months of arriving in Britain, he was imploring Louis XVI and his chief adviser and foreign minister, the Count de Vergennes, to intervene on the side of the American colonies and actively support them in their bid to win independence. Then he returned to the French capital and continued to plead his case in person.

But in Paris, the king was deeply reluctant to go to war. 'I think we should pay all our attentions to preparations ... in order to avoid war', as he had written to the king of Spain the previous year. Above all Louis was deeply conscious of the warnings of his finance minister, Turgot, who argued consistently that 'war ought to be shunned as the greatest of misfortunes'. Louis XVI was also on cordial terms with his British counterpart, George III, and had good reason to sympathise with him: if British subjects in the American colonies could rebel against London, then there was no reason why French subjects, on the mainland or in his colonies, could not revolt against his own rule. Nor was there any compelling reason for France to go to war at this time. Britain did not pose any immediate threat to France, and was too embroiled in its colonial struggles to pick any unnecessary fights.

But Beaumarchais' despatches from London played into the hands of a war lobby in Paris whose most influential member was Vergennes. His chief motive for going to war against Britain was based not on any compelling reason of state but a desire to satisfy a lust for revenge. France had lost most of its overseas empire to Britain in the Seven Years War (1754–63) – another occasion when Paris had severely, and quite unnecessarily, provoked the British into a war that it had virtually no chance of winning. Now it could exact some revenge, even if it had no chance of ever winning back most, or even any, of its possessions when the Royal Navy was so formidably strong. In the French capital, representatives of the American colonies, notably the flamboyant, bearskin-clad Benjamin Franklin, did everything they could to capitalise upon such sentiments and help Beaumarchais and Vergennes to sell the case for war.

Eventually the pleas of Beaumarchais and Vergennes won the day, and by March 1776 most of Louis' key advisers supported intervention, with the glaring exception of Turgot, who remained painfully aware of the financial burden it would impose and who resigned shortly after the decision was taken.

Beaumarchais and Vergennes initially planned to give the American rebels only covert support, enough to sustain the rebels' struggle and gradually wear down the British, who were, in Beaumarchais' estimation, already 'at the point of despair'. Using sham companies that helped them to evade detection, French ships now supplied the Americans with huge quantities of arms and supplies that helped to swing the balance against the British. After General Burgoyne's surrender at Saratoga in 1777, the British no longer looked invincible.[8]

If the French had been able to hide their support to the colonies, then Beaumarchais' tactics may have worked. The British were desperate to avoid a war on two fronts, fighting in both America and in Western Europe. But the French were on a slippery slope. British spies picked up on their 'secret mischief' and the ambassador in Paris, Lord Stormont, angrily confronted Vergennes. The French knew that the British, despite their American commitments, still had the resources to confront them and relations between the two countries quickly began to spiral out of control. France formally recognised the thirteen United States and signed a defence treaty with them in February 1778, infuriating London and prompting the prime minister to order his ambassador, Lord Stormont, 'to quit Paris without taking leave'. Great Britain was now at war with France and the American colonies.[9]

Over the next five years, French and British forces fought bitter battles, mainly on the high seas but also as far afield as India, where

British soldiers managed to capture a number of French outposts. The Franco-American forces had their most victorious moment at Yorktown in October 1781, when a British force, blockaded by French ships, was forced to surrender. Territorially Louis did quite well out of the peace treaty that he signed with Britain in 1783, but the Americans were not reliable allies for France in the long term, and they had already made their own separate peace with London.

France had also paid very heavily for the limited acquisitions it won in 1783. Supporting the colonists' war effort, and keeping both the army and navy on a permanent war footing, had cost vast sums of money that France simply could not afford. Not surprisingly, disillusionment with the war had grown steadily in Paris, and many influential voices, including Marie Antoinette and the king's brother, had long urged Louis to sue for peace. Even Vergennes had warned the king, at the end of the first year of conflict, that if the war continued then it might 'lead to the ruin of your navy and even your finances'. Jacques Necker, Turgot's successor as finance minister, was forced to borrow vast and ever increasing sums of money from foreign lenders.[10]

If Louis' chief aim had been to tie the British down in America, then he could have done this in other, much less bloody and expensive ways. He could have started by doing nothing at all, and simply waiting to see how the war progressed. Giving the American rebels such strong support so soon merely helped to hasten the end of the war: if the rebels had lost their battle at Saratoga, they could still have kept fighting and denied the British a conclusive victory and thereby tied the British down in a protracted war. Louis could also have despatched not arms but advisers, whose presence would have been much harder for the British to detect but whose involvement could have made a real difference to the course of the war.

Instead of investing such vast sums in a war effort, Louis could have done much more to defend his country and challenge the British by allocating more resources to building up France's navy: by 1776 it was still hugely overshadowed and outclassed by the Royal Navy, but he could have made efforts to bridge the gap and develop a naval force that was at least capable of making the

British wary of attacking France. And if Louis had intervened in the conflict to win back a degree of national glory that had been lost in the Seven Years War, then he could have found other, more peaceful ways of doing that. France could have made more effort, for example, to discover areas of the New World that it could claim for itself rather than pushing other countries out of their own territories (see also *Louis XIV*).

There was yet another way of challenging the British and winning political concessions from them. Louis could have exploited British vulnerability in Asia, particularly their very vulnerable sea routes to and from India. The Royal Navy had no base for refuge, supply and refitting between St Helena in the South Atlantic and Karachi in the Gulf, whereas the French held the key islands of Bourbon and Mauritius. In 1785, the French naval minister, the Marquis of Castries, wrote a paper in which he argued that Louis should concentrate his resources on Asia, which had now become the main source of British power, but by this time it was too late. Nine years before, even the mere threat of disruption to its sea lanes would have forced London to give some ground to France.[11]

Instead Beaumarchais' belligerence helped to steer France onto a path towards a revolution that began just six years after the ceasefire. Of course the French Revolution had complex causes but the monarchy's virtual bankruptcy was central to the crisis. 'Hasten to admire Necker, for some day your children will curse him,' a nobleman had cried in 1783, referring to the minister who had been responsible for the nation's finances during the war. Maybe, too, the hearts of some French soldiers and sailors had been set alight by the flames of America's revolution, and they had returned home to spread them. Perhaps this was why, in 1789, as France slid into a state of political chaos, Marie Antoinette reputedly sighed that 'today we pay dearly for our infatuation and enthusiasm for the American war'.[12]

Unlike the king and queen, Pierre Beaumarchais survived the revolution, although he was briefly imprisoned by the new regime before being released and making his way to Holland. He was alive to see the success of his best-known and most successful play, *The Marriage of Figaro*, which was published in 1782. The play, which Louis' ministers banned for some years, is often said to have helped bring down the French monarchy because it had a subversive message about the damaging effect of traditional social structures. But it seems unlikely that the damage it inflicted on the monarchy was even remotely as extensive as that caused by the author's warmongering.

Napoleon's Invasion of Russia (1812)

By 1811, after a string of victories against a succession of enemies, Napoleon Bonaparte was transfigured in the eyes of many of his contemporaries. The poet Heinrich Heine wrote that Napoleon reminded him of Jesus Christ riding into Jerusalem on Palm Sunday, while the philosopher Friedrich Hegel called him 'the world-spirit on horseback'. The great general and self-appointed emperor of France seemed to be following in the footsteps of such figures as Alexander the Great and the Emperor Charlemagne.

In one sense, such hero-worship was wholly understandable. Even Napoleon's many enemies grudgingly conceded the astonishing skills of a battlefield tactician who was capable of destroying much bigger armies, sometimes at lightning speed. At the Battle of Austerlitz in 1805, for example, his soldiers had destroyed much larger Russian and Austrian adversaries. Soon his empire extended well beyond France and incorporated present-day Luxembourg, Holland, Belgium, northern Germany, northern Spain and western Italy.

But anyone who enjoys such stunning success, and such reverence, will struggle to maintain their level-headedness. And in 1812 Napoleon began a war that he never needed to fight and never really wanted to undertake.

His target was Russia. On the morning of 24 June, the soldiers of his vast, 600,000-strong *Grande Armée* boldly marched eastwards through the Grand Duchy of Warsaw and into Russia. They were supremely confident of victory. 'Never has an expedition ... been more certain of success,' proclaimed their leader, with a conviction that his men shared. 'There was enthusiasm, a great deal of it,' recalled one of Napoleon's commanders. 'The army's confidence in the genius of the Emperor was such that nobody even dreamed that the campaign could turn out badly.' But soldiers in war are always superstitious, and when Napoleon was thrown off his horse on the opening day of the campaign, they were suddenly not quite so sure what lay ahead. The incident seemed like a bad omen.[13]

But the emperor soon discovered that Russia did not resemble his earlier enemies. He was now confronted by an elusive foe that constantly retreated, denying him the opportunity to inflict a decisive defeat while drawing his soldiers ever deeper into Russian territory as a ferociously cold winter set in. By the middle of November, with temperatures as low as -23°C outside Moscow, the fighting spirit and morale of the French army had begun to plummet. Soldiers started to openly disobey orders in their desperate bids to find warmth and shelter. Horses and men began to die of frostbite and starvation as food became harder to acquire and, over such vast distances, extremely difficult to move from the west. Napoleon's men defeated their enemy in every battle they fought, but still the Russians kept coming, drafting hundreds of thousands of recruits to replace their massive losses and using hit-and-run raids and other insurgent tactics to devastate the enemy and inflict growing casualties. Napoleon had invaded Russia with a huge army, but six months later pulled just 120,000 men out. The great emperor had finally overreached himself in the east, just as *Adolf Hitler* was to do more than a century later. He had become a victim of his own warmongering.

By 1812, the emperor was probably suffering not just from complacency and hubris but also from a degree of exhaustion. He had been fighting constant battles ever since his military career had first begun, as a young artillery officer at the age of just twenty-four. Perhaps exhaustion explains why, for example, the forty-three-year-old Corsican wore a different expression from before. His eyes had lost their intense piercing quality, he articulated more slowly and he was also more hesitant in making decisions. He still had an explosive temper but was not as quick to fly into a rage as he once was. His secretary also noted that 'his cheeks were of a matt white, giving him a full, pale face'. Perhaps Napoleon Bonaparte was suffering from a medical condition that was eroding his powers and clouding his judgment. Or perhaps he was simply worn out.

Whatever the reason, the emperor made serious errors of judgment in dealing with the Russian Czar. He had already fought and defeated the Russian army before, at Austerlitz, and had subsequently signed an alliance with Czar Alexander I. But it was not long before tensions erupted. In particular, the Russians were infuriated and alarmed when Napoleon created an independent state, the Grand Duchy of Warsaw, within present-day Poland. The Czar felt that the independent Grand Duchy incorporated lands that belonged to him, and he was concerned that it could expand further, taking yet more land that was rightfully his.

Admiration and reverence for Napoleon in Russia quickly mutated into contempt, hatred and fear. In St Petersburg, the Czar wondered if the Polish population inside Russia's borders would soon start to act as Napoleon's fifth column and instigate rebellion against his rule. Orthodox traditionalists speculated that the Roman Catholicism of the Polish population might prove contagious and therefore challenge Russia's established religion. Russians were gripped by a growing sense of paranoia that the 'satanic' Napoleon wanted to subvert their people or invade and seize their lands.

It was at this point that Napoleon could have taken some measures to prevent his relations with Russia disintegrating even further. He was aware of Russia's growing fears, since his ambassador in St Petersburg, Louis de Caulaincourt, had a close rapport with the Czar and in 1810 informed Paris of the change of attitude in the capital. But Napoleon did nothing to alleviate them.

Napoleon never wanted to fight the Czar. He badly needed Russia's support to take on the British, who were his main enemy. Above all, he needed the Czar's support to enforce commercial sanctions ('the Continental System') against Great Britain. He had nothing to gain from attacking Russia but everything, including his reputation, to lose. And his forces were hugely overstretched elsewhere in Europe, notably in Spain, where local guerrillas were harrying his soldiers with great success. 'I have no wish to make war on Russia,' he told a Russian delegate in May 1811. 'It would be a crime on my part, for I would be making war without a purpose, and I have not yet, thanks to God, lost my head. I am not mad.' Yet he did not take the simple steps that would have led him along a path of peace with the Czar.[14]

Napoleon could have stopped one of his kinsmen, Jean-Baptiste Bernadotte, from taking up an offer to become the heir presumptive of the Swedish king, Charles XIII. Bernadotte, who had been chosen by Swedish officials to succeed an aged and childless monarch, was a relation of Napoleon, and although the two men had little to do with each other, his election to the Swedish throne immediately inflamed Russia's fears about its national security. In St Petersburg, it seemed that Russia was threatened by a multi-pronged Napoleonic attack launched from Polish lands in the west and from Sweden in the north. But Napoleon made little or no effort to dissuade Bernadotte from taking up the post, treating the matter as one of peripheral importance or even as an absurdity. But he could easily have approached the Swedes and lobbied on behalf of a neutral candidate. Perhaps he was showing his anger towards the Czar, who had abandoned the Continental System against Great Britain in a bid to win back his commercial stake in one of his most important export markets.

The emperor could also have alleviated Russia's growing fears by declaring the Grand Duchy of Warsaw a neutral zone, while also giving the Czar a guarantee that France would keep its troops out of the duchy except in the event of a national emergency, such as a Russian invasion. A more drastic solution, one that Caulaincourt put forward, was to simply hand the duchy over to the Czar, perhaps in return for guarantees about the rights of its Roman Catholic population. Instead, Napoleon pitched an unconvincing argument against ceding ground over the duchy, claiming that it would only feed the Czar's appetite for more acquisitions in the west – even though Russia had limited resources to wage further wars, particularly at a time of growing unrest at home, and its armies would have become very overstretched and vulnerable.[15]

By January 1811, Russia's hostility was obvious to see. Czar Alexander had now started to gather troops close to the border with the Grand Duchy, although it seems unlikely that he ever really wanted war. He was, noted Caulaincourt, 'very afraid' of the French emperor, and might only have wanted to threaten

Napoleon into making compromises. But still Napoleon failed to address Russia's concerns, or even take them seriously. Despite further warnings from Caulaincourt, Napoleon dismissed the Czar as 'false and weak' and thought that his ambassador had given him too much weight. France and Russia were like 'two blustering braggarts', he later wrote, 'who are only seeking to scare each other instead of fighting'.[16]

As tension continued to mount over the course of 1811 and 1812, Napoleon could also have avoided war not only by making concessions to the Czar but by activating a series of alliances with some of Russia's enemies. But he infuriated the Swedes by invading and seizing one of their territories, Pomerania, on 20 January 1812 in a bid to enforce the Continental System. Other potential allies – Austria, Prussia and the Poles – were also all cold-shouldered. Instead, Napoleon voiced increasingly hubristic rhetoric about wanting 'to throw back for two hundred years that inexorable threat of invasion from the north'. Other comments he made, for example about how 'barbarian peoples are simple-minded and superstitious', were contemptuous.[17]

If Napoleon's ends had been essentially defensive, then he could easily have taken such measures to avoid going to war. He could also have simply moved his army as far as the border between Russia and the Grand Duchy, which would have defended his own territories in the west. There was no reason for him to order a vastly more ambitious attack into Russian territory. As soon as he did so, his *Grande Armée* was vulnerable to fighting a very confused war that had no clear target. Napoleon never succeeded in defining the objectives of his much more ambitious conflict; like *Adolf Hitler* a century and a half later, he discovered too late that the bigger the target, the more difficult it is to know where to stop. As a result, his army had a myriad of targets and he risked committing his troops to fighting battles for which they simply weren't prepared. As the great Prussian strategist Carl von Clausewitz remarked, Napoleon was bound to fail because his ends were unlimited. If, on the other hand, his aims were based more on grandeur and acquisition, then he could have turned to other, more limited targets that would have been much easier to capture than such a vast landmass.

Napoleon paid the price of his warmongering. Not only did he lose around half a million soldiers but, in the eyes of his enemies, he no longer seemed invincible. He also lost the respect and confidence of his own troops. On the eve of the invasion, his empire was at its zenith. Six months later, it had been mauled and pushed into a rapid state of decline.[18]

James Madison's 'Matter of Marching' (1812)

In the summer of 1812, a small number of warmongers in the US Congress finally had their chance to drive forward an ambitious agenda of militaristic aggression. A crisis with Great Britain had erupted which they could use as an excuse to fight a war of territorial aggrandisement. The congressional warmongers won the day and on 18 June America began an unnecessary war that was to have calamitous results, not least upon its relations with Canada.

The man who bears ultimate responsibility for the conflict was the president, James Madison. Three years after entering the White House, Madison had a reputation for being astute and cautious, and did not seem like someone who would lightly commit his country to a conflict that it did not need to fight. In his manner and character, he also seemed to lack the passion and aggression that a natural warmonger might have. He was, noted one contemporary, 'a very small, thin, pale-visaged man of rather a sour, reserved and forbidding countenance'. He seemed to be 'incapable of smiling, but talks a great deal and without any stiffness'.[19]

But surprised though some of his contemporaries would have been, Madison nonetheless dragged his country into a war that it was wholly unprepared for and which was also quite unnecessary. The United States had just a handful of ships, whereas the Royal Navy had hundreds on active service at any one time. On land, its army could boast only around 7,000 soldiers who were commanded by just eight officers, nearly all of them advanced in years but inexperienced in battle.

The war that began on 18 June was originally intended to resolve two issues that had confronted the new president as soon as he had taken office in March 1809. Both concerned America's relations with Great Britain, which still overshadowed its former colonial territory more than three decades after American independence in 1776.

In particular, the British exerted a strong grip over America's trade with the rest of world. Deeply embroiled in its war with Napoleon since 1803, London had tried to impose a trade blockade on France, and this meant stopping merchant ships of every country, including America, from doing business with Napoleon's regime. 'Our commerce has been plundered on every sea,' lamented the president.[20]

Another point of contention was the Royal Navy's habit of seizing American sailors and forcing them to serve in its ranks. This was generally not something British sailors did intentionally. They wanted to find deserters from the Royal Navy – desertion from the harsh sailor's life during the Napoleonic Wars was rife – and force, or 'impress', them back into its ranks. The British also knew that some deserters had joined American merchant ships, which they frequently stopped and searched. But on some occasions they had mistaken American citizens for British deserters and forced them off ship. British vessels, as Madison told Congress, 'engaged in the most lawless proceedings in our very harbours'.[21]

Madison's predecessor, Thomas Jefferson, had resisted any temptation or pressure to take on and fight Great Britain over these two bones of contention, knowing that Britain was simply too strong to engage. Not only did the Royal Navy rule the seas but the British had a sizeable military strength in Canada, which was still a colony ruled from London. So in the event of war or dispute with the United States, the British would doubtlessly move south and attack. But after a serious incident in 1807, in which a British warship had fired on an American frigate that refused to let British sailors on board to search for deserters, Jefferson had retaliated by imposing foreign trade sanctions on Britain. These measures didn't work, however, because they penalised American traders much more than Britain, which simply found other suppliers.

Over the two issues, British sanctions and impressment, Madison correctly predicted war, even if he didn't initially advocate it. In his final days as secretary of state, in March 1809, he had written that as a result of British trade embargoes 'hostilities on the part of the United States will ensue', and on another occasion that 'war (with England) is inevitable, and will be clamoured for in the same quarter which now vents its disappointed love of gain against the embargo'. But in fact it was probably not necessary to use force at all.[22]

There were numerous British export companies that had everything to gain from an end to the embargo on American trade with France, and they were lobbying the government in London to relax its sanctions. Madison could have reached out to these traders, perhaps by promising them preferential rights if their efforts were successful. More importantly, Madison did not need to continue the war once it began: two days after he declared war, the British government moderated its policies and revoked its restriction on American trade with France. As soon as news arrived, Madison could have ordered an immediate ceasefire and proclaimed a victory. But instead of brokering a peace, the president allowed Congress to expand the war.

Several 'war hawks' were elected to Congress in the elections of 1810, and they wasted little time in pressing home their private agenda on the president. Amongst them were the thirty-five-year-old Henry Clay and twenty-nine-year-old John Caldwell Calhoun. Young and idealistic, they were full of hope about what they and their country could achieve. Above all, they had a vision of America expanding northwards and seizing the British colony of Canada.

On 22 February 1810, Clay had spelt out his vision of America's northwards expansion and how this could be achieved. 'I prefer the troubled ocean of war, with all its disasters and desolation, to the calm decaying pool of dishonorable peace,' he noted. 'The conquest of Canada is in your power. I trust I shall not be thought to be bold when I state that I truly believe that the militia of Kentucky are alone competent to place Montreal and Upper Canada at your feet.' If America attacked, he continued, then the people of Canada would rise up to join them. It would be a 'cakewalk'.[23]

For many people south of the border, Canada had long been a tempting prize. American colonial soldiers had made their first incursion there at the beginning of the American Revolutionary War, marching as far north as Quebec City before being checked and pushed back. Thirty-six years later, it still looked like easy prey. Its population of just half a million was heavily outweighed by 7.5 million Americans. And the British were so busy with Napoleon's forces that they had left only a bare minimum of soldiers to guard Canada's towns and cities from any American attack.

As a result, it was not just the 'war hawks' who had been turning an acquisitive eye on Canada's prizes. When the war started, former president Thomas Jefferson wrote that 'the acquisition of Canada this year, as far as the neighbourhood of Quebec, will be a mere matter of marching, and will give us experience for the attack of Halifax the next, and the final expulsion of England from the American continent'. This is a revealing statement, suggesting that the war hawks were curiously complacent about the battles that lay ahead and felt that they could win them with a very insignificant armed force.[24]

In June 1812, after the British had offered to give ground over the impressments issue, Madison was carried forward by the agenda of the war hawks and within weeks had ordered an invasion of Canada. This expansionary war was justified, he told the British quite unconvincingly, not because Canada was 'an object of the war' but because it was 'a means of bringing it to a satisfactory conclusion'. Unless the British quickly sued for peace, he claimed, then it would be 'difficult to relinquish territory which had been conquered'.[25]

But expanding the conflict was a costly mistake. Like their descendants, who planned some of America's later wars, the war hawks had spent much more time and effort inciting war than in planning and preparing for it. In February 1812, Congress had ordered an expansion of America's army to 50,000 men. But this was an aspirational figure and four months later their commanders still only had only a fraction of that number at their disposal. Short of numbers, new recruits were sent to fight with little or no training.

Although Congress had voted for war, it was reluctant to spend any extra money on the equipment and supplies to fight it, knowing that this would incur extra taxes. But this was particularly important, partly because of the vast distances that American soldiers were moving – transporting supplies was and remains an expensive and difficult business – and because they soon needed extra clothes, blankets and food to deal with the harsh Canadian winter.

The war hawks had also managed to delude themselves about the strength of British opposition they would encounter. Although relatively few in number – just a few thousand – the British contingent in Canada, commanded by General Isaac Brock, was formidably well trained and efficient, highly experienced in battle and very familiar with the local terrain. In particular, the British controlled the Great Lakes, allowing them to move troops and supplies much more quickly and easily than their opponents. And they had the support of ordinary Canadians, as well as Native Americans, who saw the invaders as a threat, not as the liberators that the war hawks imagined themselves to be.

Before long, the war had caused serious rifts within America, as more and more people began to question why a conflict with Great Britain that was supposedly about trade rights and impressment had somehow led to the invasion of Canada. 'Quite too small a portion of public opinion was in favour of war to justify it originally,' lamented Daniel Webster in Congress. 'A much smaller portion is in favour of the mode in which it has been conducted … public opinion, strong and united, is not with you in your Canada project.'

But Madison would still not take firm action to end the war, even when his men suffered serious defeats. On 28 August, General Hull suffered a military disaster when he surrendered his entire army of 2,500 men without a shot being fired, but still Madison took no action to cease hostilities, even though he was paying a huge personal price for the conflict. 'I find myself much worn down,' he noted, 'and in need of an antidote to the accumulating bile.'[26]

America paid a price for its bellicosity. Although its forces did eventually score some impressive victories, it suffered the humiliation of suffering a determined British counter-attack during which Brock's soldiers entered Washington and ransacked the White House. And the war badly strained and stained its relations with Canada, which suffered ten major incursions by American soldiers before a peace deal was signed in 1814. The war energised and radicalised anti-American sentiment in Canada, and immortalised figures like the Native American chief Tecumseh, who lost his life defending Upper Canada against the Americans, and Laura Secord, who struggled through almost twenty miles of swampland in 1813 to warn British and Canadian troops of an imminent attack. The war of 1812–4, in other words, did the exact opposite of what the war hawks hoped: it pushed America and Canada further apart.

Instead of launching a war that America was woefully unprepared for, Madison and the war hawks could have turned to other, peaceful options to bring whole regions of Canada under their orbit. They could have done this by building closer economic relations, perhaps creating an 'ever-closer economic union', with Canadian traders, who needed America's large markets. Prior to the war, there was also a free flow of people across the border, which would have helped to create trans-national loyalties. Instead, 1812 stirred up so much anti-American sentiment that the Canadian settlers immediately stopped more migrants moving northwards. Had Madison taken this more peaceful approach, then the two countries may well have merged together over time. 'When the pear is ripe,' as Madison himself had commented about a possible union with Canada, 'it will fall of itself.'[27]

3

THE POST-NAPOLEONIC ERA

Sir William Macnaghten's 'Perfect Tranquillity' in Afghanistan (1839)

In 1838, a senior civil servant called William Macnaghten persuaded the governor of British India, Lord Auckland, to undertake a full-scale invasion of Afghanistan, which began the following year.

Macnaghten, an Ulsterman who was described by a contemporary as 'a dry, sensible man who wears an enormous pair of blue spectacles', was undoubtedly a highly talented individual. 'He is cold and reserved,' wrote a British general who met him in 1841, 'but I believe very clever.' A brilliant linguist and formidably erudite, he had been a very respected judge in Ireland before starting a career in the civil service. But he also suffered from his fair share of faults, notably vanity coupled with a lack of humility, and a searing, ferocious personal ambition. 'He is a man of no experience and quite unskilled with natives,' wrote one of the great explorers of the day, Captain Sir Alexander 'Sekundar' Burnes, 'and very hasty in taking up and throwing off plans.' He was also dismissive and even contemptuous of those who knew better than him, and regarded Burnes, despite his outstanding achievements and reputation, as little more than an overrated teenager.[1]

Just a trace of humility would have prompted Macnaghten to admit that he was the last person who ought to pass judgment on British policy towards Afghanistan. He had never even been close to the Afghan–Indian border and had only read the despatches of one or two people who travelled into the country. He was therefore not familiar with its difficult terrain and harsh climate, or with the sheer complexity of its tribal affiliations. Yet he assured Auckland that his protégé, a tribal chief called Shuja ul-Mulkh whom he wanted to restore to the Afghan throne, would be warmly welcomed in his native country.

Nor did Macnaghten have any military training, since he had gone straight from his English public school into the ranks of the Bengal Civil Service. As a result, he could not easily imagine the sheer difficulty of moving an entire expeditionary force into Afghanistan, let alone of defeating, or even finding, the enemy. But he nonetheless gave assurances that the conquest of Afghanistan would be wholly within Britain's reach. At the same time, however, he was quite willing to cast aside the advice of experts, notably Sekundar Burnes, who were well aware of the difficulties of intervening in Afghanistan and who counselled caution against any encroachment. Perhaps Macnaghten did not want to listen, particularly to a maverick explorer who had such a different style and taste from his own. Besides, the Afghan venture was probably his best chance of winning some personal glory that would help him climb the rungs of power in British India.

By persuading a reluctant Lord Auckland to order an invasion of Afghanistan, Macnaghten had scored a big success for his 'forward' approach to countering the growing power and influence of Russia. After the defeat of Napoleon's France in 1815, Russia had become Great Britain's chief adversary. Not only had the Czar's armies defeated *Napoleon in 1812* but they had subsequently seized a great deal of additional territory in central Asia, steadily taking them closer and closer to Britain's most revered colonial asset, India.

If the Russians were going to march on India, then they would have to contend with Afghanistan first. But in 1838 they seemed to be doing just that, for British spies reported that Russian officers were leading an attack, carried out by the Persian army, on the besieged Afghan city of Herat. At the same time, Afghanistan's leader, Dost Mohammed, refused to sign a treaty of cooperation with Britain. Macnaghten and other hawkish advisers now urged

Lord Auckland not to continue keeping its distance but to invade Afghanistan and restore to power its former leader, Shuja ul-Mulkh, who had previously signed a treaty with the British. Lord Auckland concurred and on 1 October issued his 'Simla Manifesto', which was, in effect, a declaration of war on Afghanistan.

Macnaghten's views capitalised upon, and were shaped by, a wave of anti-Russian sentiment that had begun to sweep through Britain from the late 1820s. It had first surfaced in 1828, when a little-known soldier called Colonel George de Lacy Evans had written a much-read pamphlet called *On the Designs of Russia*. By 1837, when the Persian army began its siege of Herat, Russia had become a fashionable bandwagon for the British press to climb on. The Czar, argued papers like the *Herald* and *Standard*, had 'underhand activities' and 'nefarious' designs on India and was showing 'unparalleled aggression'. It was no use, they continued, just to 'watch' Russia expand. Bolder and more decisive action had to be taken to keep it in check.

Such hysteria hid a more mundane reality. Russian commanders never seriously entertained the idea of moving such a vast distance into British India, particularly through Afghanistan's hostile and mountainous terrain. But they did enjoy, just as Napoleon had, the idea of frightening the British and prompting them to send more troops to India than they needed. 'The more unrealistic the expedition is,' as Napoleon once said, 'the more it can be used to terrorise the Englishmen.'[2]

Most British experts in India recognised the limits of the Russian 'threat'. One adviser argued that any Russian invasion of India 'would amount to little more than the sending of a caravan'. And when, in 1838, the Persians abandoned their siege of Herat and retreated, the arguments for British intervention in Afghanistan seemed even more tenuous than before. In the words of one historian, writing in 1873, the end of the siege 'cut from under the feet of Lord Auckland all grounds of justification, and rendered the expedition across the Indus at once a folly and a crime. But by this time it was too late, and Auckland's decision had been taken.'[3]

In March 1839, Auckland's 'Army of the Indus' moved from the plains of India's Baluchistan province and up through the mountain passes that led into Afghanistan. It was a vast enterprise, comprised of nearly 60,000 soldiers and support staff and accompanied by nearly 30,000 camels. But, judging by their merchandise, some members of the expeditionary force were curiously complacent: instead of bringing extra ammunition, several hundred camels carried bottles of wine and vast packs of high-quality cigars. One officer had even arranged to bring a pack of foxhounds that he intended to use for hunting. As for Lady Macnaghten, Sir William's notoriously demanding wife, she had arranged to bring crystal chandeliers, expensive gowns, several pets and scores of servants: one of her servants was even given the sole responsibility of making sure that her cat did not attack her pet parakeet.

Eventually, after an arduous trek of many months, the British column reached the capital, Kabul, and reinstated Shuja ul-Mulkh after overthrowing and imprisoning Dost Mohammed. But although William Macnaghten had given Lord Auckland an emphatic assurance that Shuja would be given a rapturous welcome by the Afghan people, almost no one turned up at a spectacular military parade that the British arranged for the inauguration.

Over the coming months, the British garrison in Kabul gradually became more and more isolated, and its morale sank lower and lower. In a bid to raise spirits, Macnaghten allowed his soldiers to bring their families from India to live with them in the Afghan capital. Some of the higher-ranking officers and wealthier officials even brought a grand piano and a variety of domestic pets. The local market for prostitutes thrived and their prices soared. But his relaxation of the rules proved to be a serious error because it fostered the impression of a British invasion and occupation as well as of a challenge to local ways of life, something that was bound to immediately infuriate and provoke the locals.

Macnaghten now made other serious errors. Perhaps out of complacency, he ordered most of the British soldiers to return to India. And in Kabul, he agreed to move the entire British force out of the secure confines of the Bala Hissar fort and into hurriedly constructed cantonments that were impossible to defend and where they were much more vulnerable to attack. At the same time he sent a series of extraordinarily delusional messages back to

India, commenting on the 'perfect tranquillity' of Afghanistan even though there were growing reports of local restlessness.

By now anti-British violence had started to break out in Kabul. In January 1846 the British top brass decided to evacuate the remaining members of the original expeditionary force, most of whom were women and children. But in an act of monumental folly, General William Elphinstone agreed that his men would lay down their arms if, in return, the Afghans offered them a safe passage back to India. The result was mass carnage. Just one member of the British contingent survived, a surgeon called William Brydon whose arrival at the British-held fort at Jalalabad in eastern Afghanistan was famously depicted in Elizabeth Thompson's 1879 painting *Remnants of an Army*.

It was an extortionate price to pay for a war that was always completely unnecessary. Not only was the 'Russian threat' to India a chimera but there were, in any event, simpler and more effective ways of exerting influence inside Afghanistan. In 1838 'Sekundar' Burnes had argued that Dost was highly amenable to a deal with Britain. If Dost was given a territorial concession over the Indian city of Peshawar, Burnes continued, then he would become a 'powerful pro-British ally'. But Burnes did not have Macnaghten's close proximity to Lord Auckland and his advice was cast aside. Had his counsel been taken, then even in a worst-case scenario – a Russian invasion and occupation of Afghanistan – the British could have undermined the Czar's armies.

Equally, Macnaghten and Auckland could have exploited the religious wrath that any Russian invasion of Afghanistan would have stirred. They knew that just a few years before the British attack on Afghanistan, the Russians had been confronted by a holy war in Georgia waged by infuriated local Muslims who had heard rumours that the occupiers were disrespecting their religion. Entire Russian garrisons and outposts had been overrun and their soldiers were indiscriminately massacred.

If William Macnaghten had sponsored the Afghan invasion in a bid to enhance his career, then his tactic succeeded, for in August 1841 he was offered an impressive promotion – the governorship of Bombay. His penchant for audacious and big ideas had doubtless impressed his superiors. But the very measure that had pushed him forward also held him back. For as the security situation in Kabul deteriorated in the weeks that followed his good news, Macnaghten had entered into secret negotiations with a representative of Akbar Khan, his chief adversary and the son of the deposed king, Dost Mohammed. Macnaghten acted duplicitously and paid a heavy price for doing so: he was stabbed to death and his corpse was paraded through the streets of the Afghan capital.

Nicholas I's 'Holy War' against the Ottomans (1854)

In November 1852, Abdülmecid I, the Sultan of the Ottoman Empire, issued a new ruling that seemed, to most onlookers, to be virtually inconsequential. Henceforth, proclaimed his new order, Catholic priests in Jerusalem would be allowed to hold a key to one of the world's most holy sites – the Church of the Nativity in Bethlehem. The Ottoman leader, who ruled so much of the Middle East as well as vast swathes of the Balkans and central Europe, held ultimate sovereignty over these places; as a result, although he himself was a Muslim, he had many Christians, and other non-Muslim subjects, within his enormous empire.

In Russia, the issue had long been one of enormous interest and importance. Access to these holy sites was both a symptom and a cause of the traditional rivalry between the Catholic and the Orthodox churches. 'Palestine,' as one Russian theologian wrote, 'is our native land, in which we do not recognise ourselves as foreigners.' Every year, huge numbers of Orthodox pilgrims visited these shrines, and members of different sects often jockeyed to light their candles before others lit their own. Fights often broke out in the process. One Englishman who visited Jerusalem in 1834 was astonished to witness 'a scene of disorder and profanation' in which the pilgrims, 'almost in a state of nudity, danced around with frantic gestures, yelling and screaming as if they were possessed'.[4] Catholics gaining access to this most holy of sites was the cause of great concern among Orthodox Christians.

From his palace in St Petersburg, the Russian Czar, Nicholas I, quickly escalated the issue into a full-scale crisis that led to all-out confrontation with both Britain and France. The Crimean War, which was the only occasion in the century between 1815 and 1914 when British soldiers fought on European soil, was brutal and extremely bloody for all sides but particularly for the Russians, who lost around 150,000 soldiers and suffered a far greater number of casualties. And when the war ended in early 1856, after two and a half years of hard fighting, Russia had no territorial gains to show for it. But had he approached the crisis of November 1852 with shrewd diplomacy instead of blatant warmongery then Nicholas could have gained much for his country.

In his younger days – he had become emperor in 1826, at the age of just twenty-nine – Nicholas had understandably been cautious and conservative, and keen to find and maintain foreign allies. But a quarter-century on, this sense of caution had disappeared and he began to acquire a reputation for impulsive, even reckless gestures. 'He is a man inclined to give away too much to impulse and feeling, which makes him act wrongly often,' noted Queen Victoria in 1844. Some wondered if he had inherited a psychological problem from his father, Alexander I, who had suffered from an undiagnosed mental disorder in his final years. Nicholas' character traits were aggravated by the fact that he was insulated from the outside world – he rarely left the luxury of his palaces, let alone Russia itself – and was therefore exposed to the viewpoints only of self-serving and often sycophantic advisers who competed to win his favour.[5]

If he had been more level-headed in November 1852, then Nicholas could have defused and resolved the disagreement over the Holy Lands. What he could have done, at this early stage, was simply exert quiet diplomatic pressure on Constantinople while striking a bargain with the leader of France, *Napoleon III*, who needed Russian support to balance the increasing weight of the Austro-Hungarian Empire and to meet the growing power of Prussia. Besides, the French leader was not a devout Catholic: he once confessed that he was ignorant of the finer details of the dispute in the Holy Lands and thought that it had been 'blown out of all proportion'.

The Czar also knew that if he took action against Constantinople, then many British people would sympathise with his viewpoint: the Ottomans were, after all, Muslims, and they had an atrocious record of persecuting Orthodox and Latin Christians in their own lands. At this time, there was a lot of reluctance in London to support the Islamist Sultan: even the viscerally anti-Russian ambassador in Constantinople, Stratford Canning, had been shocked by the 'atrocious massacres' of Christians by the Turks in Rumelia in 1850. The British also knew that France had sparked the crisis by asking the Sultan to grant concessions to the Catholic Church in the Holy Land. In London, Russia would therefore be seen as the victim, not the perpetrator, of the crisis.[6]

It was just such a level-headed response that Nicholas' predecessor, Alexander, had shown in 1821, when the Greeks had risen in revolt against the Ottomans. The Czar had resisted calls to intervene and instead held his faith in the Concert of Europe, established in 1815 by the great continental powers, whose leaders had agreed to work peacefully together to solve such crises. And Nicholas must have known that quiet diplomatic pressure would reap rewards. After all, the Sultan had caved into Russian pressure before, notably in 1833 when he signed a deal with the Czar that secretly gave him control over the crucial Strait of Bosphorus, which Russian ships had to sail through from the Black Sea to reach the Mediterranean.

Instead, Nicholas exploited the dispute over the Holy Lands to pursue an agenda that was much more ambitious and at times completely hubristic. By doing so, he pulled his country into a conflict with two other continental powers, Britain and France, which he could have easily avoided.

In the 1840s, he had started to fall prey to his more extreme and fanatical counsellors, who conjured images of creating a Pan-Slav empire that would stretch all the way from Siberia to the Holy Lands. 'Russia from eternity has been ordained to illuminate Asia and to unite the Slavs,' as the leading missionary at his court wrote. 'There will be a union of all Slav races.' But realising this dream would also involve capturing and abolishing the Ottoman Empire.

Its capital, Constantinople, had been the seat of the Orthodox Church before Muslim armies had dramatically seized it in 1453, and it also ruled much of the Middle East.[7]

By meddling in the Ottoman Empire, Nicholas risked provoking the French and the British, who were committed to preserving it. And by supporting Slav nationalists, he was provoking the Austro-Hungarians, who ruled so much territory in the Balkans.

Instead of recognising these risks and working around them, the Czar committed a number of key errors, all avoidable, that then led to war.

The first was appointing a highly aggressive and inflexible envoy to Constantinople. Prince Alexander Menshikov was certainly a highly experienced warrior: he had fought *Napoleon*'s army outside Moscow in 1812 and had later been castrated by a Turkish cannonball. But he was not a natural diplomat. 'The choice of a soldier has in itself a certain significance,' wrote the British ambassador, since 'the negotiator may readily become the commander.' Menshikov was a man of threats and action, not tact and diplomacy, at a court where protocol and finesse really mattered: he infuriated and insulted his hosts, for example, by turning up at court in civilian dress rather than in his full regalia. He even used 'hostile language' when addressing Ottoman officials, as one foreign envoy noted.

Nicholas's second unnecessary error was to instruct Menshikov to deal with much more than the dispute over the Holy Lands. That dispute became an excuse for his far more ambitious plan, which would effectively turn the entire Ottoman Empire into a Russian protectorate. The Czar now wanted a new treaty with Constantinople that would give him an unfettered right to protect the Ottoman Empire's entire Orthodox population. But there was absolutely no reason why he needed to link the two issues – the Holy Lands dispute and the freedoms of the Sultan's Orthodox subjects.

The Czar backed up these outrageous demands with a number of threatening gestures, such as a troop build-up along Russia's Black Sea coast. Foreign envoys also noted 'vast naval preparations' at the port of Sebastopol. But he should have known that his demands would be unacceptable to Britain, France and Austria. For example, if the Ottoman Empire had fallen under Russia's grip, then the British would have feared for the security of their colonial possessions, notably India: some of the Sultan's territories in the Middle East looked, on the map, to be too close to India's western borders.

Perhaps Nicholas convinced himself that he would win the support of both Austria and Britain. He had, after all, made a highly successful trip to London in 1844 and established a particularly good rapport with Queen Victoria. He felt sure that the Austrians would not regard him as a threat: just a few years before, in 1849, he had helped them crush the Hungarian uprising. And without British and Austrian support, the French would not dare to do anything.

In fact, news of Nicholas' next move caused political panic and chaos in London, Vienna and Paris. This was his decision, in June 1853, to invade the Ottoman principalities of Moldavia and Wallachia (which today are incorporated into Romania and Moldova). By doing so he massively escalated the crisis.

Strictly speaking, the Czar had a right to get involved in the two provinces. A treaty, signed in 1774, acknowledged him as the protector of these Christian subjects and gave him special rights to safeguard them. This was a legally valid treaty that Britain, and other countries, freely recognised: the Czar's protection of the Christian population, noted the foreign secretary Lord Russell, was 'prescribed by duty and sanctioned by treaty'. Nicholas' error, his third major mistake in the course of the crisis, was to do this when it was not necessary. As a result, the Ottomans, British and French thought that he was poised to attack and dismember the entire Ottoman Empire. And one of his top generals, Ivan Paskevich, also warned him that the further his troops advanced, the more nervous the Austrians would become about the reverberations within their own borders.[8]

War fever mounted in Constantinople, where vast Muslim crowds rallied and chanted for a *jihad* against Russia. And it became more difficult for Nicholas to retreat without losing face. If he had only wanted to put pressure on Constantinople, then the

Czar could have simply mobilised an army that would have been in a position to move into these two provinces in a matter of days.

The Czar's aim was to start a religious war: he felt sure that the presence of Russian soldiers on Ottoman soil would inspire Slavs, 'our brothers in blood, language, history and faith', to rise up against their oppressors. As they moved through Moldavia and Wallachia, his soldiers forced local people to convert their mosques into Orthodox churches, and distributed bells that would ring out the good news.

But Nicholas had had other, less drastic options if he had wanted to do even this: he could have landed a force of soldiers at Galati, on the Wallachian coast of the Black Sea, and seized control over the mouth of the Danube River. Such a force would not only have guaranteed the security of the Orthodox population in the principalities but perhaps also inspired pro-Russian Slavs to rebel. At the same time, such a force would not have been sizeable enough to provoke any significant protest from London, Paris or even Constantinople.

If he had taken these much more limited and sensible steps, then Nicholas would never have stirred up the wave of anti-Russian feeling that swept through London and Paris. On 5 August, he agreed to end hostilities in the two principalities, accepting 'without modifications' a diplomatic agreement, 'the Vienna Note'. At this point war could and should have been avoided, and it was the role of warmongers in the two Western capitals, notably *Lord Palmerston*, who now aggravated the crisis.

Knowing that London and Paris were on the verge of joining the fray and ready to fight to save the Ottoman Empire, the Sultan appears to have devised a trap. If he sent a fleet to the Caucasus to supply Muslim rebels, then the Russians would attack his ships. The British and French would then come to his rescue. Nicholas should have been aware of the likely outcome when, on 30 November, his Black Sea fleet obliterated the Turkish ships at Sinope, off the Anatolian coast, killing nearly 3,000 Turkish sailors in almost no time.

This was Nicholas' final error. He could have ordered his much bigger and more powerful fleet to simply surround the

Turkish ships and then forced the Sultan to back off. Instead, by obliterating the entire fleet – Admiral Nakhimov's warships used explosive shells to finish the Turks off in just ninety minutes – he played into the hands of his British and French critics who argued that this 'massacre' was not only a sign of Russian 'barbarism' but also that he was trying to destroy the Ottomans before launching a full-scale attack on Constantinople. On 22 December the British cabinet decided to commit a combined fleet to protect Turkish shipping in the Black Sea.

Nicholas had wanted war with the Ottomans but never with the two Western powers. He had gambled recklessly and lost. He had become too immersed in elevated talk about 'Pan-Slavism' and a religious war – that had divine blessing – to free his 'blood brothers' from the chains of Ottoman rule. In the process, he had developed an exaggerated sense of what he could achieve. His writings of the time also reveal a curious obsession with the events of 1812, when his ancestors had struggled so desperately with *Napoleon*'s armies. 'If Europe forces me to go to war,' he wrote in one letter shortly before war broke out, 'I will follow the example of my brother Alexander in 1812.'[9]

But had he taken a less heavy-handed and provocative approach, then he could have achieved much more at almost no cost. He could, for example, have used the crisis to split Britain from France. There was growing suspicion in London about the motives of France's new leader, *Napoleon III*, and some ministers in Lord Aberdeen's cabinet were concerned that French steam power posed a threat to the maritime supremacy of the Royal Navy. In 1852, there was also widespread fear in Britain of a French invasion 'under the banner of the pope' by an enemy that was 'surrounded by parasites, pimps and prostitutes'. Napoleon III, many felt, would want to follow in his uncle's footsteps and restore his country's lost fortunes. Nicholas could then have made his move, a much more limited move than those he tried to make in 1853, in Moldavia and Wallachia while Britain and France were at loggerheads.

Instead, Nicholas' inflexible and belligerent approach played into the hands of British warmongers, notably Lord Palmerston.

Lord Palmerston 'Champions Justice and Right' in Crimea (1854)

On 25 October 1854, a senior French officer watched with a mixture of horror and admiration as British cavalry hurtled towards a well-defended Russian position. As any civilian bystander could easily have foreseen, the attacking force was cut to pieces, losing around half of its number killed or wounded. 'It is magnificent but it is not war,' bemoaned the shocked witness, who was stunned by the futility as well as the bravery. 'It is madness.'

The Charge of the Light Brigade, whose commanders had been given the wrong information and attacked the wrong target, reveals much about the Crimean War. All three of the participants – Russia, Britain and France – lost vast numbers and their great armies fought in atrocious conditions: when the British nurse Florence Nightingale arrived on the peninsula in November 1854, field hospitals suffered from a staggering death rate of 44 per cent. Outside the besieged city of Sebastopol alone, the two Western armies suffered the loss of around 100,000 men, the vast majority of whom were French. The outcome also caused lasting bitterness among the Russians, who felt betrayed and resentful that two Christian countries should side with an Islamic empire and fight against them.

During the Crimean War, incompetence, as well as bravery, was certainly rife. Sixty-six-year-old Lord Raglan, the British commander in the Crimea, was a veteran of Waterloo who absent-mindedly referred to his French allies as the enemy. He had been chosen to lead the operation mainly because he spoke French, although the French commander, Saint-Arnaud, had been chosen by *Napoleon III* because he had fluent English. Unfortunately Saint-Arnaud did not have much experience of battle: he had worked in London as a dancing and fencing instructor, fled England to escape his debts and then worked as a comedian in Belgium under an alias before returning to Paris to help bring Louis Napoleon (later Napoleon III) to power. And by the time he arrived in Crimea he was dying of cancer.

In both London and Paris, not many people were quite sure why a war for Turkey was being fought in a remote part of Russia, or indeed why it was being fought at all. In the words of Tennyson, '... the soldier knew / someone had blundered / theirs not to make reply / theirs not to reason why / theirs but to do and die'. Or, as the communist philosopher Frederick Engels remarked, 'The war and its causes were a colossal comedy of errors in which at every moment the question was asked, "Who is being swindled here?"'[10]

Several parties deserve to shoulder responsibility for the outbreak of the conflict, including the bellicose French and the provocative, inflexible Russians, but the protagonists of war in London also bear a sizeable share of the blame. It was pressure from this lobby that brought Britain into a conflict that it did not need to enter at all and which should have been avoided altogether just by the exchange of diplomatic notes.

In particular, one man with much to answer for was the home secretary, Henry John Temple, better known as Lord Palmerston. Although, ironically enough, he owed his meteoric political rise to two leading pacifists, Richard Cobden and John Bright, who both strongly criticised the Crimean War, Palmerston was one of its guiding forces.

When, in March 1853, the Russians prepared to strike the principalities in Wallachia and Moldavia (see preceding chapter), Palmerston joined other parliamentarians in calling for pre-emptive action: the Royal Navy could seize Constantinople before the Russians did, he and these other interventionists claimed, and then take on and defeat them in the Black Sea. When the Russian army then moved into the two principalities, Palmerston again advocated an armed British response. The occupation, he argued, was 'a hostile act' that would require an immediate reaction 'for the protection of Turkey'. And when, in October, the Turks sent an ultimatum to the Russians, advising them that they would declare war unless the Czar's troops pulled out, Palmerston again proposed sending a British fleet into the Black Sea to protect the Ottoman army as it advanced. But the prime minister, Lord Aberdeen, initially rejected his proposals, pointing out that this would contravene an 1841 treaty obliging Britain to keep its ships out of the Bosphorus Strait, and would therefore infuriate and provoke the Russians.[11]

For Lord Palmerston this was a very moral crusade, the kind of fight for right over wrong that had long been close to his heart. In 1848, as foreign secretary in Lord John Russell's Whig administration, he had argued that 'the real policy of England ... is to be the champion of justice and right' and to give 'the weight of her moral sanction and support wherever she thinks that justice is and wherever she thinks that wrong has been done'. And war, in his eyes, was a very legitimate means to further these righteous causes. 'A moral influence', he once pronounced, could only be effective if it was 'backed up by arms'. He once told Prince Albert that 'there are many things more valuable than peace, and many things much worse than war'. He later admitted that 'the main and real object of the war was to curb the aggressive ambition of Russia. We went to war not so much to keep the sultan and the Muslims in Turkey as to keep the Russians out of it.'[12]

It was, however, very easy for Palmerston to hold such views. Like so many other warmongers, he had never seen or heard a shot fired in anger but had instead lived a life of luxury and privilege. During his time at Harrow School and then Cambridge, he heard much about the horrors of the French Revolution and of the wars that followed. But his daily life had been completely unaffected by such tumultuous events, although he did win a school prize for composing a piece of Latin verse commemorating the Battle of the Nile in 1798. In the later years of the Napoleonic Wars, when so many of his contemporaries fought the French armies in atrocious and terrifying conditions, Palmerston was a young parliamentarian, often referred to as 'Lord Cupid', who soon acquired a reputation as a ladies' man. Perhaps his main discomfort during the long years of conflict against revolutionary France was his sense of regret at not being able to return to the continent after visiting Italy as a schoolboy: 'the Grand Tour' of Europe's great cultural sites had been very fashionable among young men of his class until the French Revolution had subsequently rendered the trip too dangerous to make. By contrast, Lord Aberdeen, a leading voice in the anti-Crimean War lobby, had personally witnessed the horrors of war when he travelled across Europe in 1813, during the Battle of Leipzig, to take part in peace talks.

Nor did Palmerston have many scruples about the allies who stood alongside him in his 'moral' struggles. The Ottomans had a record of committing atrocities against some of their Christian subjects, while the French had killed huge numbers of Arabs during their pacification of Algeria in the 1830s. One of the French commanders in Crimea was Marshal Aimable-Jean-Jacques Pélissier, a man of 'violent temper and rough manner' who was known to have ordered the suffocation of several hundred Arabs by sealing them alive inside a cave.

But Palmerston's moral posturing was above all a popular gesture. He capitalised upon the strident anti-Russian feeling that had started to sweep through Britain after the Napoleonic Wars (see *William Macnaghten*). By defending the Turks, it seemed that Britain was undertaking a highly moralistic mission that it was chosen, 'by Providence', to perform. Britain was fast becoming a mass democracy, and like the US president Abraham Lincoln, Palmerston instinctively grasped the importance of capturing the public imagination and climbing to the top of the moral high ground, or what looked like it.

This was why, as foreign secretary in 1849, he had sent a British war fleet to the Dardanelles to fight for a cause that had become wildly popular in Britain, even if it did not directly impact upon the national interest. The cause was the fate of Polish refugees who had fled their homeland after taking part in an uprising against Austrian rule. When the Russians, who had intervened on Austria's behalf, ordered the refugees to return, the issue immediately became a *cause célèbre* in Britain. By sending an entire fleet to support them, Palmerston brought Britain to the brink of war with Russia, although the situation was defused when the Ottoman Sultan offered to relocate the exiles away from the Russian and Austrian border. But simple diplomatic pressure would probably have been enough to secure this outcome.

The following year, he took a similar line. In a somewhat demagogic 1850 speech, he had said that 'as the Roman, in days of old, held himself free from indignity, when he could say *Civis Romanus sum*, so also a British subject, in whatever land he may be, shall feel confident that the watchful eye and the strong arm of

England will protect him from injustice and wrong'. Doubtlessly it pleased the crowds but Palmerston was becoming a bit too moralistic.

It was in just the same populist spirit that, five years later, Palmerston went on to champion the Ottoman cause. As with the Polish refugees, he portrayed the Turks as underdogs who were being threatened by a brutal and ruthless Russian bully. Newspapers and activists across the land urged the government to get tough with the Czar, but when explosive news of the dramatic events of Sinope leaked out – the entire Turkish fleet had been destroyed in just minutes – popular enthusiasm for war reached fever-pitch. It was a 'violent outrage' and a 'massacre', fumed the press, 'and we shall draw the sword'. Palmerston was not at this stage a member of the cabinet, since he had resigned shortly before over disagreements about parliamentary reform. But he spoke passionately in favour of war before returning to the cabinet on 24 December.

But Palmerston never needed to take the hawkish measures that he did. At each and every stage of the crisis, there were much more moderate options that would have defused tension and avoided war.

The most important of these came after the conference in Vienna in 1853, when the Russians had stood down and agreed to withdraw their forces from the two principalities of Wallachia and Moldovia. It was at this crucial juncture that war could have been avoided in the same way as an earlier crisis in 1839, when the British had brokered a face-saving compromise. But fourteen years on the British Ambassador, Lord Stratford, appears to have encouraged the Sultan to reject the 'Vienna Note' and to declare war on Russia, promising him British support if he did so.

Whether Stratford did this at the instigation of Lord Palmerston remains unclear. But Palmerston could have reached out to the Sultan and Stratford to put as much diplomatic pressure on them as possible to enforce the Vienna agreement, while at the same time presenting the Russian retreat as a victory for his diplomacy, satisfying the wave of anti-Russian feeling that swept through Britain.

The British and French also inflamed the Czar's worst fears by sending warships to the Bosphorus Strait and then into the Black Sea. Not only was this a violation of their treaty obligations but it also impinged on Russia's most important interests: the Black Sea was vital to Russia's trade and its national security, and the Czar was prepared to fight hard to keep his grip on it. Moving warships there in January 1854 was a clear provocation. The British could instead have put a fleet on standby at a close but safe distance from Constantinople and then ordered it to attack and seize the city if it was in danger of falling into Russian hands.

When conflict did break out, Palmerston's final major error was to wage such an ambitious war. Despite all the public euphoria, some politicians wondered why British and French military operations were being undertaken in Crimea when the crisis emanated from Wallachia, Moldova and Constantinople. The British plan was to seize Russia's great naval base at Sebastopol, which commanded the Black Sea, and then hand Crimea back to the Ottomans, who had ruled it until 1783. But opening up such a wide front was supremely risky: it meant moving soldiers and supplies over very long distances and in bad weather.

Challenged on this point, Palmerston had simply shrugged and said, 'You need not be in the least anxious! With our combined fleets and our combined armies we are certain to succeed.' But such an ambitious venture was unlikely to yield lasting results, since the Russians would have been determined to recapture the Crimea and re-establish their control over the Black Sea even if, in a best-case scenario, the British and French had taken it. Such a disproportionate reaction also risked engendering long-term distrust and bitterness among the people of Russia, a natural ally for both Britain and France against Germany and Austria-Hungary.

By taking these steps, Palmerston could have avoided war but still kept the Ottoman Empire intact, keeping out Russian influence. Instead, the terrible human toll of the Crimean War ensured that, as in 1914, the fashionable popular enthusiasm for war soon disintegrated into disillusionment, bitterness, recrimination and anger. Perhaps not surprisingly, no British soldiers set foot on European soil again for nearly sixty years.

The Empress Eugénie's 'Sacred Bayonets' in Mexico (1860)

In February 1863, Prince Klemens von Metternich held a meeting with the Empress Eugénie, the wife of the French leader *Napoleon III*. During their conference, she had picked up a huge atlas and boldly outlined her vision of a new Europe. Poland, Saxony, Bohemia and Silesia, Venetia, central Italy, the Ottoman Empire – all of them could be redrawn, reassigned or even abolished, she asserted. But France, she added emphatically, 'would give nothing away!' Her guest had remained silent, as if stunned by the fanciful vision that she was conjuring, and later described the extraordinary 'flight over Europe' that the empress had taken him on. 'What a flight, and with what a bird!', as he wrote to the astonished Austrian foreign minister, Count Johann von Rechberg. In his reply, the minister commented that he was 'far from treating as a joke the journey which you made through three-quarters of the world in such august company', adding that 'we prefer to keep a grip on reality'.

But then Eugénie had often got carried away. Highly strung and emotional, she was frequently in a state of nervous collapse, particularly in her youth. As a young woman, living in Spain, she had twice attempted suicide after the collapse of relationships, and on the second occasion came perilously close to death before finally taking the antidote to her self-inflicted poison. For all her beauty – her auburn hair, attractively shaped head, blue eyes and pale skin won her lots of admiration wherever she went – she had temperamental faults to go with it.[13]

The same character traits started to manifest themselves after she married the French leader in 1853. They help to explain, for example, why in 1861 she became the high priestess of an entirely unnecessary intervention in a distant land, on the other side of the world, where France had no obvious interest and nothing much to gain.

In April that year, soldiers loyal to a radical politician called Benito Juárez had captured Mexico City and established a new government. The state he took over, however, was bankrupt and owed foreign governments, among them those of Britain, France and Spain, large sums of money. Juárez refused to pay, and his creditors weighed up their options.

The three governments decided to use force, a response that most European countries of this time would have used against a developing country that owed them money. Their joint plan was to send a task force to seize the main Mexican port of Veracruz and take their share of its tariffs and customs duties. When they had raised enough money, which they expected to do after a few months, they would simply sail home.

But at dinner one evening in September, Eugénie and her husband aired a more ambitious idea. The presence of a European force at Veracruz, they argued, could be used to place a European monarch on the Mexican throne. A small force of French and Spanish troops could then be permanently stationed there to guard him.

There is no record of how their guests reacted to this suggestion but it is a fair guess that most were stunned into silence. It was difficult to see how France or any other European country could support their appointee in Mexico City when it was so far away, or even get any precise idea of what local conditions were like. The emperor probably had no idea, for example, of just how war-torn and war-like Mexico had become over the preceding few years, when it had endured a long and constant civil war and become rife with armed bandits and revolutionaries. Nor was there much in Mexico that was worth fighting for: true, it was a big producer of cotton, but France had lots of other suppliers to turn to. Besides, any involvement in Mexico would antagonise the United States, whose leaders regarded Latin America as falling within its own natural sphere of influence. French policy became yet more difficult to understand when the American government offered to reimburse the three European governments for the money they had lost in Mexico.

But Eugénie had succeeded in stirring her husband's interest in the inconsequential affairs of this distant land. Perhaps her own interest went back to her teenage years, when she had mixed with a number of Mexican exiles who had taken refuge in Spain from the growing chaos in their homeland. After marrying Napoleon she had lost touch with her Mexican friends until, as she was driven through the streets of Biarritz one day in 1858, she happened to recognise one of them – a conservative politician called José Hidalgo. She invited him into her carriage and they immediately got chatting.

Eugénie was soon won over by Hidalgo's special pleas. She heard horror stories about the barbarism of the Mexican radicals and the atrocities they were committing, particularly against the Catholic Church. And she was enthralled to learn that many ordinary Mexicans were hanging portraits of her husband on their walls and regarded him as the saviour of Roman Catholicism. Napoleon III had already saved the pope in Rome, argued Hidalgo: in 1850, he had sent troops to restore papal power in Rome, and as a result his popularity amongst the French public had soared. Now he could do the same for his faith in Mexico. He would have immense popular support in Mexico if he did, he continued.

Much of this, however, was really just a clever sales pitch. Hidalgo wanted French support to win power for himself in his homeland and was doing everything he could to enlist Eugénie's support. He gave her no proof of this 'popular sympathy' for French intervention because it probably never existed on any meaningful scale. But the sales pitch worked. In the months that followed Juárez's coup, Eugénie pressed the case for French intervention in Mexico and, at a dinner in Biarritz in September, Napoleon informed Hidalgo that he was willing to carry out regime change there. Delighted, Eugénie suggested that Archduke Maximilian of Austria would be a suitable candidate to become Mexico's new king. Although initially reluctant, Maximilian accepted the offer. Shortly before Christmas 1861, he joined the invasion fleet which set sail with nearly 10,000 European soldiers, most of them Spanish, and headed for Veracruz.

Hidalgo had recognised several traits inside Eugénie's heart and mind that he was able to exploit. She probably shared something of the conviction held by many French people that their country was a civilising influence on the outside world. *La mission civilisatrice*, as it became known, was a heady mixture of Christianity and patriotism that fuelled France's acquisition of an empire, notably in the African continent, in the nineteenth century. Some French diplomats were even convinced that rational discourse could only ever be undertaken in their own native language and that other foreign languages simply led to 'degeneracy'. As a result Eugénie found it hard to understand why any foreign people, in Mexico or anywhere else, would want to oppose France's intervention.

If Eugénie shared such a magnanimous, altruistic vision, then it was also because she was a very giving person. Her character, noted one contemporary who met her when she was an adolescent, was 'good, generous, active and firm'. She also had a certain sensitivity as well as generosity: as a twelve-year-old she had been so shocked by the sight of a pauper's funeral that was unattended by a single relative or mourner that she had followed the hearse to the cemetery so that the deceased person would not die alone and unnoticed. In the same way, she was probably moved by Hidalgo's horror stories of Juárez's cruelty.

Perhaps more importantly, however, she was a devoted, lifelong member of the Catholic Church and was keen to support it. 'I am Catholic to the roots of my being,' she once said. It was no coincidence that at the same time that she was pushing her husband towards a Mexican intervention, she was also devising an imaginative but highly ambitious scheme to rebuild the church of the Holy Sepulchre in Jerusalem, constructing two new places of worship, one Roman Catholic and the other Orthodox, right next to each other. The scheme was eventually abandoned but does reveal much about the scale of her religiously inspired vision.

She may have had other personal motives that help explain her enthusiasm for a Mexican project that was so ambitious but at the same time seemed to promise so few rewards. 'The public judge by superficial appearances and thought I was only interested in smart parties and fashion, dresses and jewellery,' she later recalled. 'If only they could have seen my notebooks.' Perhaps she felt that the Mexican venture, and the wider foreign policies that she seemed to trying to shape while her husband looked away, would make her critics take her more seriously.

There was probably one other reason why she wanted France to get involved in Mexico. Eugénie and Napoleon, as well as the British prime minister, *Lord Palmerston*, were alarmed by the rapid pace of America's territorial expansion and wanted to keep its acquisitive hands off central America. Ever since the *American Revolution of 1776*, many progressively minded Frenchmen advocated an assertive foreign policy that would allow France to carve out its own empire, giving them the chance to rival the British and at the same time heal internal divisions. Mexico, in particular, seemed the key to central America, a possible canal route to the Pacific and potentially a vast new sphere of political and economic influence.

Whatever lay behind the Mexican intervention, it was clear that both the emperor and the empress suffered from hubris and harboured a ludicrously idealistic vision of what French intervention might achieve. Eugénie later said that she had been inspired by a wish to civilise an undeveloped country and claimed that 'Providence has called upon us to spread across this earth the benefits of civilisation'. Her husband spoke in similarly utopian terms. Years earlier, in his book *Les Idées Napoleoniennes*, he had committed himself to the restoration of France's natural frontiers and to liberating 'oppressed people'. Latterly, he had spoken about 'rescuing a whole continent from anarchy and misery', 'setting an example of good government' and promoting 'a wise liberty and sincere love of progress'. Curiously, he added that all this needed to be done 'in the face of dangerous Utopias'. The emperor wanted France to spread 'the values of 1789', preferably by setting an example for the rest of the world to follow but if necessary by the force of what some people called 'sacred bayonets'.[14]

But hubris led to wishful thinking, and the architects of war disregarded the warnings of Westerners on the ground (including, notably, the British ambassador) that a foreign presence on Mexican soil, particularly an imported king, would not be welcome. 'We were misled,' as Eugénie later said. 'We were told that the Mexican people would welcome the proclamation of a monarchy ... several times we had cause to think that the expedition would be a success.' But on arrival, the European troops quickly encountered hostility from the local population as well as a ferocious fighting spirit from Juárez's men. And as the 3,000-strong French force made its way towards the capital, it came under a sudden and unexpected attack, losing 500 men killed and wounded in just one battle on 5 May, as well as suffering an outbreak of yellow fever. When he heard of the disaster, a panic-stricken emperor censored the news but could not stop rumours from spreading fast, nor prevent questions being asked about why France was fighting a war for no obvious reason.[15]

The French sent reinforcements that eventually took the capital and helped to put Maximilian on the throne. But Napoleon and Eugénie privately admitted that their intervention in Mexico had been a serious mistake, while French parliamentarians openly attacked their record there, deploring 'the bloodshed in Mexico for a foreign prince'. Heavy fighting continued and the French army tried and failed to stamp out Juárez's resistance, despite taking increasingly brutal measures. By this time the French also faced heavier pressure from the Americans, whose attention was no longer diverted by their civil war and who stepped up pressure on Paris to pull its forces out altogether. In 1866, recognising that he had no alternative, Napoleon brought his troops home, and the following June, just three months after the French pull-out, Maxmilian's regime crumbled to Juárez's forces. Maximilian stayed behind in Mexico and met his fate while his wife left for France and lost her sanity.

It was a huge, humiliating blow to Napoleon, Eugénie and France. The emperor and empress should have taken up the American offer to repay Mexico's debts and then found less risky ways of supporting the Catholic Church in Mexico. A much more realistic solution would have been to strike loose alliances with local factions, perhaps buying their support with generous trade terms and subsidies. And if Napoleon had wanted to carve out a 'French India' to rival the British Empire, then he would have done better to reinforce his existing colonial possessions or find easier acquisitions rather than so drastically establishing an imperial presence in a region, already wracked by civil war, where he had none.

Napoleon III Tries to 'Finish the Job' against Prussia (1870)

On 19 July 1870, amid exultant cries of *A Berlin! Vive la Guerre!*, France declared war on Prussia. In Paris, the prospect of battle filled its leaders and generals, supremely confident of victory, with relish. The prime minister proclaimed that he had accepted the declaration 'with a light heart', while senior officers rushed to take command of their forces. One observer was taken aback by the strength of popular feeling and watched vast crowds, 'men pale with emotion, children hopping around in enthusiasm and women making drunken gestures', come into the streets to demonstrate their support.[16]

The French leader, the self-styled and self-declared 'emperor' Napoleon III, had always viewed war as a useful means to a political end. He was a driving force behind the *Crimean War*, which he regarded as a way of consolidating his tenuous position as France's new leader. Then he had led an ambitious operation of regime change in *Mexico*, a country that he knew almost nothing about and which lay thousands of miles from home. 'Napoleon,' the Prussian statesman Otto von Bismarck had commented, 'was vaguely aware that he needed a war', one that would rally the nation behind him and add to his personal prestige as the true heir of his illustrious uncle, *Napoleon Bonaparte*.[17]

Napoleon had been trying to follow in his uncle's footsteps ever since his *coup d'état* of 2 December 1851. On that day, the forty-seventh anniversary of Napoleon Bonaparte's own coronation as emperor, he had overthrown France's constitution and effectively made himself dictator of his 'Second Empire'. But he had always been an unconvincing successor. Queen Victoria, who met him for the first time in 1855, described him as 'extremely short but with a head and bust, which ought to belong to a much taller man', while others thought that, with his impressive moustache, goatee beard and large torso, he bore a closer resemblance to a successful and well-fed financier than to Europe's greatest warlord.[18]

Unfortunately for himself and for his fellow nationals, Napoleon shared his wife *Eugénie*'s rather tenuous grip on reality. In his younger days, he had written tracts about 'abolishing poverty' by 'introducing the masses to all the benefits of civilisation', setting up 'model colonies' in France and then perhaps 'one day invading the world'. Later, he had committed his country to war but then found his army to be hopelessly inadequate. In the Crimea in 1854 and at the Battle of Solferino against Austria five years later, his soldiers had often arrived in the wrong places, days or even weeks late and, above all, totally devoid of sufficient resources. In 1859, as they moved through Italy, some troops had been forced to beg local villagers to give them food and shoes, and others had used their shirts as bandages. One officer who took part in the campaign described how his counterparts 'loudly proclaimed their contempt for the military art'. Napoleon, who had led the campaign from the front, could hardly deny the fiasco he had brought about. 'We have sent an army of 120,000 men into Italy before having stocked up any supplies there,' he bemoaned. 'This is the opposite of what we should have done.'[19]

But Napoleon managed to look away from the glaring deficiencies that the Austrian campaign had exposed. 'Nothing is too difficult for the soldiers of Africa, the Crimea, China, Italy and Mexico,' he shouted out to French troops on the first day of the conflict. But more than a decade later, when he declared war on Prussia in 1870, the lamentable state of France's armed forces once again became immediately and unmistakably clear. Soldiers lacked arms, supplies and training. Without up-to-date maps, some commanders either went to the wrong place or didn't even know where they were heading. A force of 400,000 was supposed to have assembled at the onset but less than half that number turned up. There were chaotic scenes at railway stations that experienced an influx of departing troops. Meanwhile, in Berlin, the Prussian military chief, Helmuth von Moltke, wondered why the French had declared war two whole weeks before they were ready to take the offensive.[20]

The emperor was still showing all the same signs of staggering self-delusion, not only about France's army but about himself. He was determined to set an example and lead from the front but was quickly struck down by severe stomach pains – he suffered from a gallstone – and had to be taken to the front by train. And he convinced himself that other European countries would quickly come to his assistance once the war began in earnest. But despite the Catholic faith they shared with France, the states of southern Germany looked away. Nor did the British, Austrians, Russians and Italians want to get involved with a leader they did not trust and in a war that did not directly concern them.

Napoleon's capacity for self-delusion probably had something to do with his family origins. Growing up immersed in stories about Napoleon Bonaparte, he began to convince himself that only he, as a descendant, had a right to rule France. In his eyes it followed that, as the great man's nephew, huge numbers of ordinary French people would support him if he tried to seize power. But his first coup attempt, in Strasbourg in 1836, was thwarted when a loyalist army unit surrounded his garrison and forced him to flee back to Switzerland. After long years of dreaming, the fiasco brought him crashing back down to earth.

So many years later, in 1870, Napoleon III's army was confronted by a supremely efficient, well-trained and experienced army, and he did not have any foreign allies to help him out. France did not last long, for just six weeks into the campaign disaster struck. At Sedan, the encircled French army suffered punishing losses – 100,000 men and 400 guns, nearly ten times those of its enemy – before Napoleon surrendered the town and fled into exile. Then the Prussians marched towards Paris, laying siege in a bid to starve its populace into submission and the provisional government into surrender. A harsh winter set in, forcing the starved citizens to catch and eat rats to stay alive, but on 26 February the provisional government finally surrendered. It agreed to pay Berlin an indemnity of 5 billion francs and to surrender the province of Alsace, and a section of Lorraine, to the Prussians.

News of the defeat traumatised the French, who could now no longer deny that France was in a state of decline and overshadowed by the formation of its eastern neighbour Germany. Émile Zola described the deep-seated sense of malaise that overwhelmed the French nation in his celebrated novel *The Debacle*. 'Who can describe the consternation written on every face, the sound of aimless steps pacing the streets at random, the anxious conversations?' asked another great writer, Edmond de Goncourt.

Darkly, he also noted that 'there is the threatening roar of the crowd in which stupefaction had begun to give way to fury'.[21]

The damage to French national pride was considerable and enduring, and the country turned inwards to find an explanation for its defeat and decline: it was due, wrote the great statesman Léon Gambetta, to 'twenty years of corrupting power which quashed all the sources of greatness'. Others blamed a loss of religious faith, or pointed an accusatory finger at a 'degenerate' aristocracy. Whatever the cause, some cities of this shocked and humiliated nation degenerated into a state of political anarchy that bordered on civil war.

But for the former emperor and his nation, the outcome of the war was all the more tragic for the simple reason that it was completely unnecessary. Conflict had broken out partly because Bismarck had provoked it but also because Napoleon had pushed for it.

The crisis between France and Prussia in 1870 was sparked by the burning question of who ruled Spain. In September 1868, Spanish soldiers had toppled Queen Isabella II and several new candidates were considered for the throne. Among them was Prince Leopold, who was the cousin of the Prussian king. In other words, if Leopold was elected for the Spanish throne, then France would have a Prussian ally on its southern border. Such a scenario, argued a statesman and diplomat, the Duke of Gramont, would undermine Europe's balance of power and desecrate his country's honour.

But on 19 June, Eugénie and Napoleon's worst fears were realised when Leopold accepted the Spanish offer. Behind the scenes they furiously lobbied the Spanish, Belgian and British governments, hoping to win their support to find another candidate. Their diplomatic approach worked brilliantly, and on 12 July Leopold officially withdrew his candidacy. It was, proclaimed the great French statesman François Guizot, 'the finest diplomatic victory I have ever seen'. In Berlin, for a brief while, Bismarck even briefly considered resigning.

It was at this point that Napoleon made his big mistake. Instead of proclaiming this a triumph, he demanded more. He insisted that the Prussian king should permanently renounce any claim to the Spanish throne and give a written declaration that he had never meant to damage French interests.

This was a spiteful but hollow gesture, and he made things worse by publicly announcing that he was demanding these 'guarantees' of French national security. News of his demands caused pandemonium in the legislative chamber in Paris, as parliamentarians openly called for war to the sound of wild applause from members while in the public galleries ladies rose to their feet and waved their handkerchiefs. The next day the Parisian press was also in its most aggressively jingoistic form: *finissons-en*! ('Let us finish the job!') cried the celebrated journalist and politician Émile de Girardin in *La Liberté*, arguing that a clash with Prussia was inevitable sooner or later and that it was now imperative to 'get it over with'. This made it much harder for Paris to stand down without suffering a further humiliation. Years later the Empress Eugénie admitted that she herself had been carried away by the wave of jingoism that swept through the capital and suddenly shared the popular enthusiasm for a war she had not initially wanted.[22]

The crux of the issue was that the emperor and his ministers wanted to take vengeance and humiliate Prussia in retaliation for the humiliation that they thought Prussia had wanted to inflict on France: if Leopold had won the Spanish throne then Prussia would have inflicted a serious blow on French prestige. Napoleon also probably resented Prussia's dramatic victory over the Austrians at Sadowa four years before: from that moment on, France had been confronted by a powerful neighbour, a newcomer to the rank of nations that posed a clear threat to its own influence and prestige. To redress the balance, the emperor not only demanded a Prussian retreat but also insisted that William should write him a personal letter of 'explanation' about Leopold's candidature.

The emperor knew that he was risking war and may have wanted to actually provoke it. 'The country will be disappointed' that there would be no war, he wrote to his prime minister on 12 July, 'but what we can do?' The demand for Prussian 'guarantees' about France's security may perhaps have been his answer. At the very least, he made no effort to stop his cabinet voting for war on 14 July when, as emperor, he was in a position to do so. This was also true of Eugénie: at the cabinet meeting she had spoken passionately in favour of war and later insulted the French prime minister, who had voted against it.

But Napoleon would have known that even if Berlin had given him such 'guarantees', they would have been worth next to nothing: in the fast-moving world of diplomacy, Prussia's national interests, like those of any other state, were in constant flux. Even if he had really attached any importance to such 'guarantees', then a quiet, informal diplomatic initiative should have sufficed. And instead of declaring war against Prussia when Berlin failed to give the written guarantees he demanded, Napoleon could have struck up a closer relationship with prospective allies, notably Russia and Britain, whose support might have made Bismarck more cautious about attacking France. Instead, he sacrificed himself and his country in pursuit of meaningless promises.

If, on the other hand, the emperor's aim had been to boost his prestige, then he could have found other, less risky means of doing so and avoided fighting a war altogether. 'The Napoleonic idea is not an idea of war, but a social, industrial, commercial and humanitarian idea,' he had once said. The resources he invested in war, with such calamitous results, could instead have been put into delivering prosperity or building more of the impressive buildings, roads and railways that, during his two decades in office, had already helped France to take a big step forward. At the same time, he could have built up a smaller, more professional standing army that would have been in a position to fend off any aggressive Prussian attack.[23]

Another, much safer, option would have been to look beyond Europe's frontiers and build an empire. This is what France did after the defeat of 1871 when it went on to acquire Tunisia (1881), the northern areas of Indochina (1879–85) and Madagascar (1896). Overall, in the last two decades of the nineteenth century, the French Empire expanded tenfold in its surface area and population. This would have been a simpler and – potentially – less bloody way of enhancing France's prestige than picking an unnecessary fight with such a ruthless and supremely organised foe as Prussia.

If Napoleon III had avoided conflict with Germany and instead 'restored France to its proper rank' in Europe, then he might have governed France for the rest of the nineteenth century. Instead he was defeated, as one of his foreign ministers put it, by his 'immense desires and limited abilities'.

President William McKinley's 'Splendid Little War' against Spain (1898)

On the evening of 15 February 1898, a massive, deafening blast rocked the harbour outside the Cuban city of Havana. Within seconds, an American warship, the *USS Maine*, began to sink with a heavy loss of life. Two hundred and sixty sailors died in the incident and only eighty-nine survived.

The disaster sent shockwaves throughout America. In the media frenzy that ensued, incensed journalists quoted anonymous 'military experts' and 'officers' who allegedly had 'proof' that the Spanish, who were the colonial rulers of Cuba, were to blame. 'Destruction of the War Ship *USS Maine* was the work of an enemy,' declared the *New York Journal*. 'Naval Officers Think the *Maine* was destroyed by a Spanish Mine,' alleged another. Spain wanted to give the Americans an unmistakable signal to keep out of its colonies, some people claimed.[24]

The truth, however, was that no one, other than the perpetrators, had any real idea who was behind it. There was no proof, and none has subsequently ever been found, that the Spanish were to blame for this tragedy. But the 'yellow journalism', as such duplicitous, inflammatory reporting subsequently became known, had served its purpose. War fever gripped the United States as American nationalism and humanitarianism merged with anti-Catholic feeling and commercial interests. Huge numbers of Americans clamoured for retaliatory action against the Spanish.

The fifty-five-year-old president, William McKinley, was no natural warmonger. True, he had spent four long years fighting in the American Civil War and had taken part in some of its grimmest battles. But since becoming president in March 1897 he had never shown any inclination to get involved in Cuba, where the Spanish were embroiled in a vicious and protracted fight against local insurgents. Yet although America had always taken a neutral line in this war, he now did little to stop his country moving rapidly down the path of war.[25]

Perhaps the incident in Havana harbour jolted his powerful religious conscience. Born and raised in a strongly Methodist family in Ohio, the president had always been deeply devout. For some years he had wanted to be a Methodist minister, and as a young soldier his peers noted the exemplary behaviour of a man who did not swear or drink and who always lived frugally and abstinently. And during the conflict that now ensued between America and Spain, he claimed to have been guided by prayer. Maybe the fate of the *Maine* forced him to focus attention on an island that he thought needed American intervention: it was his religious duty to bring peace upon a troubled island and to 'civilise' a land that was less developed than his own. Such intervention, as he later put it, was America's 'Manifest Destiny'. America's policy of aggressively protecting its shores from the presence or intervention of foreign countries, the doctrine articulated by President James Monroe in 1823, had now started to merge with a blatantly imperial ambition to project its values elsewhere.

More cynically, the president wanted to show initiative and resolve at a time when the press had been driving forward a growing bandwagon to 'do something'. Unless he acted, he feared public criticism and electoral defeat. When the president initially counselled caution and neutrality, the undersecretary of the navy, Theodore Roosevelt, voiced loud and stinging criticisms of his approach, comparing his backbone to 'a chocolate éclair'. McKinley relented, advocating an end to Spanish rule and then asking Congress to declare war on Spain in all but name: the senators, he announced, should 'take measures to secure a full and final termination of hostilities' between Spain and the insurgents. Congress granted a huge sum of money to do this, openly provoking Spain to make a formal declaration of war.[26]

The result was a 'splendid little war', as the secretary of state John Hay called it, although, more darkly, Roosevelt described the clash as 'a bully fight'. It was over within just weeks, and on 7 August, barely two months after hostilities had begun, the Spanish sued for peace: despite a huge military presence on the island, they had completely underestimated the strength of American sea power. Four months later, after weeks of discussion, the two belligerents signed a peace deal in Paris. The Spanish effectively surrendered Cuba, which would go on to win independence after a short period of American occupation. Washington also acquired several former Spanish colonies, including the Philippines, Puerto Rico and Guam, for which they paid the Spanish $20 million in compensation.

However, McKinley's war was ultimately an unnecessary war. If he had wanted the Spanish to leave Cuba and its population to be 'liberated' from its colonial masters, then there was no need to use military force at all. Since 1895 the Spanish had been embroiled in a very bloody and bitter struggle against Cuban nationalists who were fighting for independence. But their enemy was made up of determined and skilled fighters who made very effective use of guerrilla tactics. Although the leaders in Madrid had sent an army of 200,000 men to Cuba to suppress the uprising, and were determined to defend their grip on the island 'to the last peseta and last drop of blood', their efforts had failed. In the Spanish parliament, the government was taunted by its opponents, who complained that 'after having 200,000 men and having spilt so much blood, we are masters in the island only of the territory upon which our soldiers stand'. By 1897, the financial costs and casualties were continuing to mount – perhaps 40,000 Spanish soldiers had died by this point – and proposals for Cuban home rule were being increasingly aired and soon became official policy. On the eve of the incident in Havana harbour in February 1898, the Spanish were also being hit hard by disease as well as by insurgents, and some commentators were openly predicting that 'this war cannot last more than a year'.[27]

Nationalist feeling had also been growing in other Spanish territories, and by 1890 much of Latin and south America had won its independence. And in the Philippines, radical insurgents had been steadily building up their own militia groups and were poised to unleash a major insurrection on the islands by the time the Spanish–American War broke out in April 1898.

McKinley would have done better not to fight and defeat the Spaniards in Cuba but to stand back and watch them gradually withdraw. As events increasingly turned against the Spanish army, he could have brokered a face-saving arrangement that would have allowed Madrid to beat a retreat with some semblance of honour, and then used American troops in a peacekeeping role until the Cubans were in a position to exercise full autonomy. This would have allowed him to pacify the strong popular clamour for action against Spain: although there was also a powerful anti-imperialist lobby within the United States, the 1898 intervention was cheered on by a great many Americans, and even progressive voices like the theologian Walter Rauschenbusch and the feminist Charlotte Perkins Gilman had good things to say about it. However, McKinley could still have satisfied these enthusiasts for war by making political demands backed up by veiled threats of action: he could have demanded that Spain give an autonomous Cuba certain guarantees of political freedom and then presented the outcome as a political victory for America. At the same time, this much more restricted approach would have satisfied the powerful, and relatively united anti-imperialist lobby that saw strategic dangers in the seizure and occupation of Cuba.

McKinley could also have allowed Spain to take responsibility for the foreign security of its colonies, which would have been granted increasing powers of autonomy. Spanish soldiers and ships could, for example, have prevented another foreign power with imperial ambitions – Germany, for example, or perhaps France and Britain – from trying to take its colonies. Instead the Spanish were soundly defeated and not in a position to exercise any such control.

As a result, the Americans stepped into Spanish shoes in another part of the former Spanish Empire, the Philippines, essentially to prevent anyone else from doing so. They now became embroiled in a part of the world that was a very long way from home – the distance from Manila to America's West Coast is 7,000 miles – and on islands that seemed to have little to offer in return. Soon they were confronted by growing resistance to their rule, and a bitter insurrection and insurgency began in 1899. Over the next three years, Emilio Aguinaldo's 50,000-strong guerrilla army killed around 4,000 Americans, although far more Filipinos, perhaps ten times that number, also died in the conflict. Many Americans had started to openly question the wisdom of acquiring the Philippines and drawing their country into the affairs of the Far East. McKinley's elevated and hubristic rhetoric, about how God called upon America to 'educate the Filipinos and uplift them and civilise them and Christianise them' by means of 'benevolent assimilation', suddenly seemed very hollow.[28]

The war had other downsides. It helped to stir anti-American sentiments in the wider region, and created, or reinforced, the impression that the United States was a meddling bully. For example, the Uruguayan writer José Enrique Rodó wrote a highly influential and much-read book, *Ariel*, in which he claimed that Latin America was confronted by a new enemy with an insatiable appetite for expansion. Among the Filipinos, it did not help matters that the Americans even staged a sham battle for control of Manila to give the Spanish garrison a pretext for immediate surrender: many locals would have wondered how they could trust their 'liberators'.

In Spain itself, military defeat hastened a strong sense of decline. Once it had been a great empire which, in its 'Golden Age' of the late sixteenth century, had ruled over huge swathes of the American and European continents. But now it had suffered a swift and humiliating defeat at the hands of an 'upstart' country. 1898 now became known as the year of *el desastre*, and news of the defeat created serious rifts between civilians and soldiers and triggered a desperate and ruthless hunt for scapegoats. 'Why have these incompetent generals not been shot?' asked one critic in the national parliament. Spain was in a state of crisis that was to last until and beyond the advent of civil war in 1936.[29]

'The Emperor of the Pacific' Takes on Japan (1905)

In August 1903, Czar Nicholas Romanov had appointed one of his most trusted commanders, Admiral Yevgeni Alexeyev, as his envoy to the Far East. The region was of great importance to the Czar and his advisers, who badly wanted access to the ice-free 'warm-water' port at Port Arthur, on China's southern mainland. But although Alexeyev was responsible for a vital region, no one was quite sure of his role. He was not affiliated to any government ministry, instead reporting directly to Nicholas, and was therefore neither a diplomat nor a statesman. But at the same time he was much more than just a military man. The exact purpose of his mission was never defined, and he had been heard to comment that he was himself uncertain of his own role.

Perhaps it was not altogether surprising that both men led their own country towards disaster. On 6 February, Alexeyev had sent a message from Tokyo to St Petersburg stating that, in his view, Japanese threats of war were just bluff. Japan, he argued, would not risk a fight with a nation as advanced and powerful as Russia. True, the Japanese had withdrawn their ambassador from St Petersburg, but he felt sure that was just a gesture and nothing more.[30]

Quite why he held this view, or put it forward, remains a mystery. Since his role was unclear, perhaps he never expected anyone to attach much weight to it. Maybe he was badly informed, lacking the impartial, experienced advice of seasoned diplomats. Or, as some people have argued, he might have wanted to deliberately mislead Czar Nicholas, pulling him into a conflict that he felt sure would inflict a savage defeat on an inferior, 'yellow' nation.

The Czar did not want, and had never wanted, a war with Japan. But he now placed too much faith in the judgment of a man who either tragically mistook Tokyo's intentions or else deliberately misrepresented them. As a result Nicholas made no last-minute effort to avert conflict, and four days later Tokyo formally declared war on Russia.

It is easy to see why Nicholas and his advisers had wanted to expand Russian influence into the Far East but much harder to grasp why they allowed their country to become embroiled in war. In 1897, a year after his coronation, the Czar had won rights to lease Port Arthur from the Chinese government. Russia badly needed a naval base to guard its eastern territories because sea ice rendered his port at Vladivostok useless for much of the year. And a powerful business lobby in St Petersburg also wanted to expand into the Far East, which it regarded as a major, growing market that offered a lot of opportunity.

But the Japanese had been alarmed by Russia's ascendancy in the Far East even if, to begin with, they were prepared to live with it. Still the Russians came closer. After rebellion broke out in China in 1900, Nicholas's army mobilised and occupied Manchuria. When Tokyo voiced strong protests and struck a treaty with the British, who were also alarmed to watch Russia's position grow so suddenly, St Petersburg backed down. The finance minister Sergei Witte and the foreign chief, Count Vladimir Lamsdorf, urged the Czar to rein his soldiers in. Russia, they exhorted, simply could not afford to fight a war. Their arguments proved persuasive and the Czar decided to evacuate Manchuria on condition that the Chinese authorities guaranteed the security of a critical railway that ran from the Russian border down to Port Arthur.

But hawks and doves jockeyed constantly for influence in the Russian capital and the most audacious voices now became the loudest: as one of Russia's ambassadors explained to a French colleague, his country could not just throw away all the time and money it had already invested in Manchuria. The Russians began to provoke both China and Japan by leaving many of their soldiers in Manchuria, and then demanding more concessions from Peking. At the same time, they violated another agreement, drawn up and signed in 1898, that 'assured the independence of Korea'. Far from respecting the deal, Russian workers, businessmen and contingents of soldiers had started to arrive south of the Yalu River and into the Korean peninsula.

But Nicholas and his more hawkish advisers were blundering. First, they ignored Japanese protests about Russian movements in both theatres: in St Petersburg, the Japanese ambassador made it clear that his country regarded Korea as vital to its security, and viewed a Russian presence there, as well as in Manchuria, as a clear threat. Japan's interest in Korea was obvious to see: just a few years before, in 1894, its army had fought a short but bitter war there against the Chinese, who had unwisely told Tokyo that their intervention in the peninsula was none of Japan's business.

Then the Russians disregarded Tokyo's efforts to broker a deal: on 13 January 1904, Japan had offered Russia an olive branch, stating its willingness to recognise Manchuria as a region that was outside its own sphere of interest if, in return, St Petersburg made a similar promise about Korea. But the Russians never replied and only made excuses for their failure to pull out.

Finally, they failed to take Tokyo's threats of war seriously. When the Japanese ambassador left St Petersburg, in February 1904, he told his former hosts that Tokyo would take whatever course of action it deemed necessary to defend its interests. That was clear diplomatic parlance for war. But it was not wise to ignore the Japanese war machine, which had shattered the Chinese in an eight-month campaign nine years before. In the intervening years, its admirals had worked hard to develop their navy, acquiring new ships and skills from abroad. It was at this point that the Czar and his advisers should have chosen to ignore Yevgeni Alexeyev.

Czar Nicholas would probably have avoided war if, at the very last minute, he had dispatched an urgent message to Tokyo offering to compromise, or even just to negotiate. But by 8 February it was too late, as the Japanese unleashed devastating attacks on Port Arthur that shook the complacent Russian commanders.

This was a war that St Petersburg should never have allowed to happen. 7,500 miles from the war zone, the Czar and his advisers were quite unable to fight an effective campaign against a very determined enemy, fighting on home ground, that had for some years been quietly preparing itself for this moment. But Nicholas' diary reveals a curious fatalism, as though it was not in his own power to shape the outcome of the clash: it was God's will that he frequently invoked in his daily entries and not the advice of his commanders. Just as revealing were the hubristic references he made to becoming 'the Emperor of the Pacific': he was plainly drawn to this wildly unrealistic goal and was therefore highly susceptible to the words of advisers who made him believe that it was something he could aspire to.[31]

As the Russians suffered a series of heavy blows and defeats, they could have sued for 'peace with honour' that would have spared them further humiliations. But by December, the Japanese were scenting total victory, having seized high ground outside Port Arthur that enabled them to fire at Russian ships with impunity. Nicholas had now missed his chance, for two months later, during a massive engagement at Mukden in Manchuria, the Russians lost 90,000 men before retreating. The Japanese still needed a decisive victory but knew it was well within their grasp.

Their chance came at the end of May, when the Japanese navy engaged Admiral Zinovy Rozhestvensky's fleet, which had set sail in the Baltic eight months before and made its way around the coasts of Africa and across the Indian Ocean before finally reaching its destination. Its journey had been error-strewn as well as long and arduous: in the North Sea, Russian commanders had infuriated London after they mistook British trawlers for Japanese submarines and opened fire. When they finally arrived in the Far East, they didn't last long. Operating in familiar territory and making the most of the superb intelligence that their spies had gathered, the Japanese admirals were able to launch a devastating attack on the larger but highly vulnerable Russian fleet, which was annihilated at the Battle of Tsushima.

Russia's shattering defeat was all the more painful because it had been inflicted by a country that many Russians regarded as not just smaller and weaker but as racially inferior – a prejudice that another warmonger, *Harry Truman*, and his advisers also appeared to have shared. Nicholas paid a hefty price for his errors. News of the disaster inflamed public anger towards the Czarist regime, radicalising and emboldening its critics and fanning the flames of the violent protests that were already sweeping through Russia. The naval mutiny at Odessa on board the battleship *Potemkin*, a rebellion that started soon after the peace treaty, soon became the stuff of legend. The war, in other words, was an important stepping stone on Russia's path to revolution.

But Nicholas and his advisers could easily have averted this war. There was no compelling military reason why they needed to permanently base Russian soldiers in Manchuria or Korea. Russia's worst-case scenario was that the Chinese would fail to safeguard the railway line to Port Arthur, which they had undertaken to do. But they could have prepared for this eventuality simply by deploying an armed force close to the border with China that could have intervened at short notice if the need arose. And while Korea did offer some tempting commercial opportunities, including plentiful supplies of valuable minerals and timber, St Petersburg might have been able to exploit them if it had first approached Tokyo to inform them of its plans and strike a deal. In this scenario, no Russian nationals would have entered Korea, or even Manchuria, without the prior agreement of the Japanese. This could well have allowed Japan to see Russia's plans for expansion in the region as a commercial opportunity rather than as a threat. Alternatively, Russian merchants could have looked away from Korea and instead concentrated on China, which not only offered vast commercial opportunities but had a more diverse power structure that they could have exploited.

4

THE RUN-UP TO THE FIRST
WORLD WAR

President Wilson's 'Wonderful Opportunity' in Mexico (1914)
In April 1914, one of the most extraordinary exchanges in diplomatic
history took place. An American admiral, Henry T. Mayo, had
demanded that the Mexicans give a twenty-gun salute to the Stars
and Stripes as a token gesture to show their respect for the United
States. The Mexicans initially agreed but had then quibbled about
such details as the number of rounds involved, and when and
where they should be fired. Then they made a further demand,
insisting that the Americans fire their own 'reciprocal' volleys to
salute the Mexican flag.

This ludicrous dispute had been triggered by an equally minor
incident, one that would not normally have attracted any real
attention. On 9 April, some American sailors had left their
gunboat, anchored off the Mexican shore at Tampico, and sailed
in a small landing craft to pick up supplies from the mainland.
But because they had arrived without a permit, they were briefly
arrested before being released by a profusely apologetic Mexican
commander.

Such incidents were relatively commonplace but for President
Thomas Woodrow Wilson this 'insult' was the excuse he needed
to wage war against President Victoriano Huerta's regime. Over
the next few days, as the two countries exchanged missives about
the gun salute, the president ordered his entire fleet to head for

Tampico and sent Huerta a message warning of 'the very serious character of the present situation and the very grave consequences which it may involve'. At the same time, the press was briefed about Mexico's 'contemptuous' behaviour towards the United States.[1]

But by 19 April there was still no sign of compromise, prompting Wilson to break off negotiations and to ask Congress to approve the use of force. Huerta, he told senators, had shown 'disregard for the dignity and rights of this government ... making (them) free to show in many ways their irritation and contempt'. By a huge majority, of 337 to 37, Congress quickly nodded its approval. But elsewhere, such a disproportionate response nonetheless raised eyebrows. 'Surely a question of etiquette may no longer be considered justification for an aggressive war,' one bemused newspaper editor pondered.

A short, brief war between America and Mexico was about to erupt yet no one, not even in Washington, seemed quite sure why. On the contrary, in Mexico City Ambassador Henry Lane Wilson and several American business leaders urged President Wilson to recognise Huerta as Mexico's best chance of enjoying some semblance of law and order after years of unrest, insurgency and civil war, while European leaders were also openly supporting Huerta and wanted Wilson to do the same. By the time of the Tampico incident, Huerta had also managed to win the blessing of Mexico's Catholic Church as well as the support of many of his own country's business leaders.

But by the spring of 1914, 'Wilson the Just' was losing sight of things. His lofty language was so saturated with reference to 'oppression', 'human rights' and 'liberty' that the world's imperfections seemed all the more glaring and unacceptable. In April, as tensions with Huerta rose, he told a reporter that 'my ideal is an orderly and righteous government in Mexico; but my passion is for the submerged eighty-five per cent of the people of that Republic, who are now struggling towards liberty'. The ensuing crisis was a 'wonderful opportunity to prove to the world that the United States of America is not only human but humane' and that his only motives were 'the betterment of the conditions of our unfortunate neighbour, and by the sincere desire to advance the cause of liberty'. Not surprisingly, he struck some onlookers as being 'like a Nonconformist minister (whose) thought and temperament were essentially theological not intellectual'. Others commented that talking to him was 'something like talking to Jesus Christ'.[2]

In one respect, it was easy to see why Huerta should have grated on Wilson's conscience. Far from being a champion of democracy, as Wilson always proclaimed himself to be, the Mexican was a revolutionary who in the course of 'Ten Tragic Days' in February 1913 had toppled, and was accused of assassinating, his predecessor, Francisco Madero. In the months that followed, Wilson had urged Huerta to hold elections but his pleas, or demands, fell on deaf ears. Tensions had increased and on 3 February the president had lifted the arms embargo on Huerta's enemies, the Constitutionalist forces led by Venustiano Carranza, thinking this would allow them to sweep into power without American intervention. He was wrong, and Huerta not only survived but prospered.

Perhaps there were deeper psychological reasons why Wilson could not tolerate Huerta. This was not just because most Americans had, for some while now, regarded Latin America as their own sphere of influence in which native people were deemed to have no right to act defiantly. It was also because some contemporaries felt that Wilson was incapable of accepting criticism and suffered from a deep-rooted inferiority complex. Perhaps because he had spent his formative years experiencing 'the frustrations of the post-[Civil] war South', remarked one observer, the president had 'a constant need' to 'maintain his own sense of superiority. This was the great compulsion which finally wrecked him.' Perhaps Huerta's indifference to Wilson's demand for elections touched on this raw nerve, or maybe Huerta had ventured some personal criticism that reached the president's ears.[3]

Whether Wilson was genuinely carried away by the force of his own liberal rhetoric, or was simply stung by Huerta's refusal to comply with his demands by holding elections, is unclear. But what is certain is that the Tampico incident gave him the excuse he wanted to launch an attack on Mexico. At just the same time that the incident flared, a German transport ship happened to arrive off the port of Veracruz, on Mexico's east coast. It was carrying a supply of arms, and Wilson ordered his commanders to attack the port and seize its customs houses. This needed to be done, he reckoned, before the arms reached Huerta's men and made his army too strong for Carrenza to overwhelm.

On the morning of 21 April, 1,000 American marines left their warships, anchored offshore, and stormed the port. At first everything went smoothly and they were completely unopposed. But then, all of a sudden, shots were fired and heavy fighting broke out. Resistance was soon so heavy that the commanders on the ground had to call in reinforcements. A warship on the horizon opened up with supporting fire, pummelling the Mexican defenders with heavy salvos. The Americans had soon taken the port but lost nineteen of their own men while killing hundreds of Mexicans, civilian and military, in the process.

In one sense, the tactic worked. The American forces stayed in Veracruz for six whole months, denying Huerta the customs revenues that his government needed to survive. On 15 July, Huerta resigned as leader and soon Carrenza had replaced him. It was regime change at its most brutal but also its most effective.

Yet it came at a great cost, creating a huge wave of anti-American feeling that went surging through the wider region. Instead of breaking Huerta, it rallied and united ordinary Mexicans against the United States. 'Three years of fratricidal war was forgotten in a day,' wrote a correspondent for the London *Daily Telegraph* who witnessed opposing factions cast aside their differences to unite against the invaders. And just sixteen years after the *Spanish–American War*, the United States seemed even more of a regional bully than ever before. 'The memory of this conflict will live in the history of the relations between the United States and Latin America,' wrote the editor of an Argentine paper. In Argentina, Uruguay and beyond, mobs stormed American consulates and buildings. All over Mexico, the Stars and Stripes was put to the torch.

Newspapers and journals throughout the wider world also condemned Wilson's 'medieval' behaviour. 'If war is to be made on points of punctilio raised by admirals and generals,' opined *The Economist*, then it will be 'a bad day for civilisation'. Others seethed against the 'sinister monstrosity of President Wilson', while another argued that 'plainly speaking, there has been nothing so cruelly immoral and so cynically cruel (because) no state pretending to civilisation has ever before announced its readiness to supply the anarchical elements in a neighbouring community with the means of rapine and massacre for mere profit'.[4]

Faced with such a chorus of criticism, the president lost his nerve and refused to order a full-scale invasion of the country. 'I remember how pale, almost parchmenty, Mr Wilson looked when he stood up there and answered the questions of newspaper men,' a friend later recalled. 'He was positively shaken' by news of the fighting and of the deaths it incurred.[5]

But there was no obvious reason why Wilson ever needed to get involved in Mexico's affairs. Even if he had wanted to impose liberal values on such a country, he should have recognised the formidable difficulties of doing so. Carranza went on to make few changes when he was in office, never introducing the liberal reforms that Huerta's enemies had wanted or expected, and large parts of Mexico remained under the grip of rebel guerrillas. If Wilson had genuinely wanted to help Mexico, he could have left Huerta in power, urging him to gradually moderate his political line while helping him impose law and order over rebel lands. Wilson also had huge financial and economic clout to threaten and reward Huerta.

Meanwhile, the leaders of European countries wondered about the precedent set by Wilson's invasion. If America saw nothing wrong with intervening in Mexico, the Germans and Austrians would have wondered, then how could anyone condemn them for attacking Serbia if it was in their interest to do so? Just weeks after American troops attacked Veracruz, such an argument may have helped swing the balance towards war in Europe.

Sergei Sazonov, Russia and the First World War (1914)

On 28 June 1914, as he was driven in an open car through the streets of Sarajevo, the Archduke Franz Ferdinand, the heir presumptive of the Austro-Hungarian throne, was shot dead by a nineteen-year-old fanatic called Gavrilo Princip. Over the weeks that followed, events gathered pace with a seemingly unstoppable momentum as one country after another declared war and a bloody conflagration of gargantuan, cataclysmic proportions erupted.

Responsibility for the First World War, which in origin and course was highly complex, cannot of course be easily and fairly attributed to any particular country, let alone to just a handful of individuals. But Russia was one perpetrator, among others, that bears some of the responsibility for escalating what could have been just a regional war between Serbia and the Austrians into a much wider confrontation. While it is true that the Germans declared war on Russia before the Russians declared war on Germany, the Russian government had started to move troops and equipment to the German front more than a week before the declaration. Russia was also the first great power to order a full-scale mobilisation of its forces, and then invaded East Prussia before any German troops had even attacked Russian territory.

Instrumental in taking Russia to war was the foreign minister, Sergei Sazonov.

Czar Nicholas II's decision in September 1910 to appoint Sazonov to the enormously challenging role of foreign minister had not been his most inspired. Sazonov had until that time been a relatively junior diplomat who was largely devoid of experience in high matters of state and who had few if any qualifications or professional connections of importance, either within Russia or beyond. His peers noted that he had a reputation only for 'mediocrity and obeying orders' and felt sure that his appointment was due in large part to his family connections with the prime minister, Piotr Stolypin, who was his brother-in-law. Making matters worse, he had an excitable, irascible temperament, lacking the cool-headedness that is vital in such a responsible role.

But 1910 was not a good time for a relative novice to be cutting his diplomatic teeth. Tension was growing, above all in the Balkans, where the Austro-Hungarian Empire was gradually losing its grip over its territories. In St Petersburg a growing chorus voiced its support for 'Pan-Slavist' nationalist movements that challenged Vienna's rule there. Russia had a moral duty to support its fellow Slavs in the Balkans, argued this lobby. They were its 'blood brothers' who would also act as future allies against the Austro-Hungarians and perhaps even help Russia secure control over Constantinople and the vital Bosphorus Strait. But Sazonov and Pyotr Stolypin, his political mentor, also knew that Russia could not afford to fight another war: its clash with Japan in 1905 had ended in a military disaster that had nearly triggered revolution at home. But in 1911, after the assassination of Stolypin, who had consistently argued that Russia needed peace at all costs, the foreign minister was left to steer his own course.

Resisting this war lobby was no easy task, as its exponents constantly worked to win over ministers and ambassadors as well as the Czar himself. Alexander Izvolsky, himself a former foreign minister before becoming ambassador to France, determinedly pursued his own warmongering agenda and searched hard for allies who would side with Russia against the Austrians. To begin with, Sazonov had wobbled and vacillated but gradually began to steer Russia's foreign policy along an ever more belligerent path. And when in September 1912 the Czar ordered his army to mobilise, in a bid to warn the Austrians off intervening in a Balkan dispute, it was a clear sign of a much more militant mood in the Russian capital. At the same time, the Czar approved the foreign minister's calls for big increases in military spending, overruling more cautious voices who argued that the money simply wasn't there to finance such a spree.[6]

By this time, Sazonov had also started to absorb the collective paranoia that appears to have been so prevalent in St Petersburg. Many Russian commanders and leaders felt sure that the Austrians were determined to mobilise not against Serbia, as they said they wanted to do, but really against Russia. In 1912, Austrian troop movements in Galicia (Austrian Poland) had taken Russia completely by surprise and now St Petersburg feared that something similar could happen again. Others in St Petersburg also felt sure that the Austrian armed forces were far more powerful than they actually were. In truth, Vienna wanted to concentrate its forces only on Serbia and had no intention of attacking Russia, and its forces were far less organised and efficient than Russia realised.[7]

Two years later, the key question that confronted Sazonov and other decision makers in St Petersburg was how to respond to an ultimatum that Vienna had given the Serbs after the assassination of the archduke. Feeling sure that the Serbian government had sponsored the attack on Ferdinand and was the lynchpin of wider anti-Austrian nationalism in the region, the Viennese authorities laid down stringent conditions that would, if the Serbs accepted the proposal, allow them to crack down on dissent. If, on the other hand, the Serbs rejected the ultimatum, then Vienna would have an excuse to go to war.

At exactly 6 p.m. on 23 July, the Austrian ambassador in Belgrade presented the Serbian authorities with a list of demands. These were certainly stringent but were by no means impossible for the Serbs to accept, and did not provide Serbia or Russia with a valid reason to go to war against Vienna. More than eight decades on, for example, Nato's ultimatum to Serbia presented a much more direct violation of its national sovereignty (see *Madeleine Albright and Kosovo, 1999*).

In particular, the Austrians ordered the Serbs 'to suppress the subversive movement directed against the territorial integrity of the monarchy' and 'investigate' the assassination. But because, quite reasonably, they wanted assurances that the Serbs would do as they promised, Article 6 of their document also demanded that Belgrade should 'accept the collaboration in Serbia of representative bodies' of the Austrians. But even this should not have been beyond the pale: what mattered was just how many Austrians should be allowed into Serbia, how long they could be there and just how much power they could have. But on these wider points the ultimatum said nothing. There was no reason why Belgrade could not have accepted the ultimatum and then haggled over the finer details.

For a brief while, it seemed that Belgrade had decided to accept the Austrian demands and would avoid war by doing so. 'It was thought that in the condition that she was known to be in, Serbia could not be expected to do otherwise than yield to so terrible a threat,' judged an Italian historian, Luciano Lagrini, who later met and interviewed the former leaders in Belgrade. Nikola Pasic, the most senior single figure in the capital, even drafted a telegram to his foreign ambassadors stating that he would be 'conciliatory on all points' and 'fully satisfy' the Austrian demands.[8]

But Sazonov had by this time become fully converted to the cause of the increasingly vociferous war party in the Russian capital. Invited to lunch at the French embassy, he became extremely agitated and had fumed vociferously at the Austrian ambassador, exclaiming, 'I know what it is! You want to make war on Serbia! The German newspapers have been driving you to it! You are setting Europe ablaze!' When the Austrian delegate tried to reason with him, Sazonov would have none of it. 'You want war and now you've burned your bridges!' he cried, before storming off.[9]

The Russians now deliberately sabotaged any prospects of peace. Sazonov informed the Serbian representative in St Petersburg that Belgrade could 'count unofficially on Russian support', and later added that his country would take 'energetic measures, even mobilisation' to support a Serbian rejection of the ultimatum. Above all, urged the foreign minister, Belgrade had to stand firm over Article 6 of the ultimatum and not allow Austria to violate the Serb constitution. Other Russian officials informed Belgrade that the Czar had shown 'the greatest readiness for war' and was determined 'to go to any lengths in protecting Serbia'. Hours later, as news reached Belgrade that the Russians were already starting to mobilise their forces, the Serbs unequivocally rejected the Austrian demands, handing their response to the Austrian ambassador just minutes before the deadline at 6 p.m. on Saturday 25 July.[10]

Over the next few days, the crisis escalated. By the time the Austrians had declared war against the Serbs on 28 July, the Czar had undertaken a 'partial mobilisation' of 1.7 million men and planned 'to immediately start an energetic offensive against Austria-Hungary as soon as it attacks Serbia'. Deeply alarmed, Germany warned Russia to back down but the Czar replied that his disagreement was only with the Austrians and not with Berlin.

Hours later, on the afternoon of 29 July, Sazonov met with the 'tired and preoccupied' Czar and urged him to order a full mobilisation of his troops, making a German response virtually inevitable. After listening to his foreign minister's hour-long presentation, Nicholas nodded his assent. 'You are right. There is nothing else left than to prepare ourselves for an attack. Transmit to the chief of the general staff my orders of mobilisation.' As soon as he left the conference room, Sazonov spoke to the head of the Russian army: 'Issue your orders, General, and then disappear for the day.'

On 1 August, Germany declared war against Russia, activating a series of alliances that led to a pan-European conflict.

The Russians had played a major part in provoking and escalating this crisis. Without Sazonov's support and encouragement, the Serbs would probably have agreed, in principle, to the Austrian ultimatum and differed only about the relatively minor points of detail. Vienna would have had no reason to use force against Belgrade.

But there was no pressing need for St Petersburg to back Belgrade. Serbia, after all, was a landlocked country that did not help the Russians to secure the Black Sea or the Bosphorus Strait. And although the 'Pan-Slav lobby' had become so powerful in Russia, the costs and risks of fighting a war on the Serbs' behalf were clearly enormous. The previous October, the Czar had left Serbia to fend for itself when the Austrians had issued another ultimatum demanding its withdrawal from northern Albania. In the same spirit, Sazonov could simply have condemned Austrian involvement in Serbia but kept a distance that would have avoided the very confrontations that he knew would follow.

If he and the Czar had come under intense pressure to act against the Austrians in Serbia, then they could have persuaded Belgrade to accept the June ultimatum and then supported an insurgent-style campaign against any Austrian troops who occupied the province. This would have avoided any risk of dragging Russia into outright war that it could not afford while satisfying the need for action against the emperor. Serb insurgents would have been capable of inflicting a steady stream of casualties on any Austrian army of occupation, just as the British armed forces had suffered badly from the same tactics in South Africa during the Boer War of 1899–1902.

At the same time, Sazonov could have built up defensive links not with the Serbs but with Romania. Although Bucharest had struck up a secret treaty with Berlin and Vienna in 1883, King Carol of Romania had his own disagreements with the Austrians that gave him common ground with Russia. Amongst Romania's public and political parties, there was strong anti-Habsburg sentiment and some interest in joining the Triple Entente between Russia, France and Britain. And Carol also controlled a whole section of the Black Sea's coast, which made his support vital for Russia's security. Russia was already building up its links with Bucharest at the time of the assassination in Sarajevo. On 14 June, the Czar had visited Carol at Constanta, on the Black Sea, and the two men had agreed to cooperate against Habsburg interests in the Balkans. This rapprochement, noted a French diplomat, constituted 'a new means for Russia of applying pressure to Austria'.[11]

If, over the months and years ahead, Sazonov had built up this emerging rapport with Romania into a formal alliance, then the Austrians would have exercised a much more cautious hand in the Balkans, allowing him to claim that he had played his part in protecting the Serbs while also safeguarding Russia's security interests in the Black Sea.

Moltke Fights Russia 'Sooner Rather than Later' (1914)

One of Europe's most influential warmongers in the summer of 1914 was the chief of Germany's general staff, Helmuth von Moltke. He held considerable sway over the ultimate decision maker, Kaiser Wilhelm II, as well as upon a number of leading civilian politicians in Germany's so-called 'responsible government', notably the Reich Chancellor, Theobald von Bethmann-Hollweg, who was instrumental in forging foreign policy, and the head of the foreign office, Gottlieb von Jagow.

In the course of the two years that preceded the outbreak of war, Moltke constantly pressed these decision makers to prepare their country for a preventive campaign that would neutralise emerging threats before it was too late. Germany's enemies, he argued, were growing stronger by the day and at such a rate that the Reich would need to make a pre-emptive attack soon before it lost its chance forever. Russia, he added, was a particular menace, partly because its economy was growing at a dramatic rate, and partly because it was already building new railways lines that would bring its troops westwards far more quickly and efficiently than ever before. France, he continued, was also becoming more of a threat, having replaced two years of conscription with three years of service.

In a high-level meeting at the New Palace in Potsdam in December 1912, Moltke pressed for war 'sooner rather than later' and argued that conflict could only be avoided by a 'miracle'. The French and Russians already had 827,000 more men than Germany, he pointed out, and this figure would increase in the years ahead. But although the Kaiser initially seemed sympathetic, his proposals were quietly dropped.

Moltke, however, was undeterred and looked further afield for support. On 12 May, the field marshal met in secret with his Austrian counterpart at a hotel in the city of Karlsbad. There was no time to waste, he argued, because France was providing the Russians with low-interest loans that they could use to build new roads, railways and arms.

Such a deep, pessimistic fatalism may have been borne of the teachings of the philosopher Rudolf Steiner, whose 'theosophist' ideas and teachings, based partly on the Book of Revelation, exerted a powerful hold over the general. Perhaps it was also a legacy bequeathed by his uncle, Field Marshal Helmuth von Moltke 'the Elder', who had been the architect of Prussia's great victories against Austria in 1866 and then against France four years later. He too had also held similarly pessimistic 'worst-case scenario' assumptions. In 1875, for example, just five years after a war with France that Prussia had won conclusively, he had advocated a second invasion of France on the grounds that such an attack would neutralise an emerging threat. His advice was ignored but twelve years later, in 1887, he had then urged

Chancellor Otto von Bismarck to order a full-scale invasion of Russia on similar grounds.[12]

Such a pessimistic state of mind was not just a family affair, however, since in the years that preceded the First World War it also afflicted other military men in Berlin. Admirals like Alfred von Tirpitz and land commanders like Alfred von Schlieffen openly conjured a similarly fatalistic vision of Germany's neighbours joining forces and launching a collective strike that would force Germany to fight a war on two or more fronts that it was bound to lose. Russia was at the forefront of their minds. 'They know that this great body gains each day in cohesion; they want to attack and destroy it before it has attained the plenitude of its power,' as the French statesman Raymond Poincaré remarked to a journalist a few months before the outbreak of war.

As a result, the doctrine of preventive war became fashionable in the echelons of the German High Command: one study has even identified several dozen occasions when senior commanders pressed for war 'sooner rather than later'. For example, on one occasion Moltke's deputy, General Georg von Waldersee, wrote that Germany had 'no reason whatever to avoid' war and in fact had a very good opportunity 'to conduct a great European war quickly and victoriously'.[13]

Some political leaders shared their pessimistic assumptions. The chancellor, Theobald von Bethmann-Hollweg, was also convinced that 'the future belongs to Russia, which grows and grows and weights upon us as an ever heavier nightmare' and at the same time was 'very pessimistic about the intellectual condition of Germany'. On another occasion he noted how 'Russia's claims (are) growing (along with her) enormously explosive strength ... in a few years (it is) no longer to be warded off'. A visit to Russia in 1912 confirmed his worst fears. Noting its 'agricultural wealth as much as the vigour of the population', he departed with 'a feeling of admiration and astonishment so profound'.[14]

Developments during 1913 heightened their fears even more. Military officers in Berlin were deeply alarmed by the revelation that French creditors would soon be financing new Russian railways that would have enabled two-thirds of the Russian army – the existing figure was a relatively meagre half – to reach the German border within two weeks. And in June the following year, Russia's parliament authorised a 'Great Programme' of rearmament that would add an extra 500,000 men to its armed forces. Within just three years, calculated Moltke, the Czar's army would vastly outsize his own.

Two months later, the assassination of Archduke Ferdinand gave Moltke and other warmongers in Berlin the chance they wanted. Moltke knew that the Austrians wanted to use the killing as an excuse to impose a degree of control over Serbia, which they regarded as the true sponsor of the attack and the instigator of nationalist sentiments that were threatening the cohesion of their multinational empire. And he knew that the Serbs' ally, Russia, would then probably step into the fray if the Austrians used military force: the Russian foreign minister, *Sergei Sazonov* made this clear as soon as the Austrians gave their ultimatum to Belgrade.

But although he was well aware of this outcome, Kaiser Wilhelm nonetheless pressed the Austrians to go ahead and intervene in the Balkans, knowing that Russia and its own ally, France, would then enter the fray. On 26 July, Berlin flatly rejected diplomatic overtures.

Just briefly, it looked as though Germany would back down. On 28 July, when it suddenly appeared much less likely that Britain would remain neutral, the Kaiser wobbled and questioned the received wisdom of provoking Russia into war. Bethmann-Hollweg's nerve also seemed to falter. But it was at this point that Moltke's role as a warmonger became particularly important: he and his fellow military advisers decreed that it was simply out of the question to back down and undo the plans elaborated over many years. If they did so now, he argued, then Germany would be vulnerable to attack but not have the resources to defend itself.

Before and during those fatal summer weeks, Moltke's determination to wage pre-emptive war with Germany's eastern neighbour found support from other quarters. In Germany, as in other countries, there was a powerful arms lobby that had a vested commercial interest in any conflict. Some German social democrats were also open to the prospect of waging war against the Russian Czar, whom they regarded as the epitome of tyranny. But these influences were not instrumental in driving Germany to plan and provoke the First World War: there were just as many businesses that depended on peaceful relations with Germany's neighbours. Only a sympathiser at the very highest level, who was capable of actively pursuing a militaristic agenda, was in a position to push the Kaiser into war. And it was just such a role that Moltke played.

When Germany did mobilise its forces against Russia, at 1 p.m. on 31 July 1914, a 'State of Imminent War' was declared in Berlin. Moltke hoped that any such conflict could be resolved quickly. Perhaps Russia could be dealt a quick, humiliating blow that would have neutralised any emergent threat to Germany. But the field marshal also privately conceded that a war might escalate and then drag on for years, causing death and destruction on an unprecedented scale until the participants finally bled each other to death: the war might end, as he wrote to Bethmann, with 'the mutual butchery of the civilised nations of Europe.'[15]

Germany, as well as the other participants of the First World War, went on to pay the enormously high price that Moltke feared. By the time of the Kaiser's humiliating surrender in November 1918, after four years of total war, 1.7 million German soldiers had been killed and 4.2 million were injured.

But Germany had gone to war in 1914 on false premises. Moltke had assessed the threat from Russia in narrowly numerical terms, weighing up the vast armies of hundreds of thousands that the Czar could muster. He failed to take into account the enormous supplies and reinforcements that such a force needed, and how long, overstretched and vulnerable Russian supply lines would be. In other words, the very thing that seemed to make Russia so dangerous was also its source of weakness: the Russian army would have been hugely dependent on the operation of the railways that had brought them westwards.

Nor did Moltke foresee how poorly trained and armed many of these enemy soldiers would be if, in a worst-case scenario, war did break out between them. The abysmal performance of the Russian navy in its clash against Japan a decade before revealed these weaknesses. So too did the crushing defeat that the Germans went on to inflict, in the space of just four days in late August 1914, on a vastly bigger Russian force at Tannenberg (in present-day Poland).

Nor would a war with Russia, no matter what its outcome, have neutralised any threat it posed to Germany in the longer term: in July 1914 military planners in Berlin had wanted to 'thrust (Russia) back as far as possible from Germany's eastern frontier'. But just as in 1875 Moltke 'the Elder' had deemed a second attack on France to be necessary, only five years after the first, so would Russia have recovered from any blow that Germany's army was capable of inflicting on it.

A better solution would simply have been to strike a deal with St Petersburg that obliged Russia to pull its forces far back from the German Empire. At the same time, Moltke could have found ways of targeting Russia's supply lines through Poland if, in a worst-case scenario, war did break out. Just as 'Lawrence of Arabia' badly disrupted Turkish supply lines during the First World War, destroying the railways that ran through the Arabian deserts, so too could German undercover forces have undertaken similar operations. Perhaps with the support of anti-Russian Polish partisans, such attacks would have badly disrupted the railways on which any Russian attack against Germany would have heavily depended.

Sir Edward Grey and British Involvement in the First World War (1914)

On 26 July, the British ambassador in St Petersburg, Sir George Buchanan, sent an urgent despatch back to London. Despite the Czar's denials, he wrote, the Russians were calling up vast numbers of troops whose movements were 'doubtless' connected with 'intending mobilisation'. Russia, in other words, was on the verge of going to war against Austria-Hungary and its ally in the Triple Alliance, Germany.

In Whitehall, the foreign secretary, Sir Edward Grey, had already spoken to cabinet colleagues of the importance of 'calming' Russia and had quietly asked Russian officials, based at the embassy in London, to avoid saying or doing anything provocative. But otherwise he failed to make any effort to rein in Russia after the presentation of the Austrian ultimatum. Nor did he now act on Buchanan's urgent dispatch. He did not arrange an immediate meeting with the Russian ambassador, for example, and urge the Czar to back off. Yet Grey had leverage to influence St Petersburg: Britain was, after all, a fellow member, along with France, of the same defensive alliance, the Triple Entente.

Had he done so, then Grey might have warned the Czar that he could not count on British and perhaps French support. And if Russia really was determined to use force against the Austrians, then he could have suggested that the Czar should consider only a very limited deployment, confining the conflict to the Balkans by supporting the Serbs directly instead of widening it by attacking Austria-Hungary. At the very least, the British foreign secretary could have expressed a willingness to mediate between the Austrians and the Serbs and help broker some agreement. He could have played for time while the Germans, Austrians and Russians came to their senses.

At the same time, Grey could have given the Germans a lot more bluster, assuring them that Britain would come into the war to defend the Russians if they came under attack from Germany. This did not have to be true. Just the mere threat of British intervention might have helped swing the balance against war: 'If the British government puts its foot on the whole thing today,' bemoaned the French diplomat Paul Cambon on 24 July, 'peace might be saved.' Four days later, Cambon reiterated to Grey directly that 'if once it were assumed that Britain would certainly stand aside from a European war, the chance of preserving peace would be very much imperilled'. Only a clear declaration of British solidarity, insisted both the French and the Russians, would persuade Germany and the Austrians 'to draw in their horns'.[16]

Sir Edward, however, did none of those things. Instead, in the days that followed the assassination of the archduke in Sarajevo, he initially vacillated, expressing vague hopes of peace and making half-promises about going to war to support the other two members of the Triple Entente. This initial uncertainty helped the crisis in Europe to escalate. And then, from 27 July, it was his bellicosity that took Britain into a war that it did not need to fight in any case.

On that July day he had tried but failed to win cabinet support for British intervention in Europe's crisis. But his critics were still not swayed by this emotive appeal, and David Lloyd George, the Chancellor of the Exchequer and the most powerful opponent of war, argued just as vociferously against any involvement. Two days later Grey tried and failed again, winning the support only of four colleagues. The other members of the cabinet concurred that the crisis on the continent simply didn't pose enough of a threat to British interests to warrant intervention. One of the few enthusiasts for war was the First Sea Lord, Winston Churchill, who on 1 August put the Royal Navy on a war footing without even winning the approval of the cabinet. He was, noted Asquith, 'very bellicose' and demanded 'immediate mobilisation'.[17]

But over the weekend of 1–3 August, there was a sea-change in attitudes. 'The war had leapt into popularity between Saturday and Monday', Lloyd George later wrote, as crowds came into the streets to demand British involvement. But the decision makers probably barely even noticed what was happening in the streets outside. What moved them to vote for intervention were reports that the Germans would soon be attacking France through neutral Belgium. Its neutrality, and Britain's commitment under an 1839 treaty to defend that status against foreign attack, was not in itself of any importance: what seemed to matter, to the advocates of war, was that if the Kaiser's soldiers 'substantially violated' Belgian territory then they would pose a clear threat to the North Sea and the English Channel. In other words, they would be directly challenging the supremacy of the Royal Navy and the security of the nation.[18]

Once again, Sir Edward had pushed this argument before his critics in the cabinet, threatening his resignation in order to get his way. 'We have led France to rely upon us,' he argued, 'and unless we support her in her agony, I cannot continue at the Foreign Office.' When the prime minister, Herbert Asquith, echoed the same threats, their fellow Liberals were deeply alarmed: if they resigned, neither Grey nor Asquith would have any obvious successors.

But his single most important contribution to the cause of war came the following day, on Monday 3 August, when he spoke in front of a very tense and silent House of Commons and made the case for British involvement. Picking up the same theme that he had reiterated to the cabinet with such success, he argued that Britain had a 'moral obligation' to support France. So powerful was his address, noted the parliamentarian Christopher Addison, that it 'satisfied all the House (and) with perhaps three or four exceptions ... we were compelled to participate'.

But Sir Edward Grey was always a reluctant warmonger. He was, as David Lloyd George later wrote, 'at heart a philanthropist, a man of peace'. And he also harboured no illusions about what British intervention in the war would mean. He knew, for example, that Britain could not afford to get involved in war: on 31 July he had told the French ambassador that 'the commercial and financial situation was extremely serious, there was danger of a complete collapse that would involve us and everyone in ruin; and it was possible that our standing aside might be the only means of preventing a near collapse of European credit in which we should be involved'. And he was well aware that the conflict would flare up and create a terrible tragedy: on 29 July he warned the German ambassador in London that 'if war breaks out it will be the greatest catastrophe that the world has ever seen'.[19]

The foreign secretary's critics wondered if his warmongery was a consequence of his apparent lack of engagement with the outside world. Ever since he took charge of the foreign office in 1905, at the age of forty-three, some of his civil servants had noted that he spent more time pursuing his great hobbies, birdwatching and fly-fishing, than keeping track of events in the outside world. Apt to suddenly take leave of his duties in London and disappear into the countryside, sometimes not returning until it was absolutely necessary, he could infuriate his colleagues: one diplomat complained that Grey's nature-watching trips were getting in the way of his duties and that the foreign secretary should 'spare some time from his ducks to learn French'.[20]

But these inclinations were more likely to have made Sir Edward a pacifist than a lover of war. In times of a national emergency, few individuals are busier than a foreign secretary, and by advocating British intervention in Europe in the summer of 1914 Grey knew that he would be sacrificing the very lifestyle that he loved. He also knew that his eyesight was deteriorating, which the added paperwork of wartime responsibilities could only make worse. Instead, one explanation of his warmongery was his exaggerated sense of honour.

Sir Edward Grey, whose full title was 3rd Baronet, Viscount Grey of Falloden, was every inch the product of a class of British aristocrats who had long ruled British political life. For all his personal faults – contemporaries described him as 'devoid of personal ambition, aloof and unapproachable' – he was nurtured in a culture in which to break one's word was a matter of shame. It was an inexcusable breach of personal honour.

Grey's determination not to break his word helped to overrule his judgment. He and his Foreign Office ally, the diplomat Eyre Crowe, had argued that British involvement in the growing crisis was essentially 'a matter of honour'. His country, he continued, was under a 'moral bond ... to stand by its friends. This honourable expectation has been raised.' Since 1906 he had always assured the French that they would have British support in the event of a crisis with Germany, and he felt it was simply reprehensible and wrong to then go back on his word: within just months of taking office, he had turned the Triple Entente into a full defensive alliance that committed France, Britain and Russia to come to each other's aid in the event of an attack.[21]

But such feelings were not the only driving force towards war. Both Grey and Eyre also harboured a deep fear of Germany and its intentions. More than a decade before, in January 1903, he had written that 'Germany is our worst enemy and our greatest danger', and argued that 'if any Government drags us back into the German net, I will oppose it openly at all costs'.[22]

It was in this spirit that Grey assumed the worst about Germany as the crisis in Europe grew in the summer of 1914. And when the German army mobilised and turned westwards to attack France, he felt that British interests were directly at stake. There would be a German hegemony in Western Europe, and perhaps beyond, that would imperil the passage of British warships and merchant vessels: if that happened then Britain would be at risk of starving and its links with its empire would be cut.

But on the outbreak of war, as the British historian Niall Ferguson has pointed out, no evidence has ever been found that the Germans had a 'Napoleonic vision' that would have given them hegemony over the Belgian coast. Although both the Kaiser and *Moltke* sometimes imagined Britain losing its empire, in the summer of 1914 they never had any such policies. On the contrary, on 29 July, Chancellor Bethmann stated that he was prepared to guarantee the territorial integrity of both France and Belgium if Britain stayed out of the conflict, not least because the advent of war would strengthen Germany's liberal left and create division and dissension within its borders. And on 2 August Moltke wrote that Germany 'would act with moderation in case of a victory over France' and that such an assurance 'should be given ... unconditionally and in the most binding form', together with guarantees of the integrity of Belgium. Bethmann was interested, however, in establishing a German-dominated customs union that might have worked to Britain's commercial advantage. It would certainly not have been something that posed any clear challenge to British strategic interests.[23]

Grey's fears had also been greatly inflamed over the preceding few years by a popular Germanophobe hysteria that swept through Britain. For much of the nineteenth century, the British public had regarded Russia as the chief threat to its security and to the British Empire. By the 1890s, Russia had been superseded by France. But by the early 1900s Germany was viewed as the chief threat, as its economy and, above all, its navy began to grow at dramatic pace. In 1909 a naval arms race with Germany began, orchestrated by British naval commanders and politicians who entertained hubristic notions of Britain having an 'absolute supremacy' over the high seas and who wildly exaggerated the German 'threat'. Two years later, an incident at Agadir off the Moroccan coast nearly triggered confrontation when Grey warned Lloyd George and Churchill that the German fleet was on the verge of attacking British ships. Once again, he hugely exaggerated the danger: the German ships were scattered and its commanders had no intention of attacking.[24]

In other words, Grey's view of Germany, far from being level-headed, was tinged with a strong sense of hysteria. His Germanophobia was instrumental in taking Britain into a war it never needed to fight. Britain could have stayed out of the First World War with the same sense of 'splendid isolation' that it had enjoyed in 1870, when it had stood back and watched the Prussian army defeat the French, demand reparations and then withdraw. At the same time, he could have satisfied the demands of his more hawkish commanders and fellow politicians by beefing up the size and strength of the Royal Navy, and deploying some of its warships in British waters of the North Sea, just to warn the Germans to keep their distance and prepare to attack if they moved too far. Had he taken this defensive line, the lives of the 700,000 young British men who fell in the First World War would have been spared.

5

THE AGE OF DICTATORS

Mussolini's 'Destiny' in Abyssinia (1935)

In the spring of 1935, the Italian dictator Benito Mussolini closely studied facts and figures about the population of Great Britain. It was comprised, he concluded, of a disproportionate number of women, and a considerable number of people over the age of fifty, which he deemed to be 'the age limit of bellicosity'. It didn't really matter, *Il Duce* concluded, what Britain's leaders said in public. All that really mattered was that the general public in Great Britain would want to remain docile when the next international crisis brewed and its government would therefore end up keeping out of it.[1]

Mussolini was carefully weighing up his chances of pulling off an audacious war of aggression against the East African state of Abyssinia (later Ethiopia). He always knew that Britain and France had the power to stop him in his tracks because they both dominated the League of Nations (the forerunner of the United Nations) and also exerted control over the Suez Canal. This would allow them to enforce the one punitive measure he really feared – an oil embargo – and also to cut off the flow of troops and their supplies to and from Abyssinia. But the French had already secretly nodded their assent to his plan, offering him a 'free hand' mainly because they needed his support against Adolf Hitler's resurgent Germany. The British, on the other hand, promised to be a tougher nut to crack.[2]

In early October, Mussolini decided that the moment had come to seize Abyssinia. The British, it seemed, would stand aside, perhaps because they were intimidated by him. At a time of a crippling economic recession that had severely emasculated their armed forces, the British somehow feared that Mussolini and the members of his imaginary 'suicide squad' would carry out a 'mad-dog act' unless they looked away from his invasion. On 2 October, *Il Duce* addressed vast, ecstatic crowds in the centre of Rome and proclaimed that the invasion of Abyssinia had begun: hundreds of thousands of Italian troops were poised to cross the border from neighbouring Eritrea and seize the capital, Addis Ababa, from the clutches of the Emperor Haile Selassie.

Mussolini spoke a great deal about his 'destiny' and 'will' to 'civilise' people he regarded as 'cannibals', and perhaps he had a point. Despite Selassie's effort to build his country, it was a ramshackle mess. 'Conditions here are appalling,' as one visiting doctor wrote, 'the country is way back in the 15th century – ruled over by feudal lords.' But he also had other, more specific motives for wanting to seize Abyssinia. His invasion exacted revenge for a decisive and embarrassing defeat that local tribes had inflicted on an Italian expeditionary army in 1896. Defeat on such a scale was bad enough – the Italians lost around 6,400 men, which was nearly twice the number they inflicted on their enemy – but, in the eyes of a watching world that regarded the indigenous people with utter contempt, it was complete humiliation. For the Italians this was all the more difficult to bear because Mussolini was deeply conscious that Italy had far fewer overseas colonies than most of its continental neighbours. By seizing Abyssinia he could redress the balance and, in his truly self-delusory way, enhance his prestige as the heir of the great Roman emperor Augustus.[3]

For a time, his gambit appeared to have worked. The following May, when Italian soldiers had inflicted a series of extremely bloody beatings on the Ethiopian warriors, many of whom were using spears and swords against planes and machine guns, a wave of jingoistic pride swept through Italy. Mussolini was widely hailed, as he had always hoped, as a messiah and saviour who had restored Italy to its rightful place. 'He is like a god,' exalted one of his admirers. 'Like a god? No, he *is* a god' came the reply. As the French ambassador in Rome noted, 'Never has Italian support for Mussolini been more complete.'[4]

But the flaws in Mussolini's invasion plan, however, should have been obvious to see. Once the initial euphoria wore off, it became increasingly difficult to understand the logic of capturing and occupying a land-locked, barren and desperately poor land. Sustaining such an effort always promised to be difficult, since any invasion force would inevitably depend upon long, overstretched supply lines that ran to and from neighbouring Eritrea, which was an Italian colony, as well as the Italian mainland. Colonialism had in any case had its heyday, and Western land-grabbing raised more eyebrows, and more effective resistance, than it had at the zenith of empire in the late nineteenth century. Besides, even if Britain and France were prepared to coalesce, the invasion would only heighten the suspicions of so many people there, and elsewhere, who deeply feared the rise of fascism and regarded it, with every justification, as a true threat to peace.

It was not long before Mussolini's Abyssinian venture started to go wrong. Because the port of Massawa had very limited facilities and could only handle 3,000 tons of merchandise every day, ships queued offshore for weeks, or even months, at vast expense before they could unload. Even when they had the resources they needed, Italian generals were astounded by the vast distances they had to cover over open desert or savannah, as well as by the meagre resources at their disposal. Their ruthlessness, not least in using chemical weapons, also caused widespread alarm and indignation. 'This isn't war – it isn't even slaughter,' bemoaned a Red Cross worker, 'it's the torture of tens of thousands of defenceless men, women and children with bombs and poison gas.' Soon the British and French governments started to sharply increase their defence spending, while the Italian government struggled to meet the huge costs incurred by their campaign. The jubilation of May 1936 also quickly soured, as Selassie's followers started to wage a highly effective guerrilla war, using hit-and-run tactics to inflict a steady and growing stream of casualties on the occupying force, which increasingly retreated behind the confines of its heavily defended camps.[5]

By invading Abyssinia, Benito Mussolini had gone too far with the cult of war and violence that he had championed ever since the First World War, when he had abandoned his pacifism and instead followed the crowds who clamoured for action. From this time on, his vaguely defined 'fascism' was 'a doctrine of action' that valued prowess on the battlefield as the best way of enhancing the prestige of his impoverished, backward and politically chaotic homeland. Soon he began to consciously create a political myth that was comprised of bloody and heroic acts. In 1922 he ordered his followers to 'march on Rome' and then, invited to become prime minister, he allegedly greeted the king with a memorable line: 'Majesty, I come from the battlefield – fortunately bloodless.' It was not long before his political rule became a form of institutionalised thuggery that targeted his political opponents, such as the socialist deputy Giacomo Matteotti, who was murdered in 1924.

As the leader of Italy, *Il Duce*'s theatrical posturing as a man of war quickly got noticed. Some unimpressed visitors brushed him aside as 'a Napoleon turned pugilist', while another disliked 'the absurd attitudinizing' of a man who always seemed to adopt an artificial pose, often baring his chest to the cameras, thrusting out his chin and jaw, and gesticulating to his adoring masses with quick, chopping motions of the right hand. And he was always keen to be seen undertaking impressive feats of exercise, such as boxing, swimming, fencing and cycling. Here was a true man of action.

However, if Mussolini had wanted to use invasion and conquest as a means of winning popular adulation, and raising his country's prestige and honour as well as his own, then he had had other, much less ambitious, ways of doing so than targeting such a faraway and barren land as Abyssinia. In particular, he could have focused his energies and attention on consolidating his grip on one of Italy's few existing colonies – Libya.

Although Italy had first started to colonise its 'fourth shore' in the 1910s, Libya had only started to receive much attention in 1934, when the new governor-general, Air Marshal Italo Balbo, had undertaken a personal effort to transform it into a model colony. His efforts reaped some reward, and soon much of the capital, Tripoli, had been transformed with wide, impressive streets, and the construction of new hotels, shops and offices. Under his tutelage, a 1,500-mile road was also built, at enormous cost and toil, all the way to the Tunisian border. Tourists started to arrive, tempted by the archaeological treasures and by the impressive air and car rallies that Balbo organised to lure them.

Instead of turning to Abyssinia, Mussolini could have supported the heroic efforts of his air marshal to transform Libya into what Balbo called a 'fascist triumph'. With more resources at his disposal, Balbo would have secured his grip over a vast country that was always at risk of erupting into tribal anarchy. In his characteristically theatrical style, Mussolini could have glossed up the peacekeeping activities of his soldiers in Libya and portrayed them as a true accomplishment at arms.[6]

Libya was also surrounded by the French on one side (Tunisia and Algeria) and the British on the other (Egypt). On the outbreak of the Second World War in 1939, Balbo instead found himself in a hopeless position, particularly when the Italian navy wholly lacked the ships to establish, even just briefly, an effective link between the two shores. The resources that Mussolini squandered in Abyssinia, in other words, could have addressed these weaknesses. And because he would have been acting on land that Italy had claimed as its own for some while, Mussolini could done this without stirring up any international opposition.

Nor was it just military resources that were wasted in Abyssinia. Mussolini could have allocated more time and attention to building and developing Libya's agricultural sector. When tens of thousands of Italian settlers, 'Soldiers of the Soil', arrived in Libya in 1938 and 1939, they were dismayed by the poor or even non-existent crops they tried to grow. But with more resources at his disposal, Balbo would have been in a position to realise his dreams of creating an irrigation system to feed whole stretches of arid and barren desert. Had he succeeded, then Italy's achievements would have been heralded and venerated around the world. Instead, its naked aggression and brutality in Abyssinia were almost universally excoriated.[7]

Nor, if he had concentrated on Libya, would Mussolini have probably felt any temptation to attack Albania. His justification for invading this kingdom, on 7 April 1939, was as difficult to comprehend as his earlier attack on Abyssinia. Not only was Albania mired in poverty – a British soldier quipped that it was so poor that local people would even murder a visitor just for the lice in his shirt – but it was already, on the eve of the attack, an Italian protectorate in any event. Mussolini's only possible motive was therefore just to show off and flex muscle, although it was an attempt that backfired disastrously: the invasion was carried out so ineptly that, as a senior Italian officer commented, even a 'well-armed fire brigade could have driven us back into the Adriatic'.[8]

Adolf Hitler Fights 'Bolshevism' in Spain (1936)

In his political testament, first published in 1925, Adolf Hitler spelt out his great ambitions for the German nation. Its 'historic destiny', he chillingly argued in *Mein Kampf*, was to look eastwards and carve out *lebensraum* ('living space') in some of the territories of 'Russia and her client states in the surrounding area'.

For Hitler, war was always an inevitable means of realising his grandiose, imperial ambitions, and a means that he relished using. From the moment he became Chancellor, in January 1933, he drew up plans to reconstitute and rearm Germany's armed forces in readiness for the pending invasion, and subjugation, of the 'inferior races' that occupied the territories in the East. In his bloodthirsty eyes, 'might is right', and 'struggle' and conflict were an essential part of a 'natural order of affairs' in which only the 'strongest' survived. And far from being traumatised and horrified by the carnage and savagery of the First World War, in the course of which he had served as a humble corporal, it only seems to have whetted his appetite for conflict and battle.

Adolf Hitler, in other words, was a 'warmonger' in the simplest and most obvious meaning of the word. He wanted to fight wars for their own sake, not avoid them. But one of his mistakes was nonetheless to involve his beloved Reich in more conflict and confrontation than he needed to. There were campaigns that he could have avoided, and if he had done so then, alarmingly, he would have had a much greater chance of realising his ultimate goals in the East. In other words, he was also a 'warmonger' in the widest sense of the term because he embroiled himself in conflicts that were, from his own point of view, quite unnecessary.

This was essentially because the *führer*'s great ambition, of acquiring 'living space' in the East, had one great selling-point to his foreign audiences: his main target, the Soviet Union, was a communist state. As a result there were a lot of influential people in the capitalist democracies of the Western world, in France, Britain and the United States as well as Germany itself, who would have welcomed a German attack on a country that they regarded as a threat and a menace to their own interests. The British, after all, had tried to destroy or, as Winston Churchill put it, to 'strangle at birth', the Russian revolutionary government during the civil war of 1917–22, and Russophobia was particularly prevalent among the aristocrats of the Conservative Party. Churchill was even adamant that 'of all the tyrannies in history, the Bolshevik tyranny is the worst, the most destructive, the most degrading … far worse than German militarism'. It was, he continued, 'a plague bacillus' that was capable of destroying civilisation. By the mid-1930s, such hostility towards the Soviet Union and communism was still rife and was shared by the prime minister, Neville Chamberlain: in his view, any alliance between Britain, France and the Soviets would have simply allowed Stalin to contaminate the rest of Europe with his own very contagious, dangerous beliefs.[9]

Hitler could also have capitalised upon the anti-war feelings that were prevalent in Britain, France and America. Just two decades before, the three Western democracies had lost vast numbers of young men in the carnage of the First World War and they had no wish to go to war again. Hundreds of thousands of Britons supported a charismatic clergyman, the Reverend Dick Sheppard, who openly renounced war, and when he saw a crowd shouting for peace, in Trafalgar Square in London, King George V threatened to join in. 'I fear war more than fascism,' admitted a leading writer of the day, Vera Brittain, in a remark that summed up how many of her contemporaries felt. Senior figures in London and Paris were well aware that plans to avoid war were 'appealing to public opinion', while in July 1938, as tension with Germany rose, Neville Chamberlain powerfully evoked memories of the previous war in which 'seven million young men ... were cut off in their prime, (and) the 13 million ... were maimed and mutilated'. And in France, the generation that had experienced the First World War, and been traumatised by the experience, was known as the *génération du feu*. Opinion polls showed that a majority of Frenchmen approved of the Munich agreement of September 1938, which attempted to buy Hitler's sympathy and avoid war by surrendering whole swathes of Czechoslovakia, while the foreign minister Georges Bonnet admitted to 'a terror of war so deep' that he was 'prepared to accept any solution, however unjust or fraught with future disaster, so long as it did not impair Franco-German relations'.[10]

Hitler would have had a greater chance of exploiting these sentiments, turning them to his advantage, if he had avoided getting involved in the Spanish Civil War, which broke out between nationalist and communist militias in 1936. The nationalist leader, General Francisco Franco, quickly appealed to Germany for support and Hitler, after a two-hour rant late in the night of 25 July, agreed to provide limited assistance. Against the advice of his counsellors, the *führer* sent twenty planes to aid Franco, who had requested just ten. The airlift now gathered pace and by October 1936 almost 14,000 men, 44 artillery pieces and 500 tons of equipment had been flown – much of it in crates marked 'Christmas Decorations' – to the Nationalist rebels. Over the next three years, this significant force, not least the ace 'Condor Legion', played an important part in helping the general to capture important areas and win the war by 1939. Franco,' Hitler crowed, 'ought to erect a monument to the glory of the Junkers Ju-52. It is this aircraft that the Spanish revolution has to thank for its victory.'[11]

Hitler didn't want to risk antagonising Britain and France by openly admitting his involvement in the war, and on 24 August 1936 had signed a non-intervention agreement, pledging to keep out. Not long before, on 9 August, the Germans had also informed the British that 'no war materials had been sent from Germany and none will'. But Hitler almost immediately broke his word. His supposedly 'covert' support for Franco soon became an open secret and reinforced the impression that he was untrustworthy. Much more importantly, however, it seemed to suggest that Hitler had ambitions not just in the East but on France's southern borders, in the Mediterranean and in the Atlantic. This raised suspicions in Paris, resurrecting the same fears that had haunted French strategists during the rule of *Napoleon III*, who had been confronted by the threat of Bismarck's Prussian–Iberian alliance (see above). But it also alarmed Britain and America, both of which depended heavily on trans-Atlantic trade. German influence in Spain also posed a threat to France's colonial possessions in North Africa – Algeria, Tunisia and Morocco. And in France Hitler seemed even more of a menace because many French people identified strongly with the Spanish Republican cause: 'We saw there the symbol of liberty in peril and the prefiguration of our future,' commented the communist writer André Chapman.[12]

But Hitler gained little from fighting on Franco's behalf. He signed a treaty of cooperation with General Franco on 31 March 1939, but the two men simply guaranteed each other's neutrality if either country fought a war with a third party. And at a meeting with Hitler at a train station near the Franco-Spanish border on 23 October 1940, Franco made vague promises but offered nothing of substance, prompting Hitler to later comment that he would rather 'have three teeth taken out' than endure another nine hours of fruitless negotiations with Franco. Some senior Nazis had also hoped to make Spain into an 'informal economic colony': a document from Hermann Göring's Reich Air Ministry in 1937 declared an ambition 'not to industrialise Spain, a land purely complementary to Germany, but to exploit it as a basis of raw materials on the one hand, and to maintain and strengthen it as a recipient of German industrial exports on the other'. But they were also disappointed. Franco never surrendered control of the economy and instead continued to depend on British, French and American investors. Franco, fumed the German foreign minister Joachim von Ribbentrop, was an 'ungrateful coward'.

Nor had Hitler had any strategic or political need to get involved in Spain. Hitler always claimed that he had intervened there to stop 'Bolshevism' spreading like a 'virus' elsewhere in Western Europe. 'If Spain really goes communist, France in her present situation will also be Bolshevised in due course, and then Germany is finished. Wedged between the powerful Soviet bloc in the East and a strong communist Franco-Spanish bloc in the West, we could do hardly anything if Moscow chose to attack us.' But even if Franco had lost the war, then Hitler would have had an opportunity to rally the rest of Western Europe behind him into an anti-Bolshevik alliance. France and Britain might then have looked at his prospective invasion of the Soviet Union with sympathy. The Republican forces consistently received considerable material support from Stalin's Russia, so a communist victory in Spain, or even just a stronger Republican force, would therefore have heightened fears of communist aggression in Western capitals and driven them closer to Berlin.

Even if Hitler had been right to attach such importance to the fall of Spain to communism, then he never needed to enter the civil war. *Benito Mussolini* had a strong interest in Spanish affairs and had wanted to recruit Franco as a supporter of his new 'Roman Empire' in the Mediterranean. Mussolini soon sent a much stronger military force, comprising around 75,000 men, to support Franco, together with a vast quantity of arms and supplies. If Hitler ever did have any interest in helping Franco to win, then he could have merely stood back and encouraged the Italians to act on his behalf, perhaps finding some covert way of assisting Mussolini's efforts if *Il Duce* had ever needed any support. At the same time, he could have given Britain and France assurances that he would keep his distance from the Spanish Civil War, reiterating that he had no interest in acquiring territory in the west, and then won plaudits for keeping his word.

By supporting Mussolini's Spanish war in this more indirect way, Hitler could still have won the *Duce*'s sympathy. He needed this, above all, for his planned acquisition of Austria (*Anschluss* or 'union'), of which Mussolini regarded himself as the protector, and in October 1936 succeeded in striking up an alliance, the 'Rome-Berlin Axis'. Hitler's support for Franco certainly helped him to win Italian support but no more so than an indirect involvement that would have placated the Western powers. Besides, Hitler could have won Mussolini's heart in other ways, notably by helping the Italian armed forces subdue Abyssinia (see above), which they had invaded in 1935 and which had quickly become a festering sore of insurgent activity. Like Spain, Abyssinia would also have provided German forces with a testing ground to practice the arts of war, although it would have probably have been much less costly: around 300 Germans died fighting alongside Franco's forces. Mussolini would also have welcomed German involvement in Libya, where Italian farmers and agriculturalists were struggling to cultivate the land and were in dire need of more expertise and resources.

Harry Truman, 'The Gadget' and the Japanese Surrender (1945)

Shortly after eight o'clock on the morning of 6 August 1945, an American bomber flew over its target at an altitude of 31,600 feet and dropped a single bomb. In a carefully practiced manoeuvre, the pilot then immediately forced the plane sharply up into the air, desperately pushing it as fast and as hard as it would go. It was his only chance of escaping the blast that he knew was imminent.

Seconds later, a vast fireball erupted which, in several brief but terrible moments, shone more brilliantly than the sun. The tremors from a huge shockwave rocked the plane as a vast mushroom cloud began to form and started to climb high into the sky with a terrifying, unstoppable momentum.

The *Enola Gay*'s mission had been accomplished. Its atomic bomb had struck and virtually annihilated the Japanese city of Hiroshima. Around 75,000 civilians, perhaps many more, died instantly. And in the months and years ahead, tens of thousands were destined to fall victim to the deadly effects of radioactive fallout.

The man who had ordered the mission, the American president Harry S. Truman, was well aware of what was going to happen at Hiroshima that day. 'The Bomb' had already been tried out, at a test site in the deserts of New Mexico on 16 July. Truman himself had not been present on that ominous day: he was at the Potsdam Conference with other allied leaders to discuss the future of a post-Nazi Europe. But he immediately received a detailed description of what had taken place. The bomb, noted the president in his diary on 25 July when he heard the details and saw footage, 'may be the fire destruction prophesised in the Euphrates Valley era, after Noah and his fabulous ark ... it was the most terrible thing ever discovered'. But such dark fears for humanity did not stop him from feeling gleeful on hearing of the *Enola Gay's* success. 'This is the greatest thing in human history!' he exultantly proclaimed.

Truman wanted to use such overwhelming force to bring a swift end to the Second World War, or rather to the war against Japan in the Far East. The fight with Nazi Germany had already been won – the Germans had surrendered on 7 May – but the Japanese had fought on with ferocious determination. But although the American president felt confident that the attack on Hiroshima would immediately force his fanatical enemy to its knees, he was disappointed. In the hours that followed, there was only one major development: a declaration of war against Japan by the Soviet Union, whose army was already moving against Emperor Hirohito's forces. There was no word from Tokyo.

Truman now ordered a further attack, and on 9 August, at eleven o'clock in the morning, an American warplane dropped another atomic bomb on the city of Nagasaki. There were fewer casualties than at Hiroshima, but tens of thousands still died. Hours later, the Japanese surrendered. 'I swallow my own tears and give my sanction to the proposal to accept the Allied proclamation,' declared an emotional Emperor Hirohito. He was forced to 'bear the unbearable'.

Truman's tactics had worked. The Second World War was at last over. The American president, and his senior advisers, later congratulated themselves on how they had brought long years of hostilities to such a swift end. Unless they had used the atomic bomb against a fanatical enemy, they claimed, American forces would have been compelled to invade the Japanese mainland and would have suffered horrendous casualties in doing so. When the US Army had tried to capture just one Pacific island, Okinawa, from the Japanese they had lost 20,000 men and suffered 55,000 casualties in the process. In the past five months alone, the American army had lost 50,000 soldiers in the Pacific. An attack on the mainland, Truman continued, would have cost the lives of 100,000 American troops, maybe 250,000. Or even 500,000. So the two atomic bombs had effectively saved lives, even if they had killed around 100,000 innocent Japanese civilians.

Perhaps Harry Truman's decision to use the atomic bomb against such a determined and skilful foe was the right one. What he never explained, however, was why he used them in the way he did. Why, in other words, had two bombs been dropped in such quick succession? And was it really necessary to drop even one bomb on any civilian target, let alone a big city? In the months before the attack, he appears to have completely failed to ask such probing, difficult questions.

Truman's decision to use the newly developed atomic bomb against Japan was based on the advice of his 'able and conniving' adviser and secretary of state, 'Jimmy' Byrnes, and of an Interim Committee that had met in secret over the preceding few weeks. 'The gadget,' as the committee experts called the atomic bomb, should be dropped 'in the centre of the selected city' rather than upon specific military or industrial targets which were 'quite dispersed'. Three Japanese cities were named as possible targets: Kyoto, Hiroshima and Niigata. Then, on 1 June, its members presented Truman with their findings, arguing that the bomb should be dropped on these cities without giving Japan any prior warning.[13]

Truman had accepted its recommendations without questioning them. He then issued an ultimatum to the Japanese that made reference only to 'the utter devastation of the Japanese homeland' and 'the complete destruction of the Japanese armed forces' that he would inflict unless they surrendered unconditionally. When Tokyo failed to reply, Truman gave the order to drop the bomb and the *Enola Gay* had made her deadly move.

There were, however, several steps and measures, all of which were far less drastic, that the Interim Committee could have recommended and which Truman could subsequently have taken. They could have made the Japanese aware of the full, terrifying power of the atomic bomb, which the secretary of war Henry L. Stimson called 'the most terrible weapon ever known in human history'. The atomic tests in the New Mexico deserts had been filmed, and images of the explosions, still dramatic and shocking more than seven decades on, could have been shown to the Japanese authorities by representatives of neutral Switzerland, where informal discussions, 'back channels', were taking place between the Allies and the Japanese. Perhaps independent witnesses, from a neutral country, could even have been taken to New Mexico to witness the atomic test.

The assistant secretary of war, John J. McCloy, was one of the few figures who argued that the Japanese should be given advance warning of the existence of the bomb. Instead, the military chiefs wanted to take the Japanese by complete surprise and 'shock-and-awe' them into surrender. Such a threat might have yielded quick results if Truman had coupled it with a more flexible diplomatic approach: instead of demanding Japan's unconditional surrender, which was a huge sticking-point, Washington might have given Tokyo a guarantee that Japan's traditional imperial structure would remain in place.

Byrnes, Stimson and Truman would probably have wanted to veto any such move on the grounds that the outcome of the test in New Mexico was uncertain, and there was a chance that the bomb may not have detonated at all. However, they would have found it hard to lose any real credibility: the American air force was already hugely powerful and over the preceding months had obliterated Tokyo and other Japanese cities with incendiary bombs.

Even if Truman and his advisers had decided to drop 'the gadget' on the Japanese mainland without giving any prior warning to Tokyo, they could have struck a military target, or even a wasteland. Curiously, the president seems to have entertained this idea, noting that he had

> told the Secretary of War, Mr Stimson, to use (the bomb) so that military objectives and soldiers and sailors are the target and not women and children. Even if the Japanese are savages, ruthless, merciless and fanatic, we as the lead of the world for the common welfare cannot drop this terrible bomb on the old Capital (Kyoto) or the new (Tokyo). He & I are in accord. The target will be a purely military one.[14]

But he then changed his position and supported the argument put forward by his most bloodthirsty air chief, General Curtis LeMay, that 'the entire population got into the act and worked to make those airplanes or munitions of war ... men, women and children. We knew we were going to kill a lot of women and kids when we burned a town. Had to be done.'[15]

But this should have been a last resort. Truman could have ordered the dropping of a first bomb on wasteland and then threatened to follow it with a second, much more deadly attack on a city. The Emperor Hirohito could hardly have ignored the sight, sound and impact of an atomic bomb if it had been dropped near Tokyo. 'The explosion was visible for more than 200 miles and audible for 40 miles or more,' as Truman had exalted when he was told about the New Mexico explosion.

Even if, in a worst-case scenario, Hirohito had still not sued for peace after the dropping of a first atomic bomb on a Japanese wasteland, Truman could have given Tokyo more time to reach out for peace than he did. Instead, Nagasaki was bombed just three days after the first explosion on 6 August. To make Japan's defeat less humiliating than an outright surrender, Washington could have offered an immediate ceasefire and negotiations. At the very least, Truman could have waited several days longer after Hiroshima for a formal Japanese response. Instead, he paid heed to his advisers who argued that dropping two bombs in quick succession would persuade the Japanese that America had lots of bombs at its disposal: this was something that film of the New Mexico explosion, or simple bluff, could have done just as effectively. He was also concerned that the Soviet army would make rapid headway unless Japan quickly surrendered: but there was a limit to how much territory Stalin's men could seize in the space of a few more days.

Truman later recalled that 'he could think of no alternative' to the use of the atomic bomb against the Japanese mainland. But not only was there an alternative to attacking two cities, within hours of each other and without warning, but to the use of 'the gadget' at all. In the summer of 1945, there were a number of military chiefs, notably Admiral Ernest J. King, who argued that a naval blockade of Japan, enforced by America's near-total mastery of the Asiatic seas, would force Tokyo to surrender within a matter of months. Its mainland had already been heavily bombed and its economy was heavily dependent on imports.

Such an approach, however, might have cost the lives of thousands of Allied prisoners of war, held by the Japanese, and allowed Stalin's army to seize large areas of Manchuria. But for a time Truman entertained the very 'alternative' he later denied: 'I have to decide Japanese strategy,' he wrote in his diary on 17 June. 'Shall we invade Japan proper or shall we bomb and blockade? That is my hardest decision to date.'

However, Harry Truman's decision to use the atomic bomb in the way he did is certainly open to question. It reveals, in part, the uncertainty of a man who, in the summer of 1945, had only a few months of presidential experience. Having entered the White House only on 12 April, on the death of Franklin D. Roosevelt, he easily fell into the grip of the warmongers like James Byrnes who advised him.

Perhaps the president's decision was also influenced by his own experiences as an artilleryman in the First World War. Throughout 1917 and 1918 he saw and suffered, first-hand, the terrifying reality of frontline combat: 'There was more noise than human ears could stand,' he recalled months later. 'Men serving the guns became deaf for weeks afterward', while the terrain 'looked like humans, dirt, rock, trees and steel had been turned up by one plow'. Aghast, he realised just how many people had died, and wrote from his dugout that 'there are Frenchmen buried in my front yard and Huns in the back yard and both litter up the landscape as far as you can see'.[16]

But the victims that Truman saw and whose appalling experiences he shared were fellow soldiers. So when, years later, he learned of the casualties that the American army had already suffered at Okinawa and elsewhere, and of the losses they would inevitably incur in the event of an invasion of the Japanese mainland, he would have felt a deep empathy with their fate. His honourable compassion for his fellow American soldiers, however, perhaps obscured the unnecessary suffering of Japanese civilians.

But there is also another, less charitable conclusion. Truman's willingness to drop two bombs on Japan, in quick succession and without warning, was probably an act of retribution against 'the yellow man' who had so ruthlessly and effectively destroyed America's fleet in Pearl Harbour in 1941. Perhaps, too, it was a means of impressing and intimidating the Soviet Union as the Second World War gave way to the Cold War: he had met Joseph Stalin at the Potsdam Conference just days before he took the fateful decision about the use of the bomb, and recorded that the Soviet leader's demands for territory in the newly emerging Europe were 'dynamite'.

Whatever lay behind it, Harry Truman's decision to drop the atomic bomb on those fateful August days had unfortunate consequences for his own country, as well as for Japan and its innocent civilians. In particular, it confirmed all of Joseph Stalin's worst fears about America's intentions, aggravating his strong sense of paranoia. 'It was seen as a kind of anti-Soviet, a kind of sly, or cunning anti-Soviet political move,' as a leading historian has argued. 'It was seen very much as directed against the Soviet Union ... not only in order to deprive the Soviet Union of gains in the Far East, but generally to intimidate.' The Cold War between the West and the communist East had begun, and Truman's unnecessary actions had contaminated the atmosphere between the two blocs with a massive political fallout of mistrust and fear.[17]

Several months on, the leading physicist Robert Oppenheimer, who had pioneered 'the Gadget', publicly agonised about the events of those terrible days. 'I feel we have blood on our hands,' as he told the president. 'Never mind, it'll all come out in the wash,' snapped Truman, instructing his aides, 'Don't let that cry-baby in here again.'

6

THE COLD WAR ERA

Kim Il-sung's 'Biggest Mistake' with South Korea (1950)
Just five years after the end of the Second World War, Britain and
the United States became embroiled in another large-scale conflict,
one that was to cost them nearly 150,000 dead and wounded. The
venue was a peninsula in the Far East which many people struggled
to even find on the map.

In the early hours of Sunday 25 June 1950, soldiers of communist
North Korea suddenly let loose a massive artillery barrage along
the border with South Korea. Thousands of tanks then emerged
from carefully concealed positions and crashed relentlessly through
the barbed wire, brutally overwhelming any enemy force that had
dared to stand its ground. Trumpets now suddenly sounded out a
signal for tens of thousands of soldiers of the North Korean army
to surge forward. Forming four spearheads, these shock troops
encountered little resistance and by nightfall were in the suburbs
of the capital of the south, Seoul, before continuing their drive to
take the rest of city and then the entire peninsula.

This dramatic attack was masterminded by the North Korean
leader, Kim Il-sung, a short, dark man with smooth cheeks and
heavy-framed spectacles who typically wore a close-fitting Mao
suit. A former soldier who had fought with the Soviet Army during
the Second World War, he probably planned both the overall
strategy as well as some of the tactics that his soldiers and tanks
used as they swarmed southwards.

During his wartime years Kim had acquired the defining personality trait that helps explain why he undertook this invasion. For by 1950 he had not only purged, jailed, exiled or executed many of his political rivals but had also demanded the total adoration of the people he ruled. He was their 'Great Leader', and some years later would also publicly proclaim himself as 'the sun of mankind and the greatest man who has ever appeared in the world'. His control over the state gradually became total and the adulation he received increasingly absolute. Such a man was used to having his own way and probably regarded the very existence of a hostile regime in South Korea as a very personal affront. Doubtlessly, he also suffered from the same problem as his ally, the Soviet leader Joseph Stalin, and so many other warmongers: his aides and advisers were too terrified to disagree with him if he wanted to pursue a foolish idea. He completely lacked the advice and support that would have helped him to steer a more sensible and rational course.

Kim knew exactly what he wanted to achieve: the unification of two states, and then the establishment of a 'workers' paradise', under his own communist rule. The division between North and South Korea was, after all, a completely artificial one. Culturally, linguistically and historically, 'Korea' had always been a unified nation, even if for centuries it had been overshadowed by its imperial neighbours, China and Japan, and had therefore not often been a free and independent one.

During the Second World War, the Japanese had invaded and occupied the entire Korean peninsula. By the time of Tokyo's surrender, on 15 August 1945, the Soviets had invaded and occupied the north while the Americans had established a presence in the south: needing to draw a border somewhere, American officials had found an old map and noticed that a geographical demarcation known as the 38th Parallel happened to run almost exactly through the middle of the peninsula. True, it divided 75 streams, 12 rivers, 181 small cart roads, 104 country roads, 15 provincial all-weather roads, 8 good highways, 6 north–south rail lines, and even a house. But it was as well suited as anything else to act as the border between the communist north and the American-backed Republic of Korea. This was formally established on 15 August 1945 by the republic's new leader, seventy-year-old Syngman Rhee, who had returned to his homeland after thirty-four years in American exile.

Kim's plan was to seize the south, calculating that America and Britain would not make any effort to save Rhee's regime. Washington had pulled most of its forces out of the country shortly before, and the remarks made by a number of American officials also seemed to confirm Kim's impression of indifference to the fate of South Korea: in the event of an attack in this region, Secretary of State Dean Acheson publicly declared on 12 January 1950, America would initially expect 'local military forces' to stand up for themselves. And the American Joint Chiefs of Staff argued in 1949 that keeping communism out of South Korea would require 'prodigious effort and vast expenditure far out of proportion to the benefits to be expected'. But Kim still wanted the approval and support of his allies in Moscow and Beijing, visiting both Joseph Stalin and Chairman Mao Zedong in the weeks that preceded the attack. Stalin, and perhaps Mao, probably nodded approval to Kim's plan, although this has long been a matter of contention.

But Kim was wrong and had completely misjudged the strength of America's commitment to Rhee. News of the attack horrified *President Truman*, who was afraid that the conflict might spread across a much wider region and who immediately ordered an urgent deployment of American soldiers to stop the south from falling. And Kim and Stalin totally failed to see how their attack would look to the outside world: the invasion of June 1950 was pure, naked aggression and utterly lacked even the most spartan of fig-leaves to disguise its true nature. Within just hours, the United Nations Security Council was holding an emergency session in New York, where it condemned North Korea's 'breach of the peace'. Because of the absence of the Soviet delegate, who would otherwise have used his veto, the Council authorised an international mission to defend South Korea. The first American reinforcements arrived there just two weeks later and immediately checked Kim's soldiers before pushing them back to the 38th Parallel.

Kim and Joseph Stalin were in fact classic warmongers: they were using military force when they didn't need to. They overlooked a much simpler strategy: to destabilise the government in the south. Rhee's government had so many domestic enemies that Kim had every chance of sponsoring a coup against Rhee, or could have stood back and watched a new regime seizing power in Seoul and then established closer links with it. A new communist regime in Seoul could have expelled the small force of American troops that was still left in the country by 1950 – just 500 on the eve of war – and then 'officially' invited Kim to lend his support. In this scenario, Kim might perhaps have launched an invasion of the south with just enough respectability to have avoided international reaction.

If Kim and Stalin had built up a network of communist supporters in the south, then they would almost certainly have found a good deal of sympathy. Communist insurgents had a high standing among the people of both North and South Korea because they had orchestrated resistance to the Japanese occupation in the Second World War and because they could attack the exploitative, corrupt landlords who were a major source of grievance in the south: promises of setting up a 'workers' paradise' in the south fell on receptive ears. Rhee's reliance upon former collaborators with the hated Japanese made his regime highly unpopular: when the Korean War erupted in June 1950, every top commander in the South Korean Army except one was a former member of the Japanese Imperial Army.

There are plenty of indications of how much support the communists had in Rhee's territory. Vast numbers of ordinary peasants launched violent protests in late 1946, while the new South Korean Army was also shattered by major mutinies: some large towns were held for up to a week by mutineers with local support for up to a week. In May 1949 two frontier battalions defected, with their officers, to the north. And perhaps as many as 60,000 left-leaning insurgents were allegedly killed by Rhee's men on Jeju Island, off the south coast, in the months that followed an outbreak of rioting and rebellion in the spring of 1948.

There were numerous other communist-inspired riots that were crushed with a similar level of brutality, mainly because Rhee and his American patrons were fearful of communist instigation. The death toll of the 'Yeo-Su' rebellion in October 1948 was around 2,000. In the winter of 1948 and spring of 1949, the South Korean police arrested nearly 90,000 suspected dissidents, many of whom were dealt with by henchmen who had served under the Japanese Army in the war and learned the arts of torture in its ranks before finding themselves suddenly promoted into the higher echelons of Rhee's new regime. At the very least such heavy-handedness would have stirred deep animosity towards the Seoul regime amongst the families of dead and tortured. In other words, conditions were ripe for revolution.

By the summer of 1950, the communists in the south already had a substantial network of sympathisers to build on. There was a strong communist movement in South Korea in the late 1940s, and although its power had waned when Rhee's security men cracked down on its members and activities, it had fallen increasingly under the control of the north. In 1949, Pyongyang had ordered its agents to infiltrate the security apparatus in the south and to stir up unrest. 'There is no question but that communist action is actively and intelligently being carried out through our zone,' as John J. McCloy, the assistant secretary of war, wrote in 1945. But Kim was by this stage more involved in building up his armed forces, and signing up the support of Moscow and Beijing for his planned invasion, than pursuing this strategy.[1]

As a former South Korean officer remarked, years later, 'if Kim really wanted to get the south, by far his best course would have been to do nothing. His biggest mistake was to attack us.' In national elections, held just weeks before Kim's attack, Rhee's supporters had after all won only forty-nine seats, just a quarter of the total. Kim could have sponsored strikes, political protests, subversion and riots as well as, more ambitiously, assassinations and a high-level coup by communist sympathisers whose calls for reconciliation with the north would have struck a very powerful popular chord amongst a population that was clamouring for national unity. In this situation, Washington would not have had any reason, or excuse, to step in and stop Korea becoming a single country under the effective rule of the communist north.[2]

He could also have helped things along their way by broadcasting radio propaganda that was far less belligerent than the messages that preceded the events of 25 June: instead of threatening to use force against the south – threats that simply alerted Washington and Seoul to his plans – he could have instead highlighted the social injustices that ordinary South Koreans identified with.

Kim should have listened more to his foreign minister, a former wartime guerrilla leader called Pak Hon-Yong. Not only had Pak seen first-hand how effective such guerrilla tactics could be, but he had also lived and operated south of the border before being forced to flee into the north in 1946, where he appears to have pushed the case for subverting Rhee's regime, not attacking it outright.

General Douglas MacArthur 'Not Right in the Head' about Korea (1950)

Shortly after Kim Il-sung's forces had launched their invasion in June 1950, an American general visited the embattled South Korean capital. He struck, in the words of one witness, 'a sharp profile (that) was silhouetted against the black smoke clouds of Seoul as his eyes swept the terrain about him, his hands in his rear trouser pockets and his long-stemmed pipe jutting upward as he swung his gaze over the pitiful evidence of the disaster'. Around him were 'retreating, panting columns of troops interspersed with ambulances filled with groaning, broken men, the sky resonant with shrieking missiles of death and everywhere the stench and misery and utter desolation of a stricken battlefield'.[3]

General Douglas MacArthur certainly looked the part of the allied supreme commander, the man who had come to rescue South Korea from the ravaging communist army. At the age of seventy, noted one contemporary, he was 'still tall, erect, graceful and a fine figure of a man. His step is firm. His eyes are clear and alert. His face and hands are without wrinkles. His dress is meticulous.'

By the time he received news of the North Korean attack – he was at his office in Tokyo when a startled clerk had arrived with an urgent telegram – MacArthur was also a hugely experienced veteran of war as well as America's most revered soldier. After serving bravely on the Western Front in the *First World War*, winning numerous medals for gallantry, he had become the youngest major-general in the American army before taking up a post, in 1935, as the head of the Philippine army. His familiarity with the Far East had then qualified him as the ideal man to lead America's struggle against Imperial Japan on the outbreak of war on 8 December 1941, and four months later he was appointed as the Supreme Commander of Allied Forces in the region. His victories over the Japanese army made him a figure of adulation among many of both his fellow nationals and Asiatics, even among the people he had defeated when the Japanese surrendered in August 1945: every day, a small crowd of Japanese civilians gathered outside his Tokyo headquarters to catch a glimpse of him as he came and went.

But no mere mortal can be unaffected by the experience of having so much power, and such adulation, for so long. This was why, in 1950, MacArthur's critics and enemies in Washington were alarmed by his appointment as the commander-in-chief of the allied army in Korea. They pointed to his megalomania and to his complete lack of diplomacy and finesse. They were well aware of the huge, glaring defects of character, ranging from paranoia, delusions, fits of rage and threats of suicide that he had shown in the past. They knew how much he craved the hero-worship of others, surrounding himself with sycophantic staff during the war and loving the adulation – it seems the platonic adulation – of prostitutes, or indeed anyone else who could bolster his ego. No such man could be trusted, they argued, with such responsibility.

His gung-ho approach to war was just an extension of his ego. In the closing weeks of the Second World War he had advocated a full-scale American invasion of the Japanese mainland, knowing that he would be the man to lead it. But he wanted other, less drastic options, such as the naval blockade of Japan, to be sidelined (see *Harry Truman*). 'I believe the operation (invasion),' he once cabled, 'provides less hazards of excessive loss than any other that has been suggested and that its decisive effect will eventually save lives.' This was curious logic, since an embargo would not have cost any American, or even Japanese, lives, whereas an invasion would have caused mass carnage.

In fact, his vanity was obvious to anyone who met him. Even as a young but senior officer during the *First World War*, he seemed to want everyone to see how brave he was, particularly the newspaper correspondents who always seemed to surround him. In the Second World War, his cars had the first vanity number plate the Australians had ever seen – *USA 1*. He hated being photographed when wearing his glasses and carefully dyed his hair. He was immensely thin-skinned and could not bear criticism of any sort. Nor could he contend easily with the prospect of losing a battle, let alone an entire war. Every conflict had to be won outright, or else it was an affront to his name. Such an outcome was all the more unthinkable at the end of his career, which he feared would be a defining legacy that he would be remembered by.

Such personality traits help explain the unnecessary belligerence that Douglas MacArthur showed during the Korean War. Of course neither he, nor indeed anyone in London or Washington, can be judged a warmonger for wanting to defend South Korea. It is true that the Korean peninsula was probably as irrelevant militarily to America's national security as Poland had been to Britain's in 1939. And America, its forces demobilised and its attention focused on Europe, was in no better shape to defend it. But Kim's attack was not just a blatant violation of international law but viewed in Western capitals as being a test-case of who was going to win the Cold War: if they failed to show enough resolve to defend Rhee's regime, ran a convincing argument in London and Washington, then the Soviets and the Chinese, who were deemed, quite wrongly, to be in close alliance with Kim, would be emboldened and ramp up the pressure elsewhere in the world. The fate of the south had a 'symbolic significance', argued the influential American diplomat George Kennan. And in saving it from collapse, MacArthur showed audacity and brilliance by drawing up a plan to land a force of soldiers at Inchon, far behind enemy lines and then attacking Kim's soldiers where they least expected it. The tactic worked brilliantly and by October, less than four months after their offensive had begun, the communists were on the run.

Instead, MacArthur's true colours started to show themselves when the North Koreans were pushed back to where they had started: the 38th Parallel. With a certain amount of support from Cold Warriors, he wasted no time moving north of the border to destroy Kim's army, arguing that this was necessary and justified under the UN resolution 'to restore international peace and security'.

Invading North Korea dramatically extended the war. But even if it had had some legitimacy under international law, it didn't have any obvious justification. This was partly because there was nothing north of the 38th Parallel that was worth fighting for: all the best agricultural land and light industry, and more than half of the population, lay south of the border. 'Korea was of no strategic importance to the democratic powers,' admitted a British government report in November 1950. The north was even more backward than the south, where American officials had been shocked to find only horses and carts on the streets of the capital and been exasperated by the fact that virtually no one understood a word of English. So if, at the end of the war in 1945, the Soviets had simply invaded the south of Korea, then America would probably not have raised any serious protest, recognising that there were other much more important places to defend.

But MacArthur pushed his forces not just across the border into North Korea but ordered them up as far as the River Yalu, on the border with China. When he did so, he ignored warnings from his own advisers that he would risk provoking a massive counter-reaction from both China and Russia, escalating the Korean conflict on a terrifying scale and sparking the Third World War: the Japanese had used Korea as a springboard for their attacks on the both countries, ran the warnings, and both Beijing and Moscow would be afraid of America and Britain now doing the same. And he ignored, too, a warning from the Chinese army, which fired a terrifying but harmless artillery barrage close to where Western soldiers were located, as if to warn them away as they approached the Yalu. But this did not seem to deter MacArthur, who boasted that if the Chinese or Russians did join the war then they would face 'the greatest slaughter – they would be destroyed' and turned into a 'rabble'.

Instead he ordered his soldiers to continue northwards until it was too late. In October 1950, the Chinese slipped 130,000 heavily camouflaged soldiers south of the River Yalu and launched a massive assault on the Allied force. The sheer scale and ferocity of their attack immediately forced the Allied army into a humiliating flight and prompted MacArthur, hardly able to bear defeat, to be economical with the truth. His attack north of the 38th Parallel, he now commented, had only been 'a reconnaissance-in-force' and never an invasion.[4]

Even after China's entry into the war, MacArthur continued to warmonger, wanting to bomb the Chinese mainland to keep his foothold in North Korea. The only option, he argued, was to deploy an entire force of heavy B-29 'Superfortress' bombers to destroy the bridges over the River Yalu and to carry out 'the subjection of all installations in the north area ... to the maximum of our air destruction'. More alarmingly, on 24 December he demanded that President Truman deploy twenty-six atom bombs against a number of 'retaliation targets' in China and North Korea. In one interview, which was published until after his death, General MacArthur described his plan to drop thirty to fifty atom bombs at the point where Korea meets China 'to spread ... a belt of radioactive cobalt ... with an active life of between 60 and 120 years'. 'My plan,' he said, 'was a cinch.'

MacArthur was certainly not America's only warmonger at this supremely tense moment. Several congressmen and senators were also pressing the case for an atomic strike on China. Admiral Forrest Sherman wanted Truman to declare a full-scale war with China, even without a United Nations resolution, while others amongst the top brass advocated carrying out 'damaging naval and air attacks' against Mao's regime and sponsoring a guerrilla campaign that its domestic enemies would undertake. But MacArthur was the most vocal of the hawks and the figurehead of those who wanted to take the fight to China.

His hawkish position stood in marked contrast to that of the British foreign secretary, Ernest Bevin, who wanted 'to allay the reasonable fears of the Chinese lest the Western powers should occupy large areas of Asia territory under a plea of military necessity'. Even Winston Churchill, not one to ordinarily shy away from the prospect of battle, argued that 'the United Nations should avoid by every means in their power becoming entangled inextricably in a war with China'. There was a real chance, they and many others judged, that both Britain and America would be drawn into a long, unwinnable war against both China and the Soviet Union.[5]

Finally, the American president, Harry Truman, concurred with his British allies. Won over by the more moderate line of the State Department, he decided that it was 'tragically wrong for us to take the initiative in extending the war ... Our aim is to avoid the spread of the conflict'. On 11 April 1951, Truman relieved MacArthur of his command, concluding that he was a victim of his own obsessions and hubris. A famous cartoon the next day showed MacArthur incredulously reading about Truman's order, and exclaiming: 'Who does he think he is – the President?'

MacArthur, in other words, had become carried away. If he had been determined to attack North Korea in 1950, then instead of ordering his own men to cross the 38th Parallel he could have stood back and allowed only South Korean soldiers to advance. In this scenario the Korean War could have remained a purely Korean affair, and neither China nor Russia would have any reason to have felt threatened. The South Korean forces could perhaps have united their country, allowing the three great powers to strike a deal on its independence and non-militarisation. More realistically, Rhee's army could have created a neutral buffer zone, north of the 38th Parallel, that would have helped to guarantee the south's security. And there was certainly no need to extend the war into China. Not only was such a war unwinnable, particularly when American resources were so heavily committed elsewhere in the world and hugely overstretched in Korea, but there was no obvious reason to attack a country that posed no clear threat to American interests.

MacArthur's warmongery may have been driven by an addiction to battle after so many years of continuous action in the Second World War. But perhaps the most important influence was his conviction that a decisive battle between 'the free world' and communism was 'inevitable'. In his eyes the United States and its allies would have to confront their enemies 'sooner or later', and Korea seemed as good a place as any to do so. And convinced of the 'evil' of communism, his conviction more readily envisaged destroying his enemy than merely tolerating it.

Perhaps he also suffered from a curious complex about China, one that was prevalent in America at the time. The fall of China to Mao's communist army in 1949 was a huge blow to the morale of many Americans, who had a deep attachment to a country that they had fought alongside in the Second World War, when Chiang Kai-shek's nationalist forces had confronted the Japanese. China had also been a favoured venue for many American missionaries, who had pursued their evangelical mission there for many years. George Kennan, for example, noted that many Americans had a 'certain sentimentality towards the Chinese', while after 1949 Senator Joseph McCarthy carried out his infamous 'witch hunts' against American officials who were deemed to have 'betrayed' China. MacArthur was probably suffering from just such a 'China complex' when he chose to take the war to the Yalu River and then to the Chinese mainland. After the entry of China into the fray, and their dramatic battlefield successes as they routed the Allies and drove them southwards, he then became determined to exact revenge.[6]

Whatever was driving him northwards, the war continued for another two and a half bloody years, during which time thousands of soldiers and civilians died and many more were wounded. Before the guns fell silent, around 5 million people had lost their lives, including 54,000 American soldiers. It was a prolongation that could easily have been avoided if MacArthur had ordered his men to stop at the border and sue for peace. The lives of thousands of innocent North Koreans would also have been spared. Unlike the later American campaigns in the skies over Cambodia, Laos and Vietnam, the massive US bombing of North Korea was, and remains, little noticed: the US Air Force bombed every city and town and even many villages north of the 38th Parallel and eventually even ran out of targets. A Soviet post-war study concluded that 85 per cent of the state's buildings were destroyed, while General Curtis LeMay, who asked his superiors for permission to 'burn down' five of the biggest cities in the north, admitted that 'over a period of three years or so, we killed off – what – twenty percent of the population', which would have amounted to nearly two million people.[7]

Later, President Truman regretted not dismissing MacArthur before he crossed the 38th Parallel. 'I've given it a lot of thought and finally concluded that there were time when he [MacArthur] ... wasn't right in the head ... he just wouldn't let anybody near him who wouldn't kiss his ass ... I should have fired him.'[8]

Abu Jihad (Khalil al-Wazir) Provokes the Israelis into Gaza (1955)

In the summer of 1955, a twenty-year-old Palestinian radical called Khalil al-Wazir conceived an audacious plan to redraw the map of the Middle East. His idea was to attack Israel and provoke a massive response that would force Egypt into a fight with the Jewish state. Other Arab states would then be drawn into the fray, he calculated, and the Jewish state would be forced to make concessions or even be completely overrun. At the very least, the clash of arms would focus international attention on the forgotten plight of the Palestinians.

Al-Wazir, who later became better known by his *nom de guerre*, Abu Jihad, had been determined to wage war with the Israelis ever since, as a child, he and his parents had fled their native city of Ramlah, which became part of Israel on its formation in 1948. Taking refuge in a city of tents in Gaza, he joined a group of lightly-armed insurgents, known as *fedayeen*, that made pinprick raids against the Israeli border or, more daringly, deeper within its territory.

In February 1955, al-Wazir and several fellow *fedayeen* slipped through the porous border between Israel and Gaza. This was something a lot of Palestinian refugees regularly did, often because they wanted to return to their former homelands to search for lost family members and possessions. But on that night the *fedayeen* had a darker intent as they headed for a reservoir near the town of Fallujah. 'We used a lot of TNT and the explosion made a big flood,' as he later revealed. 'I saw seeds and plants from Jewish settlements being swept along by the floodwaters. We were happy.' The Israelis claimed that a Jewish farmer was also killed that night.[9]

The insurgents knew exactly what savage reprisals Israel would take. Just a few months before, on the night of 14 October, hawks in Tel Aviv, notably the prime minister David Ben-Gurion and his chief of staff General Moshe Dayan, who described retaliation as a 'life-drug', had ordered a massive raid on the Jordanian village of Qibya. In retaliation for the killing of three Israeli settlers, a commando unit under Major *Ariel Sharon* had attacked this settlement, detonating forty-five buildings and killing sixty-six civilians, many of them women and children: even the pro-Zionist *New York Post* was reminded of Lidice, the Czech village that Nazi troops annihilated in retaliation for the assassination of Reinhard Heydrich. Al-Wazir was under no illusion that another attack, like the one he and his accomplices carried out that February night, would provoke a similar level of 'massive retaliation'.

They did not have to wait long to get the results they wanted, for on 28 February Ariel Sharon carried out Operation Black Arrow, striking the Egyptian army and Palestinians in Gaza. The Egyptian army lost thirty-six soldiers and suffered twenty-nine casualties wounded, against nine dead Israelis. The outcome was deeply humiliating for the Egyptian leader, President Gamal Abdul Nasser.

But al-Wazir's calculations were wrong on all counts. There had never been any chance that Nasser would want to fight Israel and engage in a conflict that he knew he was going to lose. By 1955 it was obvious that Israel's armed forces were supremely well trained, equipped and organised, far more so than any of the Arab countries, perhaps even if they were all acting together. The Egyptian leader had visited Gaza shortly before Israel's attack and declared that he didn't want the Gaza–Israel border to become a battleground, adding that the Israelis probably felt the same way.

In fact, al-Wazir's warmongering was to have even more dire consequences for the Arab cause he championed. Until the Gaza raid, the Egyptians had tried hard to curb *fedayeen* attacks into Israel, even if it was impossible to exercise full control over such a long and porous border. After Gaza, Cairo completely changed tack and decided to organise, train and arm these insurgent units for Egypt's self-defence. The growing capabilities of the *fedayeen* contributed to a vicious spiral of violence, causing even more ill-feeling in Israel and heightening demands for an all-out attack on Egypt that led to the *Suez war in 1956*. Nasser also looked to the Soviet Union for arms, dramatically escalating tensions in the region and driving the United States even further away from the Palestinian cause.

And although al-Wazir wasn't aware of it, Nasser had been conducting secret talks with the moderate Israeli leader, Moshe Sharett. The dialogue had started the previous October and then faltered when Sharett cancelled a top-secret meeting between the two countries in Paris. By February, as a historian of the period writes, 'The dialogue was severely strained ... but not irretrievably lost. The Gaza raid, on the other hand, dealt it a fatal blow.' An opportunity to heal the rift between two countries, and take a big step towards the resolution of the Arab–Israeli dispute, had been missed.[10]

Had he been more astute, al-Wazir would have avoided violence altogether. Instead of being a warmonger, he could have used entirely peaceful means to highlight the cause he cared so much about – the plight of Palestinian refugees. He could have done this, for example, by driving a wedge between Israel and the United States, which at this time was a very real possibility. In 1954 there was a growing rapprochement between Cairo and the Americans, who wanted to recruit both the Egyptians and the Iraqis into a new security alliance that could confront the Soviet Union. This was a development that deeply alarmed Israel, which was desperate not to be sidelined by Washington, and its secret service embarked on a covert dirty tricks campaign, codenamed 'Operation Susannah', to discredit Egypt in the eyes of the Americans.

Al-Wazir could have cultivated sympathetic Western officials, perhaps inviting them to Gaza or to Palestinian refugee camps, in a bid to persuade them of his case. In particular, there were many powerful and wealthy figures in the American oil industry who were keen to get a foothold in petroleum-rich Arab countries and who would have lobbied for the Arab cause. Just such an individual was a US State Department chief called Henry Byroade, an assistant secretary of state who had already caused offence in

Tel Aviv by criticizing some of Israel's laws. Appointed American ambassador to Cairo in 1955, Byroade worked hard to secure American support for Nasser and to increase the sluggish rate at which British and French arms were arriving in Egypt. His speeches and views, argued Moshe Sharett, 'aimed an arrow at the very pupil of Israel's eye'. But belligerent rhetoric from insurgents like al-Wazir made his task even more difficult. By contrast, placing stories and photographs in the Western media of Israeli actions against Palestinians, whether Israel's actions were justified or not, would also have created or accentuated a gulf between Israel and Western governments.[11]

But al-Wazir was a classic warmonger, reaching for the trigger instead of other less drastic but much more effective measures. He was blinded by the rawest emotions, not least a hatred towards a state that he felt had robbed him of his own homeland. Ultimately he failed to see that the Arab–Israeli dispute was, and remains, a political dispute, not a military one.

Sir Anthony Eden 'Goes Bananas' over Suez (1956)

At a high-level meeting held at his official residence, Chequers in Buckinghamshire, the British prime minister Sir Anthony Eden heard the dramatic news that France was secretly colluding with Israel to attack Egypt and oust its leader, President Gamal Abdul Nasser. It was October 1956 and after several long, frustrating months, Eden at last had an excuse to destroy his opponent. He could 'scarcely contain his glee' at the prospect of toppling Nasser, as one eyewitness, the minister Sir Anthony Nutting, later recorded.[12]

The Suez Canal crisis was one of the most turbulent and traumatic episodes in British post-war history. On 29 July, the Egyptian leader – 'Grabber Nasser' as a British tabloid called him – had stunned the world by nationalising the Suez Canal Company. 'From the strictly legal point of view,' the cabinet noted, 'his actions amounted to no more than a decision to buy out the shareholders.' But more seemed to be at stake. Owned by British and French shareholders, the company had exclusive rights to steer international shipping along the canal. But under Nasser's plan, the company would fall under the control of the Egyptian government, which therefore had the power, at least on paper, to turn some, or all, ships away if it wanted to.

The Egyptian leader, in other words, effectively had the capability to blockade something that both Britain and France were hugely dependent on: Middle Eastern oil. He seemed to have, as Eden put it, 'his finger on our windpipe'. Nasser had already tried blockading Israeli ports so it seemed quite possible that he could also hold the Western world to ransom if he wanted.

In the weeks that followed, Eden became obsessed with destroying Nasser but lacked a clear excuse to attack because there was no immediate threat to British national security that could justify an assault under international law. But at Chequers on that autumn day, Eden heard about an Israeli proposal that he felt would give him the clear justification he needed.

The idea was simple but supremely duplicitous. The Israelis would launch a major attack on Egypt, claiming to the outside world that they were retaliating against a border raid carried out by local Arab insurgents [see *Abu Jihad*]. Their assault would then give Britain and France a pretext to send their own armed forces into Egypt to seize the Suez Canal. They had a right to guard the canal, they could plausibly claim, at a time when war between Egypt and Israel imperilled its security. Then, during a top secret, three-day conference outside Paris, in late October, this audacious plan was elaborated and agreed upon in the utmost secrecy. Just days later, the Israelis attacked Egypt's Sinai desert and the Suez operation began. The plan would be kept quiet from Britain's closest and most important ally, the United States, while the United Nations would be completely sidelined. 'Please let us keep quiet about the United Nations,' as Eden contemptuously scrawled on a piece of paper in the early weeks of the crisis.

But the plan was always fraught with extreme risks. Almost everyone was going to suspect the British and French of secretly colluding with Israel, even if Eden was prepared to tell parliament that he knew nothing in advance of Israel's war plans and ordered the destruction of a copy of the secret protocol that his foreign secretary, Selwyn Lloyd, had signed. And once the British-French operation got underway, it would be extremely risky and vulnerable to unexpected resistance in the towns, cities and in the stretches of desert where the Allied soldiers would land and which they would then have to capture and hold.

Even if they did seize the canal, there was the awkward question of knowing what to do next. Nasser could appeal to the United Nations and demand, with every justification, that the Allies should hand the canal back to the Egyptian government. Above all, there was a real chance that the Americans would not want to support their strongest Western allies. The chancellor, Harold Macmillan, convinced Eden that President Eisenhower and his secretary of state, John Foster Dulles, would immediately support the venture – 'they will lie doggo!' as he put it in a memorable phrase – but others were not sure.

The operation proved calamitous on almost every count. The Egyptians put up an unexpected fight at Port Said, forcing the commander, General Charles Keightley, to use a much heavier hand than he expected. There were stormy, almost deafening sessions in the House of Commons, where some members openly accused Eden and his ministers of 'an international conspiracy' and deceit: 'Will the government stop lying?' asked 'Nye' Bevan, in his distinctive Welsh accent. Others made veiled hints of such duplicity. 'Quite the most shattering experience I've ever sat through ... the divisions, the uproar, the emotion were much worse than at the time of Munich,' noted one journalist who reported on the parliamentary debate that followed. Amid cries of treachery from supporters of the action and of warmongering from its opponents, Britain was more deeply and bitterly divided than at any time since the appeasement crisis of 1938. Now the Suez invasion, as its leading historian has written, had 'convulsed the country, tearing apart every party, every class, every family, opening up the kind of civil rift which occurs in Britain not more than two or three times a century'.[13]

A storm of protest also erupted from world capitals, not just within the communist world but from the Commonwealth countries that were supposed to be Britain's allies but where memories of colonialism were recent and bitter. 'I have come across no grosser act of naked aggression,' fumed Pandit Nehru, the Indian leader. But most importantly, news of the operation infuriated the White House, which refused to support its allies with emergency economic aid as investors took fright and their currencies plunged. Afraid that the attack might push Egypt, and others, into the Soviets' hands – although some also claimed that the Americans were a little jealous of Britain and France's traditional influence in the Middle East – Washington demanded an immediate ceasefire. Britain and France had no choice but to comply and halted their advance after just eight days, on 6 November.

Perhaps such supreme risks would have been worth taking if there had been no option other than war. But, tragically, Eden had made his move long before all other options were exhausted. On the eve of the allied military operation, Nasser had not even threatened to obstruct Western oil tankers, let alone gone ahead and done so. The Egyptian leader knew that this would have been a clear provocation and he was too shrewd and skilled a political operative to fall into such a trap. In any case, he had a lot to lose from doing so, since he would have forfeited the highly lucrative transit revenues that maritime traffic brought.

Eden would have done better to have listened to the two doves in his cabinet, the minister of defence, Sir Walter Monckton, and the First Sea Lord, Lord Louis Mountbatten. Both men gave prescient warnings about the dangers, both military and political, of using force against Egypt. 'I can only see the consequences of choosing force rather than negotiation as establishing a second and more dangerous Cyprus,' predicted Monckton, as he pointed to the possibility of a guerrilla-style campaign against an occupying army. He added that Nasser had not as yet sabotaged the canal but might well be tempted to do so if the outside world used force. Monckton also pointed out that even if in a worst-case scenario the Suez Canal was closed, then shipping could still move around the Cape of Good Hope. New 'supertankers' were already being pioneered, he continued, and Britain could also stockpile larger reserves of oil in case of a crisis.[14]

The American president, Dwight D. Eisenhower, also wrote to Eden and advised him of the less drastic options that confronted him, as well as of the dangers of using force. 'We can expect the

Arabs to rally firmly to Nasser's support (if) there should be a resort to force without thoroughly exploring and exhausting every possible peaceful means of settling the issue.' It was better, he continued, to 'concentrate on deflating him through slower but sure processes [such as economic pressures, Arab rivalries, a new pipeline to Turkey, more oil for Europe from Venezuela]'.[15]

Instead, he urged Britain to simply stick with its allies, most obviously the United States, which could not afford to sacrifice or alienate its closest friends, Britain and France. Monckton saw what Eden failed to see: that the security of the Suez Canal was in the interests of every country, not just Britain. The canal was, as the 1888 Convention of Constantinople had put it, 'a waterway economically, commercially and strategically of international importance'. Together the three Western countries could have gently cajoled Nasser into striking a mutually acceptable agreement, one that would have given London the guarantees it needed while offering him generous terms that, as Mountbatten argued, 'would be patently unreasonable and provocative for him to reject'. Winning guarantees from Nasser required patient dialogue and enlisting foreign support instead of using force that would inadvertently aggravate the situation and drive him further away. As Herbert Hoover, an under-secretary of state in Washington, argued, the United States and its Western allies needed guarantees from Nasser about the canal's security to stop the West's position in the Middle East being 'cut down'.[16]

That such a hugely experienced and talented prime minister should have made such errors is astonishing. Anthony Eden had decades of experience as a diplomat and politician, having started his career in the mid-1920s as a debonair, immaculately dressed aristocrat who had the polish and self-confidence of an Eton and Christ Church scholar. As Britain's wartime foreign secretary, he had served and helped save his country in its darkest times, and worked alongside a supremely demanding, bullying and cantankerous prime minister. And he showed his inner steel by shouldering his hugely demanding political duties even during times of extreme personal crisis, such as the loss of a son in the Second World War and a subsequent divorce.

But for some reason and at some point Eden became a warmonger and spectacularly misjudged the Suez operation. Some historians think his bad decisions, like those of *Napoleon*, were the result of the ill-health that had dogged him ever since a botched gallbladder operation nearly three years before. Just a few weeks before the war, he had suffered from a blocked bile duct that had sent his temperature soaring and forced him to undergo emergency surgery. Worn out by the intense diplomacy and stress of the Suez crisis, which lasted throughout the long months of the summer and autumn, his closest aides watched the emotionally and physically exhausted prime minister lose his grip and his terminology and references become increasingly hysterical. 'If we lose out in the Middle East we shall be immediately destroyed,' as he fumed in a typical outburst at the height of the crisis. 'He has gone bananas', as one of his advisers, Sir Dermot Boyle, told a colleague in that tumultuous summer.[17]

More specifically, he had become so obsessed with the Egyptian leader that his judgment had become clouded. Although he had met Nasser, at a dinner in February 1955, and been struck by his charm, energy and dynamism, Eden's imagination seemed to draw an increasingly distorted image of the man. In private conversation, he often compared Nasser with *Napoleon*, *Hitler* and, more typically, *Mussolini*. His analogies with Munich, appeasement and the Second World War increasingly saturated his rhetoric and conversation, a classic case of a condition that the political philosopher Leo Strauss termed *Reductio ad Hitlerum*. His adversary was 'a Muslim Mussolini', as he told Eisenhower, 'who must be dealt with as the dictators in the thirties'. He saw the hand of Nasser wherever something seemed to go against British interests, notably the sacking of a British military adviser, General Sir John Glubb 'Pasha', by the Jordanian king in March 1956. One British minister later revealed that Eden had even secretly called for the assassination of the Egyptian. 'I was horrified to get a telephone call over an open line,' Anthony Nutting recalled thirty years later, 'in which Anthony Eden said, "What's all this poppycock you've sent me about isolating and quarantining Nasser? Can't you understand – and if you can't understand it will you come to the Cabinet and explain why – that I want Nasser", and he actually used the word "murdered".'[18]

Nasser was like the Iranian leader Mohammed Mossadeq, who had infuriated and alarmed London five years before by nationalising the Anglo-Iranian Oil Company. Both men unmistakably embodied and exemplified the fact that Britain was no longer an imperial power. Nasser, in particular, interfered with a waterway, the Suez Canal, that had resonated strongly in the British imperial consciousness. The canal, as Eden said, was 'our great imperial lifeline', one that had linked Britain with its great colonial possession, India.

The end result was that the Americans assumed the role of peacemaker and negotiator while trying to rein in their bellicose European allies. Eisenhower urged restraint, pointing out 'the unwisdom even of contemplating the use of military force at the moment' and its 'far-reaching consequences'[19].

Whatever lay behind it, Eden's warmongery wrecked his own, and his country's, reputation. 'We had not realised that our government was capable of such folly and such crookedness,' wrote a highly influential newspaper editor in a piece that both captured, and helped to shape, the mood of the moment. Such accusations gained credence when it later emerged that Eden had even despatched two officials to Paris to destroy written evidence of his secret agreement with France and Israel. Meanwhile, in the House of Commons, one backbencher taunted the somewhat effete prime minister by claiming that he had invaded Egypt 'to prove that he had a moustache'. Within weeks, Anthony Eden resigned as prime minister and withdrew from public life, still strenuously denying that he had worked in secret collusion with Israel.

The outcome of the flawed, tragic and unnecessary Suez operation was no different from what Eden could have achieved by negotiation. Within days of a ceasefire, a United Nations force arrived in Cairo to secure the Canal and guard international shipping. The force also spent six months clearing the Suez Canal of damaged and sunken ships – Nasser had blocked its waters in retaliation for the allied attack – before it was eventually reopened in April 1957.

Guy Mollet Targets Nasser (1956)

Anthony Eden does not deserve to be lambasted as the chief warmonger of the Suez campaign. It was the Israeli leader, David Ben-Gurion, who wanted to attack Egypt and concocted a plan for secret collusion with France. And it was the French leader, 50-year-old Guy Mollet, who urged Eden to use force, arguing that war was the only real option to fix Nasser and settle the Suez dispute.

There was a certain irony about Mollet's role as a warmonger. A quiet, rather withdrawn man who had been a schoolteacher and then a small-town mayor before entering post-war politics, he had been a strong pacifist until the German invasion of France in 1940. But although the experience of enemy occupation made him harden his views, he is not known to have played any part in resistance activities against the Nazis and by the time he became prime minister, in January 1956, he had still hardly ventured any bellicose remarks in general, let alone about Egypt and Nasser in particular.

Within just weeks of becoming prime minister, however, his views became more hawkish. In March, Eden invited him to his official residency at Chequers, where Mollet expressed very strong views about the dangers posed by Egypt's leader. France, he argued, faced a new threat to its colonies and possessions in North Africa posed by an alliance between 'Pan-Slavism' and 'Pan-Islam'. 'All this (is) in the works of Nasser, just as Hitler's policy (was) written down in *Mein Kampf*,' he claimed. 'Nasser has (the) ambition to recreate the conquests of Islam.'[20]

Mollet's preoccupation was the security not of Tunisia and Morocco, both of which had achieved, or were about to achieve, their independence from French colonial rule. His concern was Algeria, which for the past eighteen months had been engulfed in a bitter struggle between insurgents, who demanded its independence from France, and French nationals who regarded Algeria as an integral part of France. Desperate to maintain France's grip over Algeria, Mollet's more hawkish side now started to emerge. He appointed a hard-line governor in Algiers, Robert Lacoste, and hugely increased the number of soldiers there to 400,000 men. And he may have given the approval, although his involvement has never been proven, in a daring but totally shameless kidnapping of the Algerian dissident leader Ahmed Ben Bella. What is certain is that, during his premiership, the French began to routinely use torture in their troubled North African province. One French soldier admitted that 'we make the Gestapo and SS look like children', while another, Major Paul Aussaresses, vividly described the routine tortures he and his fellow soldiers carried out, adding that the leaders at the top were 'in the know'[21].

At the same time, Mollet blamed Nasser for orchestrating the troubles. At the very least, argued officials in Paris, the Egyptian leader was stirring the agitators and supplying them with arms. They knew that the rebels hid supplies of Egyptian arms around Sollum, in the Western desert, and every night they heard Cairo Radio broadcasting inflammatory messages about the evils of 'colonialism' and the need for 'liberation'.

In the spring and summer of 1956, before he had even announced the nationalisation of the Suez Canal Company, French officials increasingly demonised the Egyptian leader. Nasser seemed to embody and exemplify France's struggle in North Africa, just as he equally embodied Britain's own loss of empire. It was upon a mental image of his person that French officials projected all the anguish and bitterness of their increasingly desperate struggle to retain their grip over Algeria.

One of those who shared this collective mindset was the foreign minister, Christian Pineau. There were only a few weeks left, as he told Dulles in early August, to save not just Algeria but the whole of North Africa from Nasser's grip. After that, France's colonial territories in Black Africa would quickly follow.

Mollet, Pineau and their ministers, Louis Mangin and Maurice Bourgès-Maunoury, were enthralled by Israeli suggestions of using force to carry out regime change in Cairo. Elaborate security plans were drawn up to hide the true identities of senior Israeli officials, including General Moshe Dayan and Golda Meir, who flew into an obscure aerodrome outside Paris heavily disguised as 'Tunisian officials' and quickly shuffled into waiting cars, to take part in a series of highly secretive meetings and draw up their plans of war.

In fact, those who met Nasser quickly found that he completely failed to resemble the distorted picture they had conjured in their imagination. Christian Pineau, who met the Egyptian in the spring of 1956, found him to be level-headed and moderate. Mollet, however, was not interested in hearing good words about a man he had come to vilify, condemning him as a 'monument of duplicity' and urging the British to join France and Israel in a collective strike on Cairo.[22]

During his talks with Pineau, Nasser had also categorically denied having any involvement, at least any meaningful involvement, with the Algerian rebels. He assured his visitor 'on his word of honour as a soldier' that Egypt was not training any of France's enemies. And although Mollet would have none of it, Nasser was in fact speaking the truth. The Algerian rebels were bitterly disappointed by the largely symbolic supplies that he was providing for them. Egypt's contribution was 'negligible', as the rebels' arms procurement chief later said, adding that 'because of the need for solidarity, we could not say so'. In fact nearly all of the rebels' arms and supplies came from neighbouring Tunisia, although some were also shipped in from West Germany and other European suppliers.[23]

But Mollet and his ministers were so determined to strike Cairo that they would probably have taken his country to war, alongside Israel, even if Britain had not been prepared to join. France secretly shipped voluminous quantities of arms and personnel to Israel while bracing itself to unleash an attack. One of Mollet's generals even suggested dropping French bombs on Beersheba and claiming that Egypt was responsible, thereby giving Israel a pretext for attack Nasser.

Mollet's warmongery against Nasser at Suez in fact proved counter-productive. Using force against Cairo simply reinforced the impression of France as a bullying power that used brutal tactics against its enemies outside Algeria as well as within. Over the preceding year France's repressive measures against the Algerian rebels had already caused their ranks to swell and attacking Egypt was now set to do the same. Far from relenting, the war in Algeria merely escalated, forcing President Charles de Gaulle to admit defeat and, by doing so, bringing France to the brink of civil war. Paris had also been desperate to avoid internationalising the Algerian dispute: it was a matter of French internal politics, Mollet and others always argued, and was therefore no business of the outside world. But by attacking Egypt, the French immediately succeeded in attracting the attention of the United Nations and the United States, which wanted to resolve it before the Soviets started to exploit the ensuing chaos.

Using force against Nasser also brought all manner of other problems. The French wanted to get rid of Nasser but they never had any clear idea of who or what would follow in his footsteps. The most likely outcome of Suez, had the operation lasted longer, was the presence of a Franco-British army of occupation that would have been terrorised by Egyptian insurgents and then forced to beat a hasty retreat, leaving behind a more radicalised and fanatically anti-Western regime. Allocating so many soldiers to Egypt would also have meant, and did mean, taking them away from Algeria, the very place that really mattered to the French. And even if the Algerian rebels had been backed by Nasser, they would simply have looked elsewhere if Mollet, Eden and Ben-Gurion had managed to depose him.

Mollet would have done much better to try and seal off the rebels' supply lines that ran closer to Algeria: the resources that were used against Egypt throughout 1956 could have been used to monitor and disrupt the arms that were smuggled across Algeria's deserts and along its coasts. At the same time, he could have made good use of Nasser's offer to open up dialogue with the rebels: Mollet had wanted to start negotiations but backed away when Pineau told him of Nasser's offer.

John F. Kennedy's Invasion of Cuba (1961)

In a top-secret meeting on 4 April 1961, America's newly elected president, John F. Kennedy, told his senior advisers that he had made up his mind to use military force against Fidel Castro's regime in Cuba. He had, according to one account, an 'earthly expression' that bore unmistakable witness to the strength of his resolution. When almost no one in the room voiced any opposition – there was just one person who spoke up against the plan – then the president was ready to give the order to send 1,400 militiamen, nearly all of them Cuban exiles, to land along a remote stretch of the island's shore called the 'Bay of Pigs' and begin their armed campaign to topple Castro.

Right from its onset, in the early hours of 17 April, the operation was a fiasco. A series of pre-emptive air raids on Cuban bases failed to materialise: forty sorties had been planned but only eight, all of which were largely ineffective, were ever carried out. By the time the exiles landed they had already lost the element of surprise and faced determined, unanticipated fire from the ground as well as relentless attack from the air. Before long several supply ships were also hit and sunk by enemy fire and radio communications were also lost. And hopes that the landing would spark a national uprising against Castro were immediately dashed, not least because he ordered a massive security crackdown as soon as he heard news of the landing. Within forty-eight hours, 140 members of the attacking force had been killed and the rest, barring a handful who escaped into thick vegetation, were taken prisoner. It was, as a senior American admiral put it, 'a real big mess'.[24]

But the attack on Cuba was also completely unnecessary. Ever since he had been swept to power, in the revolution of December 1958, Castro had never menaced the United States. Despite the proximity of the coasts of Cuba and Florida, which are little more than 100 miles apart, his armed forces were far too lightweight at the time of Kennedy's inauguration to pose even a very modest, peripheral threat to the American mainland. In the weeks that followed, the Soviets did start to send arms in greater quantities: in April 1961, for example, the Cubans received tanks, rifles and machine guns, and had been promised several war planes. But these sufficed only to defend the island from foreign attack. Even if Castro had entered into a secret alliance with Moscow – he hadn't, but the White House feared that he had – then it really would not have mattered.

Like General 'Ike' Eisenhower before him, Kennedy had also been concerned about the impact that Castro's regime would have on other Latin American countries. There seemed to be a real danger that the Cuban leader would inspire other revolutionaries across the wider region, where he would be regarded as a role model for their own armed struggles and as a potential ally when or if they did seize power for themselves. 'We could lose all of South America' unless action was taken, Eisenhower had warned, although he had cautioned that the United States had to 'conduct itself in precisely the right way'. Ike's response was to covertly fund and support a coup carried out by Cuban rebels.[25]

But Kennedy and his advisers failed to recognise that Castro would attract much more attention and admiration from America's enemies if he succeeded in resisting the kind of coercive measures that they were planning on unleashing. Or even if they did succeed in toppling him, then they would not only create a martyr but also be displaying the very aggression that other countries feared: if America was even seen to be involved, warned one adviser, then the attack would create 'a wave of massive protest, agitation and sabotage' that would sweep across a very wide region.[26]

Perhaps what really drove Kennedy to order the Bay of Pigs attack, and Eisenhower to prepare the ground for it, was a feeling of deep indignation that someone outside their control, even one who posed no direct threat and who had no known link with the Soviet Union, should exert power in a region that American leaders had long regarded as their country's natural sphere of influence. The fact that Castro was such a powerful and charismatic personality, whose speeches brought vast crowds of ordinary Cubans into the streets, aggravated this sense of violation, intrusion and indignation. So too did the fact that Castro was often portrayed as a communist, even though he had come to power as just one leader of a broad coalition and at this stage categorically denied being a follower of Karl Marx.

But this was not a compelling enough reason to launch an attack that was always hugely risky. It was true that a few coup attempts had succeeded brilliantly, notably the CIA's covert operation against the regime of Jacob Arbenz in Guatemala more than six years before, or indeed against the troublesome prime minister of Iran, Mohammed Mossadeq, in 1953. But Cuba was a different proposition altogether. The CIA had virtually no information about conditions on the island, particularly about how much opposition to Castro there really was. And the logistical difficulties of mounting an amphibious invasion were, even in the very best-case scenario, formidable. If Kennedy then tried to claim that the CIA had nothing to do with such an assault then he would hardly sound convincing, even to the most gullible.

Quite why President Kennedy overlooked these obstacles and authorised the operation remains a mystery, particularly when the relatively youthful, fresh-faced senator who was sworn into office on 20 January 1961, at the age of forty-three, was not a natural warmonger. During his presidential campaign he had not made any specific mention of Cuba, an island that he, and so many others, considered to be a matter of peripheral importance that was considerably overshadowed by wider questions of the Cold War and the American economy. The true enthusiast for war was Eisenhower, who in January 1960 had taken the decision to topple Castro and had spent his last months of office 'organizing, training and leading resistance forces'. When Kennedy had entered the White House and discovered how committed his predecessor was to using force against Castro and how advanced these preparations were, the young president had immediately voiced his strong doubts.[27]

When and why Kennedy changed his tack in the weeks between his inauguration and the National Security Council meeting on 4 April remains unclear. It seems most likely that he simply fell under the spell of a number of highly talented but misguided advisers who very effectively sold their case for military force. One such salesman of war, who cleverly packaged and marketed a very toxic product, was a CIA director called Richard M. Bissell Jr.

Like every good salesman, Bissell exuded enthusiasm, confidence and conviction in his product, and he persuaded the president that Castro's regime would collapse like a house of cards as soon as the invasion force landed. Castro had numerous enemies, Bissell asserted, who would rise up and sweep away his rule as soon as they had the chance. And he convinced Kennedy that the spring of 1961 was a unique opportunity, a 'once-in-a-lifetime' chance, to make his move: if there was any delay, he argued, then Castro would have new stocks of Soviet arms and it would be too late. He was like a salesman who tells his prospective purchaser to 'buy now' before prices go up.

Bissell had enough flaws of his own. He appears to have had a vast capacity for self-deception and always wanted the CIA to have as much freedom as possible, arguing that its officers should be subject only to 'a higher law, a higher loyalty'. At the same time, he brushed aside and suppressed any information that might have raised awkward questions about an operation which, he deluded himself, was not an invasion but really just 'an infiltration in support of an internal revolution'.[28]

Kennedy was hardly a fool and by 1961 had seen enough of the world and of political life to ask searching questions about the operation. As a Harvard University student, he had travelled across Russia, France and Germany just before war broke out, and on leaving college, in 1940, he had joined the American navy and nearly lost his life during the campaign against the Japanese in the Far East. After a brief spell as a journalist, he had entered politics and enjoyed a dazzling, rapid ascent through the House of Representatives and the Senate. But despite such experiences, he of course had his vulnerabilities. For example, he was always very sensitive to criticism that he was 'soft on communism', a charge that his Republican rivals, *Richard Nixon* and Barry Goldwater, had often levelled against him during the presidential contest of 1959/60. And he particularly feared criticism from the media and was prepared to go to great lengths to avoid it: Kennedy would be seen as an 'appeaser', as another adviser warned, because 'Eisenhower made a decision to overthrow Castro and you dropped it'.[29]

It was probably such sensitive spots that the skilled, high-pressure salesmen of war repeatedly pressed when they urged him to authorise the Bay of Pigs operation. Unless he took the risk, they would have said, then Castro would become an ever greater risk to American interests. Kennedy's enemies, in the Republican Party and in the press, would then seize their chance. Maybe Bissell also appealed to Kennedy's wartime experiences and depicted the coup as something of an adventure that would be carried out by rather romantic figures. Kennedy appears to have dazzled by the loquacious and flamboyant Bissell. As one of the president's senior advisers, William Bundy, later admitted, 'it was the stupidity of freshmen on our part, and the stupidity on their part of being wrapped in their own illusions'.[30]

Whatever and whoever lay behind it, on the eve of the assault the president and his White House staff had been given the impression that the landing force 'would get ashore and run into some militia units and beat the hell out of them' and that 'the ability of this force to pass to guerrilla activities presented no difficulty'. When news broke of the subsequent disaster, White House staff, and the First Lady, found the president distraught and in tears. Almost at once he started to wonder why he had ever authorised the operation, and vowed to 'never rely on the experts' again.[31]

But there were peaceful alternatives that Kennedy could have pursued in the weeks that followed his inauguration, even if by this stage the operation against Castro had acquired a powerful momentum that only real presidential determination would have halted and reversed. In particular, the newly elected Kennedy could have struck up fresh dialogue with Castro. And he was particularly well qualified to do this because, as a senator, he had not only made numerous trips to pre-Castro Cuba but also voiced sympathy for its people, whom he publicly referred to as 'oppressed' by colonial masters. He had also condemned the way in which America had previously treated Cuba as a colony because it was only 'interested in the money we took out of Cuba ... (rather) than seeing Cuba raise its standard of living for its people'. Until he became president, as his adviser Arthur Schlesinger pointed out, he had championed 'liberty, justice and self-determination' and this meant that, as president, there was 'extraordinary good will ... rising towards the administration'.[32]

On 13 March, less than two months after entering the White House, Kennedy had taken one step along this peaceful and promising path when he had launched an 'Alliance for Progress' that would help to meet the 'basic needs of the (Latin) American people for homes, work and land, health and schools'. The sticking point was his insistence that these countries should embrace democracy, something that all of them did except for Cuba. But this need not have prevented the White House from compromising. Castro's Cuba was at this stage in desperate economic straits, not least because the previous October Washington had imposed a full embargo that stopped much of its foreign trade. At the very least, Kennedy could have offered to lift this embargo on the condition that Castro respected certain conditions. Perhaps he could have insisted that Castro should refuse to accept any more Soviet arms and steered a neutral course between the two Cold War superpowers. But even that was more than the president needed to ask: it didn't really matter if Castro allied himself with Moscow and accepted Soviet arms, provided they weren't heavy arms that were capable of striking the American mainland.

Instead, Kennedy authorised an operation that played into the hands of his own critics at home and of America's critics abroad, who argued that it was a perfect example of Washington's tendency to use 'dirty tricks' against popular movements and to then practise deceit and deception when things went wrong. Once again, America was seen as the aggressor, as indeed it was; Castro had 1,113 prisoners he could use as a bargaining chip, and he also now turned and took several steps closer to the Soviet Union: in August 1961, Blas Roca, the secretary-general of the Cuban communist party, went to Moscow and spent three months there, working on plans to bring the two countries closer together. Soon after his return Castro made his first, open declaration that he was 'a Marxist-Leninist and shall be till the day I die'.[33]

Relations between Havana and Washington now broke down irretrievably, for in November 1961 Kennedy bowed to the pressure of the hawks and approved Operation Mongoose, a CIA plan to destabilise Cuba by any and every means. But had the president been able to seize his opportunity in those early weeks of his administration, then he would have averted the major crisis that erupted eighteen months later, when the Soviets shipped nuclear missiles to Cuba and nearly provoked a nuclear exchange with America. Relations between the two countries were not to fully recover until the end of 2014, when presidents Barack Obama and Raúl Castro broke the deadlock and announced moves to normalise relations.

Lyndon B. Johnson's 'Last Push' in Vietnam (1965)

On 28 July 1965, the American president, Lyndon B. Johnson, made a dramatic announcement about his country's involvement in a war that was being waged to stop South Vietnam falling to communist forces based in, and supported by, North Vietnam. He had decided to increase the number of troops there, he informed the American public, from 75,000 to 125,000, and there would also be a big jump in the number of Americans being drafted into the ranks of the armed forces to serve in the conflict.

Johnson had already escalated America's involvement. Five months before, in February, he had unleashed a major bombing campaign against North Vietnamese targets, adding a new dimension to an American campaign that had previously been confined almost exclusively to the south of the country. But the additional troop deployment in July meant that Johnson had now effectively crossed a new line. He had cast his die in favour of much greater American involvement in Vietnam and there was no turning back.

Until this moment, American support for the regime in Saigon, the capital of South Vietnam, had been relatively marginal. In early 1964 he could have ordered a pull-out from South Vietnam without suffering any major loss of face. There were other places, President Johnson could have persuasively argued, that were much more important to the United States, and South Vietnam would have to fend for itself against the communist onslaught of the Viet Cong guerrillas and their sponsors, the North Vietnamese government. But from that July day onwards, he committed the United States, its resources and its credibility, as well as his own career, to winning the war against Vietnamese communism.

'LBJ' came to power knowing something about Vietnam and its struggles. In May 1961, as Kennedy's vice-president, he had made a short visit to Saigon, where he made flattering remarks about its leader Ngo Dinh Diem and touted the official line about how Washington would strongly support the south against the communists. But when the fifty-five-year-old Texan had entered the White House, after John F. Kennedy's assassination in November 1963, he was initially far more interested in social justice and equality than in foreign affairs, about which he had little knowledge, expertise or interest. And in his first year as president, after being thrust so suddenly into office by such a dramatic turn of events, he was forced to delegate a great many of his less pressing foreign policy issues to more hawkish advisers while he focused on more urgent matters.

Vietnam, and America's involvement there, was one of the issues that he had little trouble in delegating but which merited much more presidential attention. In the months before his death, President Kennedy had already ramped up American involvement in the war. There were 16,000 American soldiers in the south at this time, a huge increase from the 900-strong force that President Dwight D. Eisenhower had stationed there by the end of his own administration. All the signs were present, in other words, of what later became known as 'mission creep' – a growing momentum of intervention that is difficult to stop or perhaps even recognise. Johnson needed to focus a lot more of his own attention, and that of his advisers, upon the Vietnam question before he sent even more young American men to die there.

In fact Johnson always had doubts about America's involvement there. In a recorded private telephone conversation in May 1964, for example, his uncertainty and deep personal anguish about the war are plain to hear. But under his presidency the United States became trapped in a vicious and extremely costly conflict that ended, nearly a decade on, with a disturbing death toll: 59,000 Americans and hundreds of thousands, perhaps even millions, of Vietnamese civilians. The United States military had dropped millions of tons of explosives – it unleashed more bombs in the course of 1968 alone than during the whole of the Second World War – and fired even more bullets. A country lay in ruins while the United States was embroiled in bitter internal conflict, its reputation overseas in tatters. And it was all for nothing: in 1975, less than two years after the Americans pulled out of South Vietnam, communist tanks rolled south of the border and seized Saigon, unifying the two states into one single communist state that was ruled from Hanoi.[34]

From about late 1964, the Vietnam War began to loom larger on his political agenda and Johnson focused more attention upon it. The president now became a reluctant warmonger not because he delegated too many duties but because he was unwilling to challenge the orthodoxies and assurances of his more hawkish advisers. Some of these, like Walt Rostow, were fascinated by faddish theories about 'counter-insurgency' and 'nation-building'. Another, Robert S. McNamara, produced a deluge of statistics, claiming confidently that 'every quantitative measurement we have shows we are winning the war' and that North Vietnam was 'extremely vulnerable to conventional bombing'. All the hawks assured him that just 'one last push' was needed to force North Vietnam into a compromise on America's terms.[35]

Critics of the war, like the diplomats John K. Galbraith and George W. Ball, thought they noticed some deep psychological processes that were driving the United States ever closer into Vietnam. 'There was something about Vietnam', mused Ball, 'that seduced the toughest military minds into fantasy.' Perhaps the American military wanted to prove its superiority over the French, whose armed forces had fought their own bloody decade-long struggle in Indochina and lost around 90,000 men by doing so. It was probably pride and a sense of superiority that prompted so many Americans to disregard the warnings of Frenchmen like Jean Sainteny, a leading French expert on the region, that no foreign power would ever subjugate the Vietnamese. Perhaps, too, there was a racial element, just as some Western soldiers of the Second World War had initially been contemptuous of the fighting prowess of 'the yellow man'. Traits of this racialism emerged in a comment ventured by a later warmonger, Henry Kissinger, who refused to believe that 'a little fourth-rate power like Vietnam doesn't have a breaking-point'.[36]

Such attitudes quickly snowballed and became established truths. As soon as senior officials, civilian and military, argued in favour of supporting Diem, their more junior subordinates also started to toe the line, reluctant to risk their careers by questioning the chosen course and preferring to twist logic and statistics to convince themselves and others that they were doing the right thing.

Maybe Johnson was drawn into this collective mindset, or maybe he just lacked the intellectual confidence to challenge the advocates of intervention. Johnson suffered from a strong sense of intellectual inferiority, having graduated with poor marks from an obscure teacher-training college in San Marcos. 'The men of ideas think little of me,' he later confided to one of his biographers. 'They despise me.' On another occasion, he admitted that 'my daddy told me that if I brushed up against the grindstone of life, I'd come away with far more polish than I could ever get at Harvard or Yale. I wanted to believe him, but somehow I never could.' Contemporaries noted that, in the company of clever and educated men, LBJ often acted in a way that was 'boastful, churlish and abusive', but this disguised his secret admiration and susceptibility to their views. As a result, Johnson was easy prey to war hawks like Robert McNamara, a razor-sharp Berkeley-educated intellectual who intimidated colleagues with his grasp, or apparent grasp, of official statistics.[37]

Perhaps, to some degree, Johnson also enjoyed a bit of military posturing. By escalating the war, he could sell himself to the American public as the soldier that he wasn't. During the Second World War, he had honourably left Congress to join the American army but had done little more than undertake fact-finding missions in safe areas of the Far East. In June 1943, however, he had bravely volunteered to join a bombing mission on a Japanese base in New Guinea. But while the crew were given no award at all for a regular flight, Johnson, who was just a passenger, received the army's third-highest medal. Maybe, as his critics suggested, he had volunteered for the flight only for political reasons, thinking it would enhance his career. Whatever drove him to do it, he certainly went on to exaggerate his wartime service. On one occasion he described making his way through the jungles of New Guinea and 'the horrors' he had experienced of fighting 'the Japs in the Pacific'.[38]

Doubtlessly he also suffered from the same fear as his predecessor – of being seen as weak on defence and the 'Soviet threat'. In 1963, the Republican senator Barry Goldwater had enjoyed a spectacular run of political successes, campaigning on a very hawkish ticket and making maximum capital out of the *Bay of Pigs* fiasco, the 'loss of China' in 1949 and the failure to hold *North Korea* from 1951. Goldwater, felt Johnson, was 'nutty as a fruitcake' and 'a screwball' who 'wanted to drop atomic bombs on everybody'. He felt sure that 'the people (won't) stand for that' but cautioned that, in America, they 'may do it'.[39]

But whatever lay behind it, President Johnson's announcement in July 1965 committed America to a war that was, on every count, quite unnecessary. Thousands of miles away, its fall to communism would have presented no obvious threat to the United States: the communist militia had a proven expertise only in guerrilla warfare.

Initially, the warmongers in Washington also claimed that other countries in the region might fall to communism 'like dominoes'. But this was just a worst-case scenario and only an argument for bolstering the defences of those neighbours. Yet the president echoed the hawks' argument: the question, he argued, was 'whether we are to help these countries ... or if we throw in the towel in the area and pull back our defences to San Francisco'. Nothing seemed to lie between the two.[40]

Then the hawks raised another argument, asserting that America's commitment to Vietnam was a 'test-case' of Washington's resolve to defend the 'free world' from communism elsewhere. But it was just as true that Vietnam distracted and detracted from other, much more important frontlines in the Cold War, such as West Berlin. These were inactive frontlines where young Americans didn't have to die. And there was nothing good about losing a 'test-case' by making a bloody, humiliating retreat.

Instead of using military force, a much better strategy would have been to stand back and study the relations between Vietnam and its neighbours, notably China. For centuries the two countries had had a tempestuous relationship, sparring over disputed territory and freedoms. In the early 1960s, most Cold Warriors felt sure that a shared belief in communism had superseded these long-standing tensions, and that China, the Soviet Union and North Vietnam effectively acted as one monolithic bloc. But others, notably in the State Department, dissented and pointed out that national sentiment and rivalry could not just disappear so fast and so soon. Even in the event of a communist victory, in other words, a communist Vietnam would be contained by its more powerful rival, and perhaps ways could even have been found of playing one off against the other.

This is exactly what did happen after the communist victory in 1975. Less than four years later, the two countries went to war. Angered by Vietnam's occupation of the disputed Spratly Island, the alleged treatment of its ethnic Chinese population, and its invasion of neighbouring Cambodia, the Chinese launched a ferocious assault on their fellow communists who ruled Vietnam.

On that July day in 1965, Johnson should have listened to the dissenting voices of those who tried to make themselves heard. One was George Ball, who had written detailed and powerful memos that offered a very different course of action. Arguing that the war in Vietnam would be just as costly and futile as it had been for the French, Ball wanted to set up a coalition government in Saigon, declare a general amnesty for the Viet Cong and then pull American forces right out. Quoting General de Gaulle, he thought that Vietnam was simply a 'rotten country' that wasn't worth the sacrifice of American lives.[41]

Other critics, like the senior presidential adviser Clark Clifford, correctly predicted unrest at home and abroad, as the general public protested about the draft and the unnecessary loss of American, and Vietnamese, lives. These warnings also proved prescient: America, along with some European capitals, was soon rocked by violent protest as hundreds of thousands of demonstrators took to the streets to demand an immediate end to the fighting. America was unleashing an onslaught of carpet bombing, napalm and flamethrowers in a remote and strategically unimportant corner of the world, and sacrificing its unity and stability at home, and its reputation abroad, by doing so.

Richard Nixon's 'Brutal Blows' on South-East Asia (1972)

Richard Nixon had become president in 1969 promising 'peace with honour' in Vietnam, and within four years of his election had pulled all American forces out of the country. The chief architect of his policy, his national security adviser, Henry Kissinger, even won the Nobel Peace Prize for his instrumental role in ending America's involvement in the Vietnam War in 1973.

But this version of events presents a superficial veneer that hides a brutal warmongering reality. As soon as he took office, Nixon resumed American bombing of North Vietnam, which Johnson had halted before the 1968 election. In total, twice as many American bombs fell on North and South Vietnam during the Nixon administration's three years of war than in the five years of the Johnson administration. Tens of thousands of civilians, and thousands of American servicemen, died unnecessarily as American bombers ravaged huge areas of two neutral countries, Cambodia and Laos, as well as Vietnam. And although the president publicly championed the cause of peace in Vietnam during the 1968 presidential campaign, the truth was more complex. Kissinger's memoirs reveal that, at the onset, the Nixon administration was quite unsure where it was heading. All the talk of 'peace with honour', in other words, was really just a catchy and highly effective marketing slogan to win power.

Unlike Johnson, Nixon was never a reluctant warmonger. In April 1954, as vice-president, he had argued for 'putting American boys in' Indochina as soon as the French, who had suffered a massive, bloody defeat at the battle of Dien Bien Phu, pulled out, but had been overruled by President Eisenhower and General Matthew Ridgway. Then there were whispers that he had wanted to use the atomic bomb against the Chinese to stop them moving into Indochina after the French finally left in 1955, and five years later, during the presidential race, he had openly accused John F. Kennedy of failing to commit to the use of nuclear weapons to defend Quemoy and Matsu, in the Taiwan Straits, from the Chinese. When, in April 1961, news broke of disaster at the *Bay of Pigs*, he urged President Kennedy to 'do whatever is necessary to assure that the invasion is a success' – a demand for a full-scale invasion by American troops, using an imaginary threat to American interests in Cuba as a false pretext.[42]

Nor did he play a less militaristic tune during the Vietnam years. In 1964, he had advocated a sharp escalation of the bombing in south-east Asia, urging President Johnson to attack North Vietnam – not something the US air force had at that stage done – as well as Laos while also opposing negotiations. He believed, like the bloodthirsty General Curtis LeMay, in 'bombing North Vietnam back into the Stone Age'. Then, just as the presidential electoral contest got underway in 1968, he deliberately sabotaged President Johnson's last-minute breakthrough in peace negotiations with North Vietnam, persuading President Thieu not to cooperate and thereby depriving his Democrat opponent, vice-president Hubert Humphrey, of a huge electoral boost. Nixon went on to win the election by a mere whisker, but scarcely could he have acted more selfishly, indeed treasonably.[43]

But long before he became mired in the Watergate phone-tapping scandal that later prompted his resignation as president, Nixon's judgment was often called into question. In the White House, he even used presidential memos, referring to himself in the third person, to correspond with his wife over banal issues such as his choice of bedroom furniture. He was full of complexes, deeply suspicious of and paranoid about others, and very quick to take offence. Contemporaries noted that 'he clung to the word and the idea of being "tough"', thinking that it was this quality that had 'brought him to greatness'. Others were bemused by some of the superficial but expensive changes he introduced to the presidential lifestyle, such as spending millions of dollars on moving some of the trees at his Camp David retreat. His personal psychiatrist wondered why he looked at himself in the mirror only to complain that 'it was as if there was nobody there'.[44]

If he had a distorted view of himself, then so too was his view of foreign affairs equally warped. As soon as he became president, the heavy-jowled, lugubrious Richard Nixon tried to bomb the North Vietnamese into peace negotiations. He was utterly convinced that 'measures of great consequence' – a euphemism for dropping bombs from the air – would simply force even the most determined enemy to the negotiating table. True, there were times when Nixon's conviction in bombing sometimes wavered but on each occasion he was pushed back into line by Henry Kissinger who knew how to bait him and fend off the more cautious, level-headed advice put forward by rival figures like Melvin Laird and William Rogers. 'Weakling,' as Kissinger taunted the president, 'they will think you are a weakling.'[45]

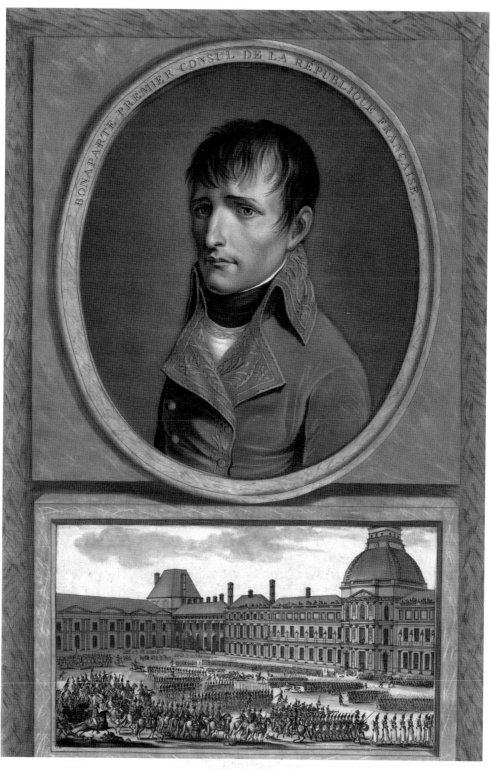

One of the original warmongers, Napoleon Bonaparte. (Courtesy of the Library of Congress)

Lord Palmerston. (Courtesy of the Yale Center for British Art)

President William McKinley. (Courtesy of the Library of Congress)

Above: Field Marshal Helmuth von Moltke. (Courtesy of the Library of Congress)

Below: No Man's Land in Flanders during the First World War. (Courtesy of the Library of Congress)

Above: President Woodrow Wilson. (Courtesy of the Library of Congress)

Left: British Foreign Minister Sir Edward Grey. (Courtesy of the Library of Congress)

Right: Benito Mussolini. (Courtesy of the Library of Congress)

Below: Clement Attlee (left), Harry Truman (centre) and Josef Stalin (right) at the Potsdam Conference in August 1945. (Courtesy of the Library of Congress)

Left: General Douglas MacArthur. (Courtesy of the Library of Congress)

Below: American soldiers take cover during the Korean War. (Courtesy of the Library of Congress)

President Lyndon B. Johnson meets South Vietnamese troops in Saigon in 1962. (Courtesy of the Library of Congress)

President Ronald Reagan in the White House. (Courtesy of the Library of Congress)

A fitting end for a warmonger? In Baghdad, Iraq, Saddam Hussein sits before an Iraqi judge who informs him of the legal investigation into his crimes. He was later executed. (Courtesy of Ssgt D. Myles Cullen, US Air Force)

Another outcome of a warmongering life. In North Korea, Kim Il-sung remains a figure of adulation. This statue in Pyongyang stands in his memory; his son, Kim Jong-il, stands beside him. (Courtesy of Nicor)

Between them, Nixon and Kissinger made a deadly, warmongering duo. If America stopped dropping bombs, they argued, then it faced 'the first defeat in our nation's history (which) would result in a collapse of confidence in American leadership'. Kissinger felt sure that victory was in their grasp. 'Give us six months,' he told an audience in 1969, 'and if we haven't ended the war by then, you can come back and tear down the White House fence.' Just a few more 'brutal blows' were required. Meanwhile, the president became increasingly exasperated by his failure to beat a 'fourth-rate power' into submission, and even considered applying his 'Madman Theory' by pretending to be an insane, unpredictable leader whose very irrationality would terrify his opponent. 'The enemy would be compelled to cower, saying "we just can't restrain him when he is angry and he has his hand on the nuclear button",' argued Nixon. 'Ho Chi Minh will be in Paris in two days, begging for peace.' But such justifications for violence, or attempted justifications, disguised the truth: that Nixon and Kissinger were vengefully lashing out against a resilient, determined enemy that was continually outsmarting and defeating them.[46]

Still the Vietnamese resisted and still Nixon's critics pointed out that aerial bombing is, on its own, generally ineffective. This was bound to be particularly true, they added, against a highly fanatical enemy that had been at war for decades and which was utterly dedicated to its nationalist cause, having never stepped back from its insistence on an unconditional American withdrawal. The North Vietnamese were also clever and astute enough to realise that America could not afford to indefinitely sustain its costly and unpopular war, fought 12,000 miles from home. All they had to do was to continue with their existing course and wait until the White House, and the American general public, finally lost patience.

Part of the problem was that Nixon had allowed his national security adviser to carve out his own personal fiefdom and to sideline the influence of more moderate, and experienced, voices in the State Department. This aggravated the vulnerability of a man who was given to shutting himself away from others – he frequently withdrew to spend long hours entirely on his own – and who was therefore vulnerable to the warmongering of Henry Kissinger, one of the few individuals who had direct and virtually constant access to the presidential office. 'The Nixon administration,' as one magazine pointed out, was merely 'a small junta, suspicious of the bureaucrats it presides over, ill at ease with Congress, distrustful of those it can't control ... and unnecessarily inhospitable to people whose ideas might occasionally help it.'[47]

Too late in the day, as Hanoi refused to buckle under the bombing and insisted on an American pull-out, both men came to realise the futility of their approach. But still they continued with a bombing campaign that became a form of therapy, externalising the sense of frustration and helplessness that years of wasted effort and lives had created. This approach only inflicted heavy losses for no tactical gain. The massive 'Linebacker II' bombing raids over North Vietnam in December 1972, for example, cost the lives of ninety-three American pilots and thousands of civilians, even though Nixon was demanding only pedantic changes to a proposed treaty that everyone knew was not likely to last for long once the Americans withdrew from Vietnam.

In January 1973 Nixon and Kissinger finally signed a peace deal which pulled American forces out of South Vietnam, recognised the border between north and south, and implemented an immediate ceasefire. But this was no different from the agreement that they could and should have signed three years before. In 1969 Nixon could have offered the communists a ceasefire and secured the release of hundreds of American prisoners-of-war in return for a phased withdrawal of the 500,000 American troops in the south. This was the advice that peacemongers like George Ball gave but which Nixon and Kissinger refused to take.[48]

Instead, the fighting that took place in the course of those three bloody years cost the lives of 20,000 American soldiers and around half a million Vietnamese, Cambodian and Laotian civilians. Some 200 young American men were dying every week. And one particularly grisly incident, which attracted huge media attention and badly denigrated America's name, would never have happened: this was the massacre at My Lai on 16 March 1968, when rampaging US troops massacred hundreds of innocent men, women and children in cold blood.

The carpet-bombing of Laos and the invasion of Cambodia in 1970, which were intended to destroy the communists' supply lines and force them to moderate their negotiating demands, further tarnished America's international reputation: even in 2015, around one-third of Laotian territory remained covered in unexploded ordnance. To describe events, Nixon used extreme language that bordered on the genocidal: 'I want everything that can fly to go in there and crack the hell out of them. There is no limitation on mileage and ... on budget ... every goddamn thing that can fly goes into Cambodia and hits every target that is open.' Making things even worse was the deceit and deception with which Nixon and Kissinger tried to hide these, and other, operations in a bid to prevent even more protests and demonstrations in America and elsewhere. During 'Operation Menu', the covert bombing of Laos, they devised a way of drawing up phony records to conceal what was really happening, keeping the operation secret even from the State Department. Bomber crews were themselves kept in the dark about their true targets. When, a few months later, the story nonetheless leaked into the press, Nixon ordered wiretaps to be placed on officials, journalists and citizen groups.[49]

By continuing the war, America also paid a high price on its home front. Its cities, and particularly its university campuses, were rocked by violent protests, while support for radical, revolutionary political parties surged. Security men fought regular and sometimes brutal battles with protestors, and at Kent State, in May 1970, National Guardsmen opened fire and killed four students.

Even after the American withdrawal in 1973, Nixon still continued to make some very bloodthirsty threats. If the communist forces violated the treaty agreement, he privately promised Thieu, then 'it is my intention to take swift and severe retaliatory action ... and that we will respond with full force'. The president was making a private commitment to a foreign leader, perhaps intonating that he was prepared to use nuclear force while gambling that Congress would support any renewal of the war. Similar remarks were made by Dr Kissinger, who advised his president in 1972 that the peace deal needed to be supported by 'evident hair-trigger US readiness, which may in fact be challenged at any time, to enforce its provisions'.[50]

After America's withdrawal, in March 1973, South Vietnam soon came under intense, relentless military pressure from communist forces. Nixon blamed Congress for not giving him the support he wanted, Kissinger later blamed Nixon and the Watergate Scandal, while the military blamed the lack of political will. But whoever deserved to take responsibility, no one could disguise the sheer scale, or the immense folly, of America's Vietnam venture. Of the 2.7 million Americans who served there, more than 58,000 had died, along with around 2.1 million Vietnamese, civilian and military. Washington had also provided South Vietnam with $138 billion in military aid and $8.5 billion in economic assistance. Perhaps some 600,000 Cambodians also perished under the 2.75 million tons of bombs that American planes dropped, often indiscriminately. And it was all in vain. On 30 April 1975, the Saigon regime finally capitulated to the North Vietnamese. The two Vietnamese states were united into one communist state ruled from Hanoi.

No amount of public relations could hide the fact that America had lost its Vietnam War. Nixon would have done much better to have simply pursued the containment strategy that his predecessor, Lyndon Johnson, had also spurned: both men could have allowed South Vietnam to fall to communism and then found ways of containing any possible threat it posed to America, not least by playing it off against its regional enemies.

President Carter, Iran and Afghanistan (1979)

Before he became president in 1977, James Earl 'Jimmy' Carter sometimes tried just too hard. During his presidential election campaign, he tried to quash concerns that he was a religious fanatic by giving an interview for *Playboy* magazine and claiming that he had 'committed adultery, in my heart, many times'. The American nation was stunned. And on 15 September 1979, ignoring the warnings of his staff, he took part in a sponsored long-distance run near Camp David during which he collapsed and was stretchered off to hospital in front of television cameras that broadcast the incident across the world. Perhaps by this time, after so much heavy responsibility and working fifteen-hour days without delegating as much of his workload as he should, Jimmy Carter was feeling the pressure.

But it was not just on the running track or in interviews that President Carter was going a bit too far. At almost the same time that he collapsed on the track, he quietly authorised Operation Cyclone – a top-secret plan to provoke a war in south-west Asia and bring the Soviet Union and its empire crashing down.

The architect of his plan was his hawkish national security adviser, Zbigniew Brzezinski. He was a true Cold Warrior who regarded the Soviet Union not as a paranoid and ailing power but as a global menace to 'the free world'. He was determined to find ways of orchestrating its collapse. And just a few years after the *Vietnam War*, Brzezinski shared the same collective sense of national failure and humiliation as so many other Americans. Destroying the Soviet Union was a way of exorcising those feelings.

Cyclone was his answer, although it was a plan that President Carter approved and must take responsibility for. Brzezinski's idea was to provoke the Soviets into invading Afghanistan, thereby embroiling them in a protracted guerrilla war that would weaken and emasculate the military threat that Moscow seemed to pose to the West. At the same time, such an outcome promised to make America feel better about itself: we lost in Vietnam, the thinking seemed to run, but so were the Soviets losing in Afghanistan.

The official version of events was that the CIA didn't start arming the Afghan militias until after the Soviet invasion in December 1979. The truth, however, was that on 3 July Carter authorised Brzezinski's plan to give secret assistance to Islamist militias in Afghanistan that would be in a position, as the national security adviser later admitted, to undermine the pro-Moscow regime in Kabul and, by doing so, 'to lure the Soviets into an invasion'.[51]

This is exactly what did happen. As the Afghan government came under increasing pressure from its enemies, in the course of the summer, it made repeated, and increasingly frantic, requests to Moscow for military assistance. Then, in December, as rumours flew around Kabul of covert American influence, the Kremlin authorised a full-scale invasion (see *Yuri Andropov*).

In Washington, President Carter kept a straight face, suppressing a self-satisfied smile beneath a veneer of shock and surprise as news of the attack broke. And Brzezinski later admitted that he wrote Carter a note 'saying, in effect, "We've now our chance of giving the Russians their own Vietnam."'[52]

With the benefit of hindsight, it is plain that the Carter-Brzezinski warmongering had a disastrous fallout. Tens of thousands of innocent Afghans were killed and millions more became refugees. Islamists became radicalised and the region militarised. But years later, Brzezinski was unashamed about the deaths and damage that he and Carter were partially responsible for. 'Regret what?', he once asked his interviewer. 'The CIA operation was a wonderful idea ... it succeeded in luring the Soviets into the Afghan trap and you want me to regret that? What is more important in terms of world history? The fall of the Soviet empire – or the Taliban? A handful of hysterical Islamists or the liberation of central Europe and the end of the Cold War?'[53]

President Carter was guilty of trying too hard to meet the 'threat', if indeed there ever really was such a thing, that the Soviets posed to Western security. He never needed to provoke the invasion of an entire country, with the hugely destabilising consequences that such a tumultuous event would have. Over the preceding two years, enormous strides had been made to nurture a spirit of détente between East and West: in 1975, America and the Soviet Union had signed the Helsinki Final Act, which set up confidence-building measures between the two countries. Afterwards there were talks – 'Strategic Arms Limitation' – to cut back the vast number of missiles that both sides had gradually built up: an agreement was signed in Vienna in June 1979 but after the Soviet invasion of Afghanistan it was never ratified by the US Senate. Instead of provoking wars and setting whole regions alight, Carter could have pursued these and other agreements that were intended to reduce mistrust between the two superpowers.

And if President Carter had, for whatever reason, really wanted to pursue a much more aggressive approach and undermine the very foundations of the Soviet Union, then there were smarter, more peaceful ways of doing so. This became clear in 1986, when a collapse in the oil price wrecked the Soviet economy, which was, and remains, heavily dependent on petroleum exports. As the oil price steadied and then dropped in 1978, Carter could have liaised with America's close allies, the Saudis, to engineer falls in the oil price that would, at the very least, have curbed Moscow's ambitions. Such a plan could have been implemented at some future point in the years ahead, when the oil price finally began to drop.

Several months later, the president was to overreach himself again. On 11 April 1980, he quietly authorised a top-secret mission to rescue sixty-six American diplomats and nationals who had been seized in Iran.

The crisis had started more than a year before, when the shah of Iran had fled his country and his leading political critic and opponent, *Ayatollah Khomeini*, had then made his return, flying into Tehran to be greeted by vast, ecstatic crowds. The Iranian Revolution was now underway but there was no reason why this needed to adversely affect the United States: the revolutionary regime had declared its good intentions towards Washington, even if the shah had been America's close ally. But despite warnings not to do so, Carter took the extraordinary decision to allow the exiled shah into America for medical treatment. This immediately sparked a vitriolic reaction in Tehran and on 4 November 1979 an armed mob of revolutionaries stormed the American embassy, seizing its staff as hostages and demanding the shah's return.[54]

Carter had initially relied upon secret dialogue with the Iranians to negotiate the diplomats' release but these talks eventually petered out and on 7 April the two countries broke off diplomatic relations altogether. What the president could have done at this stage was simply to have shown patience: the hostages gave the Iranians a bargaining chip that they could use to extract maximum concessions from Washington. But any country that has just experienced revolution is always in dire political and economic straits, as it struggles to find its feet in the turbulent months and years that follow. Carter only needed to bide his time and wait until the regime was desperate for allies and support.

Had he waited, then Carter may have found his moment within just months: on 22 September 1980, *Saddam Hussein* launched a massive invasion of Iran, striking hard into the border province of Khuzestan at a time when Khomeini's regime was at its most vulnerable. Although the Iranians bravely fought back, they were under huge pressure on the battlefield. It was in these opening weeks of Saddam's offensive that they may well have proved willing to strike a deal over the hostages in return for some American support, even if Washington had simply offered to broker a ceasefire.

Instead, President Carter gave the go-ahead for a mission that had virtually no chance of bringing any of the hostages, let alone some or all of them, back alive. On 24 April, Operation 'Eagle Claw' began as helicopters from the aircraft carrier USS *Nimitz* made their way by stealth to a remote part of the Iranian desert, where they made contact with a highly trained rescue force. The plan was to land a short distance outside Tehran and then move into the capital, storm the prisons where the hostages were held and release them.

Carter was a trained naval officer who had served in the Second World War, although he had never seen active service, and who for a time had entertained ambitions to become a chief of naval operations. He should have known, as some of his advisers knew and tried to warn him, of the huge risks he was taking, and of the virtual certainty that things would not go according to plan. 'I guarantee you something will go wrong,' lamented his secretary of state, Cyrus Vance as he put forward his resignation shortly before the hour of attack. 'It never works out the way they say it's going to work.'[55]

And so it proved when the some of the helicopters were tragically caught in ferocious dust-storms and crashed, killing eight servicemen and forcing a humbled president to abort the entire operation and make a full admission of responsibility, to a shocked American public, on national television.

In both cases, Afghanistan and Iran, President Carter had tried to do too much too soon. He could have bided his time, exerting as much pressure on the Iranians and enticing them when they were at their most vulnerable. This was equally true of the Soviet Union, which was badly affected by the oil price collapse of the mid-1980s. Instead he chose to use war and violence when neither was appropriate or necessary.

'Yuri's War' in Afghanistan (1979)

At noon on Christmas Day 1979, the Soviet defence minister, Dmitri Ustinov, gave an order that his senior generals had long expected but always feared. 'The state frontier of the Democratic Republic of Afghanistan is to be crossed on the ground and in the air by forces of the 40th Army and the Air Force at 1500 hours on 25 December (Moscow time).' Hours later, exactly on schedule, hundreds of Soviet tanks rolled south of the Oxus River along a section of the Silk Road, the fabled trade route between east and west, and into Afghanistan. At the same time, a constant stream of transport aircraft ferried thousands of combat troops and vast quantities of equipment straight into the capital, Kabul.

The decision to invade Afghanistan had been taken nearly two weeks before, at a meeting of the Politburo – the ruling clique of the Soviet regime – in Moscow on 12 December 1979. Of those present the main cheerleader of war was Yuri Andropov, the head of the much-feared Soviet foreign intelligence service, the KGB. While the ultimate arbiter of the invasion was the chairman of the Politburo, Leonid Brezhnev, Moscow's Afghan intervention was essentially 'Yuri's War'.

Before the meeting began, Andropov had presented each member of the committee with a briefing about the deteriorating security situation in Afghanistan. The principal aim of Soviet foreign policy in the region had always been to preserve Afghanistan as a neutral state, partly because the country was devoid of strategic importance but also because it was too economically backward for communism to take root. But matters had now changed. The leader of the Kabul government, Hafizullah Amin, could no longer be trusted and was carrying out brutally repressive measures that were only creating new enemies and making things even worse. Amin, he continued, was also establishing links with the Americans, who wanted to establish military bases in Afghanistan that would directly threaten the Soviet Union (see *President Jimmy Carter*). Moscow had to act now to install a more compliant leader in Kabul and establish a buffer state that would render its southern territories more secure from foreign attack.[56]

Andropov did not seem to realise, however, that launching a full-scale invasion of the country might make things worse still, stirring up a hornet's nest of the very anti-Soviet sentiment that he feared. Nor does he appear to have been aware of the fate of earlier invaders of Afghanistan, who had been badly mauled and forced to retreat (see *William Macnaghten*).

Perhaps his willingness to reach for the trigger was a legacy of the Second World War. In 1939, at the age of twenty-six, he had watched with horror as Hitler's army poured across the border with Poland and into the Soviet Union, seizing hundreds of miles within just days. For several, terrifying weeks at the end of 1941, it seemed possible that the capital, Moscow, would fall to the invader. Russia would have been much safer, he must have thought, if only it had taken a more aggressive line towards Germany long before instead of doing deals with its inherently untrustworthy leader. In other words, the Kremlin's passive approach to growing danger had rendered Russia immensely vulnerable.

After spending four wartime years as a partisan, fighting in Finland, Andropov had entered government service and been appointed as the Soviet ambassador to Hungary in 1954. Two years later, he witnessed the horrors of violence once again when an anti-Soviet revolt quickly began to spread across the country. From the embassy he was able to look out into streets and watch government officials being beaten and then lynched. Such violence was just a reminder that dissent and potential threats had to be brutally extinguished before they got out of hand, just as they had done in 1941.

Andropov's advice was now instrumental in persuading Moscow to send armed troops to crush an uprising against Soviet rule, overruling the reservations of President Nikita Khrushchev. On 1 November, Soviet forces invaded Hungary, imposing martial law and establishing a new administration. Around 2,000 civilians died in the brutal street battles that demonstrators fought, mainly in the capital, Budapest, against well-armed and trained regular soldiers. Hundreds of ringleaders were also rounded up and executed.

Andropov's credentials as a hawk were by now well established and he subsequently swiftly climbed the party ladder, returning to Moscow and joining the ranks of the KGB. As an intelligence chief, he now proved himself to be a loyal heir of Joseph Stalin, under whose rule millions of Soviet citizens had perished. With Andropov at its helm, the KGB consigned many 'dissidents' to psychiatric hospitals, and ordered the assassination, kidnap and torture of individuals who it deemed to be a threat to Soviet security. But cold and clinical in approach, Andropov only assessed the threat he thought they posed. He could not see, quantify or care about, the suffering he caused.[57]

When, in 1968, another foreign policy crisis once again erupted, the KGB chief quickly advocated an armed response. In a bid to prise the communist state out of Moscow's grip, the Americans were stirring an anti-Soviet uprising in Czechoslovakia, argued Andropov. Moscow had to act quickly and firmly, he asserted, as it had done twelve years before, if it was to contain the crisis and keep the Americans out of Eastern Europe. He ordered his KGB henchmen to fabricate 'evidence' about Washington's role in the uprising before and deliberately portrayed peaceful protests as a stepping-stone for violence and even civil war. Soviet officials in Washington sent reassuring diplomatic reports, arguing that the Americans were not involved in the Czech unrest, but Andropov made sure that these were sidelined, knowing that they would undermine the case for armed intervention against 'the Prague Spring'. Once again, Soviet tanks moved in and blood was spilled.[58]

A decade on, Andropov and the other members of the Politburo were faced by another crisis, this time on the Soviet Union's southern borders.

Afghanistan did not at first sight seem to be worth fighting over. It is a landlocked country and does not have any known natural resources. It mattered, or seemed to matter, partly because of its Muslim population. An Islamist government in Kabul, ran the thinking, might be capable of inciting millions of Soviet Muslims to rise up against Moscow's rule. In December 1979 such fears seemed very real because, just months before, Iran had experienced a tumultuous Islamic revolution that had also shaken the outside world. Leaders in foreign capitals wondered where and how far *Ayatollah Khomeini*'s radical Islamism would spread and what effects it would have.

The Iranian Revolution had also toppled one of America's closest allies – Shah Mohammed Reza Pahlavi. Iran had been a major listening post and military base for the American armed forces, and in the event of a military clash between the two superpowers, the Kremlin always expected the Americans to make the most of Iranian bases to attack the Soviet Union's underbelly. But after the Islamic Revolution, the Americans were forced to pull out of Iran, and Moscow wondered if they would look to Afghanistan instead.

Afghanistan had been in a state of domestic turmoil since 1973, when its king, Zahir Shah, had been deposed after forty years on the throne. In the political flux that ensued, Moscow lost its few allies on the ground and the country seemed to be descending into a state of lawlessness. Then, in the course of 1979, the KGB heard reports of covert American support for the Afghans and informed the Kremlin that the Afghan president, Hafizullah Amin, was turning towards Washington, meeting American representatives and signalling an interest in establishing better relations with President Carter. At the same time, Amin started to openly criticise Moscow.

As the security situation in Afghanistan deteriorated even more, in the closing weeks of 1979, Andropov performed a sharp turnaround. Some months before, in March, he had urged his fellow members of the Politburo to take a cautious line. Supported by Foreign Minister Andrei Gromyko and the prime minister, Alexei Kosygin, he warned against intervention, arguing that tanks would not resolve another country's domestic political crisis. The Soviets would be the aggressors, he continued, and be seen and treated as such by both the Afghans and the outside world. Brezhnev concurred and ordered Amin to fight his own wars instead of expecting the Soviets to do that for him.[59]

Andropov, in other words, foresaw all the dangers and risks of intervention but went on to ignore them as his growing fears and running imagination clouded his judgment. In such difficult days of East–West relations it was hard enough to maintain a level head, and Andropov had become increasingly paranoid about western intentions towards his homeland. But in the heady months that followed the Iranian revolution, it was more difficult still.

What he, and the other architects of Russia's war, could have done instead was much simpler and vastly less costly. If, in the Kremlin's worst-case scenario, an Islamist or pro-American regime had seized power in Kabul, the Soviets could have quickly identified and built links with various Afghan factions that would have opposed it. Afghanistan has always been a highly complex mixture of rival ethnic groups with different religious and political affiliations, and if any one faction became too powerful then others invariably emerged to counterbalance it.

The Soviets were well aware of these deep divisions within Afghan society, having been closely involved in the country's domestic affairs for centuries, yet curiously do not seem to have drawn up any plan to 'divide and rule'. The loyalty of some of these rival commanders could, for example, have been bought with large bribes. At the very least, such a policy would have helped to contain any foreign presence in Afghanistan, although, more ambitiously, Moscow could also have carved out its own zone of influence.

If the Kremlin feared incursions into its own territory by Islamist radicals, then a full-scale intervention of Afghanistan was also hugely disproportionate. There are forbidding natural obstacles – high mountains and wide rivers – that made any serious Afghan encroachment of the border most unlikely. And the Soviets also had a monopoly of air power since the Afghan government possessed only a threadbare air force, and they could therefore have used their warplanes and helicopters to effectively patrol the border.

These were exactly the tactics that the states of the former Soviet Union later used against the threat of encroachment by the Taliban movement that swept through Afghanistan from the mid-1990s. Russia, along with other countries, supplied large quantities of arms and supplies to its allies inside Afghanistan that fought a proxy war on its behalf. Other than a few isolated incidents, no Taliban force is known to have crossed the Oxus River.

Yuri Andropov died in 1982 and so was not alive to witness the immensely high price for the unnecessary, decade-long incursion that he had been responsible for. The Soviets lost around 20,000 soldiers – the precise number is unknown – and squandered billions of roubles before ordering a full-scale retreat. They left behind a puppet regime in the capital, which fell three years after the Soviet withdrawal in 1989. News of the invasion hugely increased tensions with the United States, making Moscow new enemies, including the American president *Jimmy Carter*, who now became even more viscerally anti-Soviet in his views, while playing into the hands of its existing critics. And, as such an ardent communist, Andropov would have been dismayed to watch the war hugely inflame domestic dissent within the Soviet Union, accentuating the tensions that erupted in the early 1990s as its empire began to crumble.

The Soviet regime paid a heavy price for an intervention that was induced essentially by panic about imaginary, worst-case scenarios.

'Good-Time-Charlie' Runs Wild in Afghanistan (1980)

In December 1979, the Soviet army invaded Afghanistan, overrunning the entire country in just hours. But almost at once it encountered resistance in the provinces from rebels who were lightly armed but skilful and determined. The Kremlin ordered its high command to bring the country under its grip as soon as it could, before the costs of the operation rose even more. But despite their determined efforts, the Soviet army suffered an increasingly heavy stream of deaths and casualties, and still its elusive enemy fought on.

Thousands of miles away, an American politician called Charles Nesbitt Wilson heard about the war.

A loud, flamboyant, garishly-dressed Texan, with a huge, constant grin and giant height, standing six foot seven in his cowboy boots, 'Good-Time-Charlie' Wilson had made a name for himself from the moment he arrived on Capitol Hill as a young representative in 1972. Many people talked about the personal life of a man who staffed his office with a team of leggy blonde young women, widely referred to as 'Charlie's Angels'. He went to wild parties, drank voluminous quantities of Scotch, snorted cocaine and shared an enormous jacuzzi with Vegas strippers who had 'long, red fingernails with an endless supply of beautiful white powder'. As for his constituents, 'they don't care if I am a single man and have dinner with a pretty lady now and then', as he once told a reporter.[60]

By the time of the Soviet invasion of Afghanistan, however, Wilson had precious few political achievements to boast of. He rarely spoke in debates and had never really championed any particular causes. But all that changed in 1980, when he had first heard about the fight that a collection of tribesmen, who were all illiterate, untrained and armed only with very few and entirely antiquated weapons, were putting up against the Russian invaders. His imagination was gripped by a television documentary and then also by the first-hand account of a fellow American who had visited Pakistan and seen first-hand what was happening. The rebels were trying to strike back at the Soviet army of occupation, she explained, but they simply lacked the resources to put up an effective fight. Their arms were sparse, simple and outdated.

'We'll be damned if we let them fight with stones,' rumbled Wilson as he leapt into action. Wanting 'to make sure that the Afghans could do everything possible to kill Russians, as painfully as possible', he immediately began to lobby Congress to provide more funding for the rebels. The CIA's budget increased in the early 1980s and then jumped considerably in 1984, when it received an additional $50 million. There was another surge the following year, when the rebels were allocated a whopping $300 million of unused budget.[61]

Charlie Wilson always said that he felt such an overwhelming need to support the Afghan rebels because they, like America, 'were fighting the Evil Empire'. Raised in Bible Belt territory, he saw the world in truly black-and-white terms that invariably portrayed communists as 'the bad guys' and their enemies, in Afghanistan or wherever, as the good. This does not, however, quite explain his enthusiasm for the cause of the Afghan rebels. There was no obvious need to fight for a country that had no obvious strategic value. Afghanistan is land-locked and devoid in any resources that are worth fighting for. Wilson and the CIA, in other words, could simply have left the Soviet forces in Afghanistan alone.

But Charlie was spoiling for a fight and finally had a theatre of war in which to act out his dream. This may have been because he had grown up in the Second World War – he was just eight years old when America joined the fray in 1941 – and heard numerous stories of the feats of heroes like Generals *Douglas MacArthur* and George Patton in a conflict that he had never been old enough to participate in. Then he narrowly missed the *Korean War*, and when he did join the navy, in 1956, he sailed the world but did not hear a shot fired in anger. By this time he was perhaps suffering from the complex that George Orwell, born eleven years before the *First World War*, diagnosed within his own self – the complex of being old enough to remember and experience a conflict but too young to participate.[62]

Some other complexes may have also been coming to the fore. During and after the Second World War, he had revered the British prime minister Winston Churchill, a reverence that became a life-long affair and one that he also shared with *Margaret Thatcher*. And so soon after the losses and humiliation of the *Vietnam War*, he probably regarded the Afghan venture as an opportunity to retaliate against communism and for America to exorcise its demons. Other congressmen undoubtedly shared this mindset: 'We lost 50,000 dead in Vietnam,' one congressman was heard to say when he was informed of Russian losses in the early years of the war, 'and that means the Soviets owe us another 40,000.'

By 1980 the Americans had another demon to exorcise. In April, President Carter had ordered a covert effort to rescue hostages who were being held in Iran by *Ayatollah Khomeini* (see *President Carter*). But Operation Eagle Claw was a major disaster and humiliation: eight servicemen died when helicopters crashed in an Iranian desert and the operation was aborted. So soon after *Vietnam*, it was a terrible blow to American prestige. Once again, something had to be done to put America back on the global pedestal it seemed to have fallen off so spectacularly.

By this time, planeloads of American arms were secretly pouring into Pakistan. Among the cargos were some of the Pentagon's latest and most effective weapons. One in particular caught the eye of the intelligence operatives who moved them. Desperate to counter the military threat posed by Russian helicopters and warplanes, which pounded the rebels' supply routes to and from Pakistan, Wilson and his CIA contacts had arranged to supply the shoulder-fired Stinger missile, which began to arrive in 1986. The hugely expensive Stinger quickly changed the course of the war. Immediately losing air superiority, the Soviet army had no chance of winning its battles on the ground. Two years later, the Kremlin concluded that the war was unwinnable and by February 1989 the last of its troops had left the country.

Charles Wilson had been instrumental in inflicting this defeat upon the Soviet Union. In an interview on American television about the conflict, Pakistan's former president Zia ul-Haq had argued simply that 'Charlie did it'.

'Charlie', however, had given little consideration to the consequences of flooding Afghanistan with so much, and such valuable, weaponry. As soon as the Soviets left, it became obvious that America had nothing in common with the ragbag of Islamist tribes that now began to viciously feud between themselves, tearing each other apart and destroying innocent lives with the arms that the American taxpayer had bought for them. Individual warlords now staked out their personal fiefdoms and waged brutal wars against their rivals. In 1991 and 1992, for example, thousands of people died in the capital, Kabul, as one faction rained rockets onto civilian areas.

Nor was it just an Afghan civil war that Charlie Wilson had fuelled. In the late stages of Russia's occupation, thousands of Islamist volunteers had started to arrive in Afghanistan to fight off the 'Godless' and 'imperialist' invader. These volunteers, among whom was Osama bin Laden, later became known as Al Qaeda, and Charlie Wilson had succeeded in lavishing enormous American generosity upon its global *jihad*. At the same time, Washington's involvement in Afghanistan exemplified and aggravated the Islamists' fears of and hostility towards the United States.

The wider region was now saturated with arms, turning whole regions of Pakistan, notably the city of Karachi, into a cauldron of political militarisation and stoking up a bitter guerrilla war in the Indian province of Kashmir. Vast quantities of American weapons had also been side-tracked by corrupt Pakistani officials or by Afghan recipients and sold to the highest bidder, one of which was reputedly America's arch-enemy, Iran, whose armed forces were well aware of the Stinger's value.

Before his death in 2010, Wilson had been asked about these inadvertent consequences of his warmongery but he had shrugged them aside, adding only that 'no one had heard of the Taliban' in the circumstances of the time.

In fact, neither Charlie Wilson, nor any other Cold Warrior, had ever needed to support the Afghan rebels at all. There was no strategic reason why the Soviets could not occupy Afghanistan, although there was a humanitarian one: the invasion caused a mass exodus of around 3 million refugees into neighbouring Pakistan, which was potentially destabilising as well as supremely miserable for the hundreds of thousands of unfortunate civilians who were condemned to living in wretched conditions. In Washington, some hawks had opined that the Soviet invasion posed a threat to the Middle East's oil fields. But there were huge stretches of desert between Afghanistan's most southern point and the Arabian Gulf. Besides, the Soviet Union already encompassed Armenia and Azerbaijan, which were not so much more distant.

An American arms embargo on the Afghan rebels would not have stopped them from fighting, since they were also supported, on a much lesser scale, by China and Middle Eastern countries. But all of these other foreign supporters channelled their arms through Pakistan, which was hugely dependent on American aid. This gave Washington considerable leverage to stop the flow of weapons into the region, even if diplomatic pressure on some of the foreign donors would have failed to reap results.

If the Soviets had been left to occupy Afghanistan, and Washington had refused to fund and arm the rebels, then there were two possible outcomes, both of which would have pleased the frostiest of Cold Warriors.

On the one hand, the Soviet Army might have remained in the country, fighting off a persistent but largely ineffective resistance. But a low-level conflict like this would have tied down the Soviet army from intervening in other, strategically important places where Washington had more reason to fear its involvement, notably the Middle East or central Europe. And it would also have drained the Kremlin's finances, making fundamental reform of the old system of communism even more of a pressing concern for the Kremlin. In other words, it would have helped America to win the Cold War.

The other possible outcome was that the Russians would have done what they went on to do in 1989: installed a pro-Soviet regime in Kabul and then retreated, leaving their puppet to fend for himself. Such a regime would probably not have lasted long, allowing the rebels and refugees to return and impose their own order. This might have happened as early as 1983 or 1984, and Afghanistan and the wider region would never have suffered from the mass influx and proliferation of weapons that have subsequently proved to be hugely destabilising. Nor would vast numbers of Afghan civilians, perhaps a million or more, have died.

Even if the Cold Warriors in Washington really were convinced that a Soviet presence in Afghanistan somehow posed a threat to the flow of oil in the Gulf, they did not need to invade the country to prevent such a worst-case scenario from being realised. Even a relatively small number of local insurgents, drawn from the tribes of Pakistan and Iran as well as Afghanistan, would have been capable of mauling any Soviet army that had swept south of the Afghan border and across large deserts towards the open sea. Washington hawks could have simply undertaken detailed surveys of who would have comprised this local opposition, assessed how it could have stopped any Soviet advance and worked out ways of helping it do so.

Ayatollah Ruhollah Khomeini, Iran and Iraq (1982)

Saddam Hussein had invaded Iran in 1980, hoping to wrest control of several oil-rich provinces at his enemy's most vulnerable hour: Iran had experienced a traumatic revolution the previous year, forcing it to turn its eyes inwards and look away from foreign threats. But the new Iranian leader, seventy-nine-year-old Ayatollah Ruhollah Khomeini, also deserves to be castigated as a warmonger. The reason is that, in the summer of 1982, he failed to seize a clear opportunity to end a war that had already inflicted extremely heavy losses on his country and which was to exact an even more devastating toll in the years ahead. Instead he chose to push the conflict into a new and quite unnecessary phase. Khomeini had escalated the war to undermine Saddam, but he could have done this in far simpler and more effective ways than using brute force.

In the late spring of 1982, the Iranians made a series of stunning advances and inflicted devastating losses on the Iraqi army. In March, Khomeini's men unleashed the *Beit al Moqaddas* ('Jerusalem') offensive, during which they recaptured huge swathes of territory, comprising an area of around 3,000 square miles, that Saddam's army had seized and occupied. Iranian soldiers, many little older than children who fought with basic arms or, in some cases, with their bare hands, formed 'human waves' that descended on the Iraqi lines, panicking the enemy soldiers and prompting many of them to flee.[63]

Then they recaptured the highly prized, oil-rich city of Khorramshahr. On 24 May its shattered defenders laid down their arms, raised white flags and walked towards the Iranians besiegers, who cried *Allah-o-Akbar* as they entered 'the city of blood'. Since his men now occupied just a few isolated pockets of Iranian territory and had otherwise been pushed right back into their homeland, Saddam announced that he would withdraw his forces from those remaining areas.

Ayatollah Khomeini, a heavily bearded, scowling, intense, turbaned cleric, could at this point have accepted a ceasefire and negotiations from a position of strength: his armed forces had the upper hand and the Iraqis were defeated, demoralised and on-the-run. The Iran–Iraq war would have been over, little more than eighteen months after it began. Incredibly, however, he ordered his generals to undertake a massive offensive into Iraq and continue the war. Up until this point, he had rejected calls for peace on the reasonable grounds that the Iraqis had to leave Iranian territory first. Now he had no obvious reason not to sue for peace. But Operation Ramadan began on 13 July, as the Iranians stormed across the Iraqi border and opened a new chapter in the conflict.

Khomeini, Iran's 'supreme leader', was showing signs of hubris and seemed to be entertaining wildly unrealistic ambitions. In Tehran, government statements heralded 'a grand, historical battle' which was about to be undertaken because 'now is the time for Saddam to be toppled and his Baath regime to die, so that the warmonger may be destroyed and the war ended'. Yet the Iranian army never had any chance of capturing Baghdad, or even seizing any significant amount of Iraqi territory: even reaching the Iraqi capital involved moving over hundreds of miles of hostile, enemy territory against a battle-hardened enemy that was fighting on home ground. Other countries in the region, notably Israel and Saudi Arabia, would also have stepped in to covertly support Saddam and stop the Iranians from becoming too powerful. True, there were many Iraqis who shared Khomeini's Shia faith. But he could not just assume that they would rise up against Saddam because of this single thing alone.[64]

After just ten miles, the Iranian advance was checked and then beaten back, but still Khomeini harboured other motives, less ambitious yet quite unrealistic. For example, he demanded reparations from Saddam to compensate for the damage that the Iraqi army had inflicted on Iran, even though the Iraqi leader, short of suffering a calamitous defeat, was never going to make any such offer. Perhaps, too, Khomeini wanted to seize the religious shrines at Najaf and Karbala, the most holy places for the school of faith, Shia Islam, to which Khomeini himself and most of his fellow Iranians swore allegiance. Yet reaching, and capturing, these cities promised to be hugely demanding, given the long distance they lay from the Iranian border. Perhaps, more simply, Khomeini just wanted to simply punish Saddam and his fellow Iraqis for the death and destruction they had inflicted on his own country.

At the very least, he wanted revenge, an emotion that is deeply ingrained in the hearts of many Shia Muslims, who have always viewed themselves as the victims of injustice and who regard it as their duty to seek revenge upon the oppressors. He had shown his vindictive ruthlessness unmistakably enough in the bloody days that had followed the Islamic Revolution in 1979, ordering the summary trials and mass executions of hundreds, perhaps thousands, of officials who had served the shah's regime and allowing his chief executioner, Sadegh Khalkhali, and his revolutionary courts enormous discretion to decide who was worthy of the death sentence and who should be spared.[65]

Unfortunately for so many innocent people on both sides of the war, such fanaticism, vindictiveness, hubris and ruthlessness were all marked traits of Ruhollah Khomeini. He had spent much of his life in the religious seminaries of Iran, Iraq and later, as an exile, in Paris, immersed in highly abstract, abstruse questions of Islamic jurisprudence and philosophy, drawing up blueprints of a new theocratic state that seemed, to the unconverted, to have no bearing upon reality. As well as showing the fanaticism of a religious zealot, the young Khomeini also became fired with loathing towards the Iranian leader, Shah Mohammed Reza Pahlavi, despising not just his corruption but his apparent indifference to Islam and his subservience towards 'the Great Satan', the secular, materialist and 'godless' United States.[66]

Above all, Khomeini derived an utter self-belief from his religious fanaticism. He regarded Iran's war against Iraq, like his own political career, as an utterly just, religious struggle fought in God's name. The political institutions that he had introduced were designed to express God's will, and Khomeini himself, in the words of one biographer, was genuinely convinced that 'he had polished his soul to such a point that his mind had become an instrument for the performance of God's will in the world'. Khomeini also regarded Saddam's regime as no more legitimate than the shah's rule, which he had overthrown: no government, he had long argued, can be legitimate unless it accepts the rule of God by uncompromisingly implementing Islamic law. For although he professed to be a Muslim, Saddam's rule was much more secular in content and style than Khomeini's.[67]

Khomeini's devout theological training and commitment also meant that he had a Manichaean, black-and-white, good-and-evil view of the world that led him to seek outright victory. In the words of one biographer, 'The struggle between truth and falsehood ... and the resulting tendency to see things in black and white is imprinted on children's minds and can remain with them for the rest of their lives. There are no grey areas and it is only through revenge that things can be put right.'[68]

The likelihood is that, in the early summer of 1982, Khomeini's fanatical and hubristic mindset was easily led astray by his senior commanders, all members of a Supreme Defence Council, with whom he held a decisive, fateful meeting on 10 June. His commanders may by this time have become so drunk by their stunning victory at Khorramshahr that their judgment had become intoxicated, quickly inebriating the supreme leader. Khomeini had not initially wanted to send his men into Iraqi territory but had relented when his commanders pressed him to do so.[69]

Khomeini's decision was a calamitous one for both countries. By the summer of 1988, when a UN Security Council resolution came into effect and imposed a ceasefire between the two armies, Iran and Iraq had suffered a total of eight, very bloody years of war. Hundreds of thousands died on both sides – it is possible that each country lost a million young men – and many more were displaced from their homes and forced to flee into the cities to find shelter and work. Both countries spent billions of dollars on the war, squandering huge earnings from the sale of oil that could have been spent on vastly more worthwhile projects. 'If the aim of the enemies was to deliver an economic blow to us, they succeeded to some extent,' admitted a senior figure in the Iranian regime, Hashemi Rafsanjani, as the ceasefire came into effect. Iraq and Iran were both weighed down by huge war debts, causing tension between Baghdad and Kuwait that spilled over into conflict and *invasion in 1990*. Another unfortunate consequence was that the wider region became even more awash with arms, fuelling wars and tensions in other countries, notably Afghanistan, Kashmir and Pakistan. But most of this damage could have been avoided if the two countries had signed a ceasefire and peace deal in the summer of 1982. When a ceasefire was eventually struck, in 1988, Iran was no further forward than it would have been if it had sued for peace six years before.

If he wanted to buttress his regime, Khomeini would have done better to have focused his time and resources on building up Iran's defences against other foreign aggressors, and finding alternative, peaceful ways of rallying the nation behind him and his cause. One such move would have been to find more support from foreign governments that would have regarded Iran's geographic position, and its oil, as strategic assets. Equally, to strike a blow against Saddam, Khomeini could have found allies among Iraq's Shia population who were in a position to wage a much more limited proxy war against the Iraqi government than the one he unleashed. Khomeini could have used such proxies to carve out his own sphere of influence within Iraq, just as the Iranian regime used such tactics so effectively against Iraq after 2003, when American forces invaded the country and *toppled Saddam.*[70]

General Galtieri and the Falklands (1982)

Just months after he had come to power as Argentina's new president, General Leopoldo Galtieri was at war with Britain, fighting a short but bitter, brutal and costly campaign for control over an archipelago in the South Atlantic.

Until the spring of 1982, few people in Britain, as well as elsewhere, could find the Falklands on the atlas, and a lot had never even heard of them. Once the war started in earnest, in May, some people also wondered quite why two countries were trading blows over islands that were sparsely populated, with just 1,800 inhabitants, and had no natural resources worth fighting over. And located 8,000 miles from Britain they did not appear to have any obvious strategic value. The islands, as the Foreign Secretary Peter Carrington once wrote, 'represented no vital strategic or economic interest for Britain'. Or, as Sir Denis Thatcher, the husband of the British prime minister, put it, they had only 'miles and miles of bugger all'.[71]

There are other respects in which the dispute over the islands is hard to understand. For if he had practiced careful diplomacy instead of using brute force then Galtieri, an impulsive man with a fondness for Scotch, would have had every chance of recapturing them. And even if, in a worst-case scenario, he had relied upon armed intervention, then he could have avoided outright confrontation and war with the British.

When General Leopoldo Galtieri had become Argentina's new president on 8 December 1981, he was determined to give the Falkland Islands, off the Argentine coast in the South Atlantic, the attention that he, and other members of his military *Junta* ('ruling clique'), strongly felt they deserved. Soon they had resolved to 'reactivate to the fullest extent all negotiations for the sovereignty of the Malvinas (Falklands)', and at the same time to 'prepare a contingency plan for the employment of military power should the first alternative fail'.[72]

Lying only 300 miles from the Argentine coast but so far from England, most Argentines had always regarded the Falklands as their own national soil, even though they had been British territory ever since 3 January 1833, when a British warship had anchored off the main harbour, Port Stanley, and a boarding party had touched ground and raised the Union Jack. The Argentines also refused to recognise Britain's claim over the island of South Georgia, several hundred miles to the east, even though it had first been discovered and claimed by Captain Cook in 1775. But Argentina's claim gradually became less convincing over the ensuing decades, as British emigrants started to arrive and colonise the land.

On that December day in 1981, Galtieri knew that progress on the issue would help him deflect his country's economic and political woes. Argentina's economy was under real pressure, with soaring inflation and unemployment. And the brutal political repression imposed by his political predecessors, notably the previous military leader, General Roberto Viola, had left a legacy of widespread, popular discontent. It would be a political masterstroke if he could win concessions from London by 1983, which would be the 150th anniversary of British rule.

If Galtieri was going to win back the Falkland Islands, then the most obvious starting point was to restart negotiations. Argentina had entered into talks over the matter in 1965 with a cash-strapped, cost-cutting British government that regarded its rule over such distant, barren land as an expensive luxury. The negotiations made good progress but a final deal was thwarted by the presence of a powerful pro-Falkland lobby in Westminster that insisted on justice for the 1,800 islanders. The 'wishes' of these islanders — not just the 'interests' that the UN General Assembly's Resolution 2065 referred to – could not be ignored and overridden, demanded their advocates in London. And every one of the Falklanders was a British citizen with British ancestry. None would even contemplate living under Argentine rule.

On coming to power in 1979, Margaret Thatcher had picked up negotiations where her predecessors had left off. Desperate to reduce the national deficit, she floated the idea of giving Argentina sovereignty over the islands and then leasing them back over a period of ninety-nine years, in the same way that the British were leasing Hong Kong from China. But when one of her ministers, Nicholas Ridley, had put the idea forward in 1980, he was subjected to fierce criticism in parliament as well as from the Falklanders themselves.[73]

At the end of February 1982 British and Argentine representatives had held talks in New York. But still there was no breakthrough and by now Galtieri was becoming increasingly impatient. On 19 March, events started to unfold with dramatic speed. In complete disregard for agreed procedures, the Argentine navy made an unauthorised trip to the island of South Georgia, accompanying some scrap metal workers, and raised their national flag. Buenos Aires then assured London that there had only been procedural errors and that the naval vessel had already pulled out. But British officials discovered that this was blatantly untrue and ordered reinforcements to sail to the South Atlantic. As the press broke the story, Galtieri ordered his army to invade the islands: he needed to strike now, he calculated, before the British reinforced their vulnerable position and it was too late.

Galtieri did not want or expect a war with Britain. He thought that seizing control over the islands would give him a stronger bargaining position, and that the British prime minister, *Margaret Thatcher*, would not want to fight over territory that she, and her political predecessors, had wanted to get rid of in any case. As his foreign minister Costa Mendez said, 'This occupation would make it possible for us to negotiate once and for all the underlying dispute. It would induce the international community ... to pay more attention to the reasons for the dispute.'[74]

But he knew, or must have known, that he was taking a risk. There was still a chance that 'the Iron Lady', as the Soviets called her, might 'prove her mettle'.

The miscalculation had disastrous results for the Argentines, as well as for the 255 British servicemen who died during the conflict and the 750 who were wounded. By the time the British captured Port Stanley, on 14 June, Galtieri's army had lost 649 dead and suffered around 1,700 casualties. Some 11,000 hungry and exhausted men of his mauled army were taken prisoner before being repatriated back to their homeland. News of the Falklands' capture had made him a national hero – on 5 April the masses had flooded into the Plaza de Mayo in Buenos Aires to cheer him – but when news of the surrender broke, weeks later, thousands of furious, bitter people came into the streets to vent their anger. Within just days, Galtieri had been forced from power. Stripped of all rank, his death penalty was commuted and he was given a lengthy jail term instead.

Galtieri had taken a gamble and lost, paying a heavy price for doing so. But there is a good chance that he could in fact have achieved his ultimate goal, and wrested the Malvinas back into Argentine hands, without using force at all.

In the talks that Argentine negotiators had held with their British counterparts since the mid-1960s, the sticking-point had always been the willingness of the fiercely patriotic Falkland Islanders to forfeit British rule and live under an Argentine flag. Margaret Thatcher and her ministers knew that sacrificing the Falklanders to defence cuts would provoke strong backbench opposition, particularly amid accusations that she had also abandoned the white population in the former British colony of Rhodesia, which became the independent republic of Zimbabwe in 1980.

But the obvious step that General Galtieri overlooked was to offer financial payments to each and every islander in return for seceding sovereignty. The cost of effectively bribing the local population was far lower than mounting an expeditionary force to capture the islands, let alone waging a war to defend them. At the same time, the Falklanders could have had the right to live on the British mainland if they had wanted to, and perhaps been given guarantees that their way of life on the islands would be respected and to some degree preserved. Had Galtieri waited just a few years, then such an offer would also have been much more difficult for a British government, cash-strapped at a time of recession, to refuse.

Galtieri also succeeded in undermining the trust of the islanders at the very time he needed to build it. In 1981, the Argentines suddenly stopped the civilian transport flights between the islands and their mainland, sending a message that they were not only unreliable but also hostile. Making matters worse were the overhead flights that Argentine jets suddenly started to make into the airspace of both the Falklands and South Georgia in early 1982, reinforcing the same threatening, negative impression of Galtieri's intentions. Designed to ramp up diplomatic pressure on London, they made the Falklanders even more mistrustful. Galtieri could have shown an impressive restraint by ensuring the Argentine navy did not overstep the mark when escorting the scrap metal workers to South Georgia in March and then ensuring they left immediately when the British protested. Instead, such menacing behaviour alienated the British: as a memorandum drawn up by Carrington emphasised, negotiations 'cannot be pursued against a background of threats from either side of retaliatory action if they break down'.[75]

What Galtieri could have done to win trust and favour was to initially offer the tiny population of South Georgia and the South Sandwich Islands, which successive Argentine governments had also laid claim to, sums of money to surrender their allegiance. By keeping to his word and giving these fifty or so British citizens what he had promised, he would have won wider trust in the Falklands, where the local population would have watched the newly founded wealth of the South Georgians with an envious eye.

At the same time, Galtieri could have done more to win American support for his policies. He knew that he had highly influential supporters in the United States, notably Jeane Kirkpatrick, America's ambassador to the United Nations, and Alexander Haig, a former protégé of *Nixon* and Kissinger. Nor did the president, *Ronald Reagan*, fully grasp why Britain needed the Falklands, describing them as a 'little ice-cold bunch of land down there'.[76]

Relations between the two countries had been steadily improving by the time the conflict broke out. Above all, Galtieri had one great bargaining chip: he knew that Reagan was a true Cold Warrior who was deeply concerned about communism making any inroads into Argentina and elsewhere in South America. Argentina was closely involved in American efforts to fight the left-leaning 'Sandinistas' in Nicaragua. In his meetings with the American diplomat Thomas Enders, Costa Mendez could have prompted the Americans to put more pressure on London to reconsider the future of the islands, and floated a proposal to pay the Falklanders to live under Argentine rule.

Even if he had been determined to use military force to capture the islands, then Galtieri could have played for time and avoided a conflict altogether. In his White Paper, published in June 1981, the British defence secretary, John Nott, had proposed some far-reaching changes to the Royal Navy. One aircraft carrier, the *Hermes*, was to be scrapped and another, *Invincible*, would be sold off to Australia. At the same time, the assault ships *Fearless* and *Intrepid* were to be disbanded and the number of frigates slashed from sixty to forty, while the British naval presence in South Atlantic and in Antarctica would be hugely reduced, or even eliminated.

Had the Argentines postponed their attack for another year, then the Royal Navy would simply not have been able to mount any effective response. Yet although the defence white paper was widely discussed in Britain and must have been seen by Argentine diplomats based in London, Buenos Aires did not act on it. Even putting stronger diplomatic pressure on London at this later stage would, in all likelihood, have reaped rewards for the Argentines. By this time, the fate of the white population in Zimbabwe had long faded as a political issue in Britain – political memories are notoriously short – and Margaret Thatcher was no longer so vulnerable to protests from her political backbenchers.

Instead, Galtieri rushed into using force, probably to alleviate political pressure at home. After unsuccessful talks with British representatives in February 1982, the Argentine government issued a communiqué saying that the British had to recognise its sovereignty 'within a time which at this advanced stage of the discussions will necessarily have to be short'. The following day, Argentine newspapers, almost certainly using leaked information, said that the timescale was no more than three or four months and that it was not negotiable. In other words, the media had raised the hopes of the Argentine general public and Galtieri knew that he would lose face if he now dashed them.[77]

But on Friday 26 March Galtieri ordered his generals to capture the Falklands. It was a huge gamble: two days before, the British parliament responded to the incident in South Georgia by passing a motion that called for a tough line over the question of sovereignty, and Galtieri later admitted that the British response showed an 'evident intention of the British government to reinforce the Falkland Islands'. In his bid to win the support of the Argentine masses, Galtieri had risked war and over the coming weeks paid a heavy price.

Margaret Thatcher's Gamble in the South Atlantic (1982)

In July 1982, Margaret Thatcher, her senior military commanders and many officials all attended a memorial service at St Paul's Cathedral in London to commemorate the end of the Falklands War, six weeks before. After a brief and bitter fight against the Argentine invaders, the islands had been recaptured and the Union Jack was once again flying over the town of Port Stanley.

It was one of Margaret Thatcher's greatest political moments, a defining moment of not just her first term in office but indeed of her entire political career. By a curious inversion of what her opponent, the Argentine leader *General Leopoldo Galtieri*, had hoped to do for his own country by invading the islands, Mrs Thatcher had fought a victorious war and rallied her nation behind her by recapturing them. During the campaign, and for some while afterwards, the British public had looked away from severe economic woes at home and held its breath as 'our boys', as she famously called them, took the enemy on. At this supremely patriotic hour, Margaret Thatcher's popularity soared and she went on to win the next general election, which was held the following year, with an overwhelming majority. To beat back Galtieri's wanton aggression against British territory, she had displayed determination and courage of the highest order.

Her achievement was all the more remarkable because the British campaign in the Falklands was, as the Duke of Wellington famously judged of Waterloo, 'a damn close-run thing'. On 5 April, a British task force, a hastily assembled armada comprised of a hundred ships carrying 26,000 men and women, had set off from Portsmouth to confront the enemy, eight thousand miles away in the South Atlantic. But the military risks were enormous. It had very limited air cover, protected only by the warplanes of the two giant aircraft carriers, *Hermes* and *Invincible*, and would have to face bad weather in the South Atlantic, where a harsh, bitter winter sets in during the month of May. And so far away from home, it would only be a matter of time before it began to run out of food and fuel. In other words, if Galtieri did not back down and a land invasion did prove to be necessary, then the entire task force, even in a best-case scenario, would be stretched to its absolute limits.

Nor were British commanders quite sure of Argentine capabilities. If Galtieri's men put up unexpected resistance then there would be a real danger that the British task force exhausted its ammunition and other supplies: in fact, in the hours preceding the Argentine surrender in June, some British units were down to their last few rounds. If the Argentines had targeted and struck just a few supply and transport vessels instead of warships, then the entire operation would have been impossible.

It also emerged that the enemy's warplanes had a much longer reach, and a more deadly strike, than British commanders originally anticipated. When, on 4 May, HMS *Sheffield* was hit and sunk, with the loss of twenty-one lives, the vulnerability of the entire operation was plain to see: if just one of the Argentines' deadly Exocet missiles struck either of the two carriers, then it would kill thousands of servicemen and torpedo the entire military effort. And Mrs Thatcher would have then been forced to resign, having spectacularly misjudged the viability of the entire operation.

Another danger was that British forces might hit the wrong target or kill more people than need be. And if anything did go seriously wrong, then Mrs Thatcher would have easily lost the sympathy of her own general public and of the outside world. This is exactly what did happen in May. Galtieri had been stunned when, hours after his invasion of the Falklands at the beginning of April, the United Nations General Assembly had passed a resolution that unequivocally condemned his actions. But then, on 2 May, a British submarine sank an Argentine warship, the *Belgrano*, leaving 323 sailors to drown in the icy seas. The Argentines claimed that it had been heading away from the islands and back to port, so it could not have posed any military threat to the British. Whatever the truth, news of the incident and the large loss of life brought about a sea change of attitude amongst some foreign governments. 'Suddenly it looked as though ... a horrid NATO country (was) clobbering poor a Third World non-aligned state ... I could see this happening,' recalled a British ambassador, Sir Anthony Parsons. The Security Council seemed ready to turn, not against Argentina but Britain.[78]

But when news reached London of the Argentine invasion, however, Margaret Thatcher had had little choice but to use military force. Galtieri's actions amounted to naked aggression against British sovereign territory, blatantly breaching Article 51 of the United Nations Charter, which embodies 'the inherent right of self-defence against attack'. The invasion, argued the British prime minister, 'has not a shred of justification nor a scrap of legality' since the islands were 'British sovereign territory' and had been ever since 1833. Even the left-wing, anti-militaristic leader of the opposition, Michael Foot, demanded 'action, not words'. It would have been unjust, as well as political suicidal, just to brush aside the interests of the 1,800 British subjects who lived on the islands. And even if no one had lived there, doing nothing would have encouraged other would-be invaders elsewhere in the world. 'A large task force will sail as soon as possible,' as Mrs Thatcher told a packed, silent House of Commons on 3 April. 'The Falkland Islands and their dependencies remain British territory; no aggression and no invasion can alter that simple fact.'

But Mrs Thatcher never needed to order an entire task force to set sail. There were other measures, militaristic but far less drastic, that she could easily have started off with. Sending an entire task force, which should have been only a last resort, instead made it much more difficult for either side to back down and compromise. Galtieri would have been accused of weakness and cowardice if he had pulled his soldiers out and accepted a compromise deal when a large British force was heading southwards. And Mrs Thatcher would have faced the same charges if she had given away more ground than she originally wanted, having sent a task force but then failed to use it.

There was, however, a more limited military alternative that she could have pursued, one that would have balanced the need to use some force on the one hand without polarising positions on the other. On 30 April, the British government had imposed a 'Naval Exclusion Zone' around the Falklands and declared that any 'Argentine warships, including submarines (and) military aircraft ... will encounter the appropriate response' if they ventured within 200 nautical miles of the islands. This was a 'blockade' in all but name, one that led to the sinking of the *Belgrano*, even if Foreign Office lawyers warned against any formal use of such a confrontational term.

But instead of scrambling to assemble and then despatch a large task force, at such vast expense and huge risk, Mrs Thatcher could simply have ordered the Royal Navy to impose this blockade and allowed it several months to yield results. Any naval blockade would have probably soon starved the Argentine army into surrender, since it did not have enough food, and arms, to last for long: on subsistence rations, reckoned British experts at the beginning of the conflict, the bulk of the occupying army could last until 18 May, although some units were better equipped than others.[79]

The Argentines could have supplied their garrison from the air, since in this scenario the British, acting without any aircraft carriers, would have had no air cover. But moving supplies by air is very costly. During the war, British bombers also pounded the islands' main airstrip at Port Stanley, and the other four, at Darwin, Kepple Island, Dunnose Head and Pebble Island, could also have been put out of use, making the Argentines' task even more difficult. Since the Argentine air force had only seven transport planes, they would have been able to drop only relatively meagre quantities. If, in a worst-case scenario, the 1,800 civilians had begun to starve, then the Red Cross would have been in a position to intervene. And if the Argentine authorities had denied the Red Cross access, then they would have faced the furious condemnation of the outside world, providing the British with a huge propaganda gift.

At the same time, the imposition of economic sanctions on Buenos Aires would have continued to exact a painful price, prompting Galtieri to accept a face-saving formula, withdraw his forces and declare that he would 'win' the Falklands back in the future. If, in a worst-case scenario, he had still refused to beat a retreat, then a British task force could have been sent later in the course of 1982, arriving in the Falklands' summer season, which begins in October, and then confronting a hungry, dispirited and isolated Argentine conscript force that would have surrendered even more quickly than it did in May and June, probably without even a single shot being fired.

The effectiveness of the naval blockade became clear by 17 May, when the Argentine air force made a desperate bid to break through the British no-fly zone to deliver desperately needed supplies. There were reports that, by this time, their land forces could last for only another ten days and their living conditions were deteriorating rapidly. As the harsh Falklands winter set in, there were outbreaks of gastroenteritis and influenza. Feelings of homesickness and boredom were also endemic among the conscripts, many of whom were just teenagers. They were suffering, as the official British historian of the conflict has written, 'from an ill-considered deployment, with many more troops sent than could be adequately supported'.[80]

Imposing a naval blockade over a period of several months would have had other advantages. The diversion of at least four NATO nuclear submarines to the South Atlantic would have alarmed Washington because it detracted from the Cold War deterrence that they were intended to mount. As a result, the Reagan administration would have put more pressure on Galtieri to withdraw, perhaps offering him more incentive to do so. On 1 April, President Reagan had held a fifty-minute phone call with a somewhat drunken Galtieri but failed to shift him. However, a promise of more generous economic aid might have helped to swing the balance if a face-saving formula, perhaps based on vague but hollow British promises of negotiations, could have been found.

Margaret Thatcher cannot take all the responsibility for having failed to pursue or even consider this much more limited option, and having instead rushed headlong into taking a wholly disproportionate response. After all, the fifty-six-year-old prime minister knew almost nothing of the military. A chemist and lawyer by training and a politician by vocation, she had only had direct contact with the armed forces once before, during the siege of the Iranian Embassy in London in the spring of 1980. On that occasion, she established a close and easy rapport with the British commanders who organised a very successful rescue mission.

Part of the blame must instead lie with the senior naval commanders who, as soon as news of the Argentine invasion broke, advised the prime minister. The head of the navy, Admiral Sir Henry Leach, had galvanised Thatcher by promising to recapture the islands by force, and assuring her that a task force could be assembled within days. His Churchillian gung-ho approach appealed to the prime minister enormously.

Unfortunately, the top brass had a vested interest in overlooking any less drastic measures. The previous year, the British defence minister, John Nott, had published a plan to drastically reduce the size of the Royal Navy. So by advising the prime minister to assemble a task force, even if everyone hoped it would not be used because Galtieri would back down, the admirals made themselves and their warships appear indispensable to British defence requirements.[81]

If in one sense such resolution and fortitude was admirable, it was also hugely costly in human life. As well as the loss of 2,000 killed and wounded on both sides, the British armed services lost six ships and twenty aircraft. Mrs Thatcher's government was always determined to slash its outgoings but ironically the immediate cost of the operation was considerable, somewhere between £350 million and £900 million, and in the longer term, taking into account the cost of replacing lost and damaged resources, it was closer to £3 billion. It would have been cheaper to have simply given every islander a million pounds to abandon their homes and relocate.

But the admirals had won their own private battle against the threat of defence cuts. After the war, the Royal Navy successfully defended itself against the onslaught of the Treasury. The sale of *Invincible* to Australia was cancelled while the patrol ship *Endurance* and two assault ships were given a reprieve. The massive reduction in the number of frigates and destroyers was also revised. The Falklands War seemed to have proved that Britain did, after all, need a bigger navy than the accountants had originally thought.

As for Mrs Thatcher, sending a task force to the South Atlantic had served another purpose. Having grown up in the Second World War – she was fourteen when war had been declared in 1939 – she had long revered Winston Churchill. During the difficult days of her early administration, long before the Falklands crisis erupted, she had even read Churchill's wartime speeches in front of bewildered staff, and the tone and language of her speeches sometimes strongly echoed those of her wartime predecessor. Sending an entire task force to the Falklands was quite unnecessary in military terms, but it did at least help her not only to reap a huge electoral boost, as she probably always hoped it would, but to live her dream of emulating Britain's great wartime prime minister.[82]

Ariel Sharon's Grand Plan for Lebanon (1982)

On 3 June 1982 the Israeli defence minister, Ariel Sharon, finally found an excuse to unleash a war that he had long been planning. News had just broken that Israel's ambassador to London had been shot and wounded by Palestinian militiamen, and in Tel Aviv prime minister Menachem Begin quickly ordered a full-scale invasion of Lebanon in retaliation.

This was not a knee-jerk response to Palestinian violence, similar to the assault that Israel had undertaken four years before, when its soldiers had made a large-scale incursion into south Lebanon in response to a number of Palestinian attacks on Israel. Instead, the cabinet decision of June 1982, which authorised the invasion, made only meagre references about pushing Palestinian guerrillas away from the border. Sharon had something far more ambitious in mind. War was his means of realising a much wider political end, and all he had needed was an excuse to fire the first shot.[83]

Up until this point, the Israelis had only once been to war when it was not strictly 'necessary'. That occasion was the *Suez invasion in 1956*. Israel had fought each and every other conflict only in response to an attack by a neighbour, notably in 1948, 1967 and 1973. However the Lebanese war in 1982 was a 'war of choice' that was commissioned, planned and executed by a warmonger who was determined to use force of arms at any price.

But then defence minister Sharon had never away shied from battle. He had first made his name, among Israelis and Arabs alike, as a young, swashbuckling maverick officer who had, in the words of a future Israeli president, 'an uncanny feel for battle'. In 1953, at the age of just twenty-five, he was tasked with organising and leading a new commando unit, known as Unit 101, that was specially trained to carry out raids behind enemy lines, a role in which he excelled. When his men killed scores of innocent Arabs during a reprisal raid on Qibya (see *Abu Jihad and Gaza, 1955*) in 1954, he remarked only that 'some Arab families must have stayed in their houses rather than running away', adding that the houses were too big to search properly before the explosives were laid. UN military observers, however, noted that 'bullet-riddled bodies near the doorways and multiple bullet hits on the doors of the demolished houses indicated that the inhabitants had been forced to remain inside until their homes were blown up over them'. Then the Israeli prime minister, Moshe Sharett, ordered him to make another attack on Gaza, insisting that it should only be on a small scale. But Sharon – 'a most difficult man to control' – and his men killed twenty-nine and injured many more.[84]

Nearly thirty years later, and as a veteran of many more engagements, wars and campaigns, Ariel Sharon had drawn up a new battle plan, one whose scope and ambition vastly transcended anything that he, or indeed most of his contemporaries, had ever even envisaged, let alone put into practice.

Instead of just pushing Palestinian guerrillas further north, putting the Israeli border beyond their range, he instead sought to completely reshape the politics of Lebanon. The Syrians, who had a strong presence in a country they regarded as their own, would then be driven out and a new government, headed by Israel's allies, would be installed in Beirut. As a result, the morale and resources of the PLO, led by Yasser Arafat, would be broken, allowing Israel to seize Palestinian territory on the West Bank without opposition. And there would be a massive flow of Palestinian refugees from Lebanon and the West Bank into neighbouring Jordan, which in turn would become a Palestinian state, thereby taking the international pressure off Israel to create one in the West Bank, which Israel could annex for itself. In other words, Ariel Sharon wanted to redraw the geopolitical map of the Middle East, and wanted an excuse to fight a war that would achieve that end.[85]

Over the preceding few months, a few of Sharon's cabinet colleagues had also shared his vision of launching a more ambitious attack on Lebanon. But they had done so for reasons that were much less ambitious: General Rafael Eytan, for example, wanted to destroy the PLO once and for all to stop it from launching more attacks on Israel. But Sharon needed more supporters in the cabinet and had to work out a way of enlisting them. At one stage he proposed bombing PLO targets in Lebanon, knowing that the guerrillas would retaliate against Israel and by doing so give him an excuse for a more far-reaching attack. But other Israeli ministers seemed to read his mind and refused him permission to attack Lebanon. Then, at a meeting with prime minister Begin in early March, Sharon and Eytan found another excuse for war, arguing that an assault on Lebanon would test the sincerity of the Egyptian government, which had just signed a peace deal with Israel. But still Begin and the rest of the cabinet were unpersuaded.

In the meantime, Sharon was also trying to shore up his position in the United States, knowing that, without American diplomatic support, any attack on Lebanon would quickly grind to a halt. In December 1981 he met senior American negotiators and, in the words of one leading historian, 'fed the Americans selective information that was intended to prove that the PLO was making a mockery of the cease-fire agreement and to establish Israel's right to retaliate'. But still he could not sell the case for war, and as he laid down his plan to drive the PLO out of Lebanon altogether, an appalled US diplomat could not contain his horror: 'General Sharon, this is the twentieth century and times have changed! You can't go around invading countries just like that, spreading destruction and killing civilians ... the entire region will be engulfed in flames!'[86]

When, on 3 June, ambassador Shlomo Argov was shot in London, Sharon and Eytan played down the fact that the attack was perpetrated only by a breakaway faction of the PLO, wanting to pin the blame on its mainstream rival. This time the prime minister concurred. 'They are all PLO!' exclaimed Begin, as he cut short one of his intelligence chiefs. The warmongers also overlooked the fact that the shooting did not breach the ceasefire agreement between Israel and the PLO, which called for a halt in hostile activities against Israel only 'from Lebanon'. And Sharon and Eytan also misled cabinet colleagues about their ulterior motives and the scope of the operation that they now prepared to unleash.[87]

Israel now launched its full-fisted attack on Lebanon, Operation 'Peace for Galilee'. Its leaders did so ignoring *President Reagan's* pleas not to widen their attack and brushing aside Yasser Arafat's offer of a mutual ceasefire and negotiations. But as the tanks rolled forward and the warplanes swooped over Beirut, casualties mounted. Around 10,000 civilians died as the Israelis fired on civilian areas with cluster bombs, which shower whole areas with clouds of metal shrapnel, and with phosphorus shells, which are designed to burn flesh down to the bones. Many more civilians, perhaps as many as 100,000, were forced to flee their homes. At the same time, Ariel Sharon proclaimed that Israel was taking 'the greatest precautionary efforts' to avoid civilian casualties, and claiming that during the entire siege of the Lebanese capital 'only forty of the almost 24,000 buildings in Beirut proper had been hit, each one of them precisely identified as a PLO base or as places where the PLO Chief Yasser Arafat was likely to be'.

But General Sharon's plans for regime change were still no closer to being realised. On the contrary, they suffered a decisive blow when his key ally, Bashir Gemayal, was assassinated on 14 September. The carnage became even worse when Gemayal's followers exacted a terrible revenge against innocent Palestinians, slaughtering thousands of innocent refugees in the camps of Sabra and Shatila. As the outside world watched in horror, thousands of ordinary Israelis came out into the streets to protest against their own government while an official report ruled that Israel should take 'indirect responsibility' for the tragedy. Meanwhile, Israeli jets continued to blast the Lebanese capital. 'Watching the Israeli air force smashing Beirut to pieces was like having to stand and watch a man slowly beating a sick dog to death,' lamented a report for *Newsweek* magazine as the campaign ran into its ninth week.

But soon Israel, as well as Lebanon, was in crisis. Ariel Sharon resigned from the cabinet in February 1983, six months before Menachem Begin announced his own, quite unexpected departure from politics. He was perhaps dispirited by the peace protestors who gathered outside his house every evening, or by the letters from the families of the 500 soldiers who had by now lost their lives in a war that seemed, to most Israelis, to be as futile as it was unnecessary. The former prime minister immediately became a recluse, his physical and psychological health broken.

Israel's international image had also taken a serious blow in direct proportion to the battering its forces had inflicted on Lebanon. Its relations with the United States were also stretched to breaking point. President Reagan ruled that Israel did not have a right to annex, or to build settlements, on the West Bank and could not exploit the bloodshed in Lebanon for its own political ends. And the crisis focused an enormous amount of attention upon, and sympathy for, the fate of the Palestinian people. 'I can't be part of this anymore,' bemoaned Secretary of State George Shultz to his president, 'the bombings, the killing of children. It's wrong. And you're the one person on the face of the earth who can stop it.'[88]

The root cause of the Lebanese tragedy was that the warmongers who unleashed the invasion of Lebanon had, at some point, lost touch with reality. When President Reagan remonstrated with Israel, as its artillery pounded civilian areas of Beirut, Menachem Begin wrote a letter that drew extraordinary parallels with the Second World War. It was, writes one expert, 'bizarre in the extreme'. Some of Begin's fellow Israelis thought the same. 'Return to reality,' urged one Israeli parliamentarian, who had herself once fought against the Nazis in Poland. 'We are not in the Warsaw Ghetto, we are in the state of Israel!' Other Israelis urged Begin to shed his 'Holocaust Complex', and some critics noted that Israel's Christian allies in Lebanon, the Phalange, had roots in European fascism in the 1930s.[89]

Equally, Ariel Sharon's grandiose, hubristic plans for the region were based on completely unrealistic assumptions. The difficulty of installing a pro-Israeli government in Beirut, in the face of the visceral opposition of highly influential neighbours such as Syria, was immense. That such a regime would last more than a few weeks, or even days, seemed even less likely. To drive hundreds of thousands of Palestinians into neighbouring states was not only callous but also completely misjudged the reaction of the outside world. As two of Israel's most distinguished military writers, Ze'ev Schiff and Ehud Ya'ari, have declared, 'Born of the ambition of one wilful, reckless man, Israel's 1982 invasion of Lebanon was anchored in delusion, propelled by deceit, and bound to end in calamity.'[90]

Sharon, however, was not finished. He returned to office, as prime minister, in 2001 and remained a proponent of what one historian has called Israel's 'doctrine of perpetual war'. As Israeli leader, he urged the American president, *George W. Bush*, to attack Iran, settling for Iraq only as a second-best option.[91]

By a curious irony, the American president also once called Sharon 'a man of peace', although this hardly fitted a man who entitled his autobiography *Warrior*, who had planned and participated in so many battles and who reminded even Israel's strongest supporters of 'the swaggering Goering'. It was as curious an irony as Henry Kissinger receiving the Nobel Peace Prize after unnecessarily destroying four countries – Laos, Cambodia and North and South Vietnam – or the UN chief Kofi Annan hailing *Tony Blair* as a 'peacemaker'.[92]

Sharon could have found much less drastic alternatives to realise the ends he championed. If he had wanted to simply defend his country, then instead of trying to drive Palestinian civilians out of Lebanon he could simply have reinforced the demilitarised zone between Lebanon and Israel. And if he had wanted to drive the Palestinians away and annex the West Bank, then he could have adopted the same policy as subsequent right-wing Israeli governments, which have encouraged or authorised the construction of Jewish settlements there. Carried out gradually over a long period of time, this media-friendly form of annexation would have attracted less attention and condemnation from the outside world than an invasion. And it would have spared many innocent Palestinian lives.[93]

Ronald Reagan's 'Lovely Little War' in Grenada (1983)

Ronald Wilson Reagan stepped into the White House on 20 January 1981 as a true Cold Warrior, deeply committed to taking a hard line against the Soviet Union and the threat he thought it posed to America's national security. Almost at once, he adopted a fierce anti-communist rhetoric and soon vowed to dramatically increase the national arms budget.

But like other warmongering presidents, notably *Jimmy Carter*, *Lyndon B. Johnson* and *George W. Bush*, Ronald Reagan was not a man with a military background. The sixty-nine-year-old president was a former actor who had spent his wartime years shooting only films. In the 1940s he was something of a star, reaping an average earning of $52,000 for each of his performances – a vast sum of money in America at that time – and receiving more fan mail than anyone except Errol Flynn. But he was so busy taking lead roles, such as a secret service agent called 'Brass Bancroft' who stops an enemy spy stealing a death ray known as 'the Inertia Projector', that he never even left his native country during the Second World

War. His closest brush with violence was witnessing a bruising confrontation among feuding workmen in Hollywood, several weeks after the end of the war.

But like Johnson, he sometimes seemed to have convinced himself that he had done rather more than he really had. 'By the time I got out of the Army Air Corps,' as he wrote in his 1965 autobiography, 'all I wanted to do – in common with several million other veterans – was to rest up for a while, make love to my wife, and come up refreshed to a better job in an ideal world.' And when asked by a French journalist about events in wartime Europe, he answered, 'I know all the bad things that happened in that war. I was in uniform for four years myself.'[94]

But in October 1983, the tall, lanky, broad-shouldered president, who always had immaculate, slick-black hair, finally had his chance to flex muscle. The invasion of Grenada, a very brief, three-day affair that involved nearly 8,000 American soldiers, was a quite unnecessary show of force to deal with a crisis that never existed. In short, the White House was determined to fight a war, come what may.

A tiny Caribbean island off the Venezuelan coast, Grenada was a former British protectorate that had won independence from London in 1974. It had subsequently been ruled by an idiosyncratic figure called Sir Eric Gairy, a dictatorial individual whose chief interests, outside politics, were UFOs and the occult. With a population of only around 100,000, covering just 120 square miles and with no known natural resources, it was a place of no real importance to the outside world other than as a rather exotic and fairly unusual holiday retreat and as a producer of nutmeg.

But in 1979, a dynamic young radical called Maurice Bishop has seized power on the island, turning to Cuba for help and implementing a socialist plan to reduce high unemployment and rescue a stricken economy. Several hundred Cubans, mainly labourers, technicians and medics as well as number of military advisers, then arrived on the island over the months that followed while Washington looked on warily. Four years later Bishop himself then suffered the same fate as his own predecessor: on 19 October

1983 he was toppled in a military coup that was instigated by more left-leaning figures. News of his arrest infuriated his supporters. Violent protests followed. The Grenadan security forces opened fire and killed dozens of demonstrators.

Shortly after 5 a.m. the next morning, two advisers woke President Reagan as he slept at his cottage in Augusta. They briefed him as he sat, still in his pyjamas, and outlined his options. 'He was very unequivocal,' recalled Robert McFarlane. 'He couldn't wait' to unleash military force.[95]

America's armed forces were already on stand-by and the White House now gave them the order to move. Early in the morning of 25 October, waves of helicopters and transport planes flew from Barbados and landed advance parties on the south-eastern tip of the tiny island. The invasion, which was America's first armed intervention since the *Vietnam War*, met barely any resistance for the simple reason that the island had barely any armed forces, just semi-trained militias that brandished outdated arms.

As news of events broke, President Reagan made an official announcement about America's intervention and what lay behind it. 'Our military forces moved quickly and professionally to restore order and democracy,' he proclaimed, but also 'to protect American lives'.

Reagan was referring to the safety of a thousand American citizens who were students at St George's University Medical School. Yet officials at the school had been in regular touch with Washington ever since unrest began, nearly a week before, and had given repeated assurances that they were safe. So had many of the students and their parents, while Grenadan representatives in Washington were also guaranteeing the students' safety.[96]

President Reagan also claimed that the students had no means of escape. Yet the international airport had remained open until the day before the invasion, and a steady flow of foreign travellers had simply flown home. If the White House genuinely was concerned about the safety of the students, then they could easily have been evacuated without a full-scale invasion. As the school's chancellor pointed out, they were safe until the invasion began, because it was at this point that law and order broke down.

Reagan then found another justification for the invasion, pointing out that the Grenadans were building a new airport runway, at Port Salines in the south, that would have been capable of hosting Soviet and Cuban bombers. The island, he claimed, was 'a Soviet-Cuban colony, being readied as a major military bastion to export terror and undermine democracy. We go there just in time.'[97]

In fact, President Bishop had wanted to upgrade the island's airport facility to attract more tourists. Grenada was, and remains, highly dependent on tourism, and this was particularly true in the early 1980s, when it had been hit hard by the global economic slump. Its airport was too small for passenger jets, forcing tourists to fly to neighbouring islands before completing their journey on smaller planes. Even then, they touched down at an airport that was dangerously outmoded and completely lacking in the latest safety equipment and standards.[98]

Even in a worst-case scenario, it was difficult to see quite what danger the island posed to American security, since it lies much further away from the American mainland than even Cuba. And after the invasion, the reality of Grenada's 'Cuban threat' became clear, although Washington tried to hide it. There were in fact only 700 Cuban personnel on the island, and nearly all of these were civilians, who were working with Western counterparts, mainly from Canada, to develop its infrastructure. Less than 100 Cuban military personnel were on the island, and their role was to train the island's sparse and largely ineffectual armed forces. The Cubans had brought weapons with them, it was true, but these were very outdated pistols and rifles.

Reagan warmongered at a price. In the UN Security Council, American diplomats had to exercise their right of veto against a hostile resolution but, more importantly, news of the invasion caused serious rifts with his strongest allies, notably Canada, which had business interests on the island, and above all with Britain: the British prime minister, Margaret Thatcher, was infuriated that she had not been consulted in advance about an attack on a former British colony by an ally with whom she supposedly had 'a special relationship'. The president did his best to placate her in a difficult phone call that he made soon after the attack got underway, explaining that he was deeply concerned about any such information being leaked. 'If I were there, Margaret, I'd throw my hat in the door before I came in,' implored Reagan as he started the awkward conversation. The rift was healed but the British prime minister failed to see how the regime that Reagan had toppled was any different from its predecessor.[99]

The operation also bequeathed another legacy, one that very nearly had catastrophic results. It was not just coincidence that, a few days after the invasion, the world came to the brink of nuclear war. Convinced that the United States and its Nato allies were about to launch a nuclear attack against the Soviet Union, the Kremlin came within a whisker of launching its own pre-emptive assault: only the desperate last-minute intervention of an undercover agent, Oleg Gordievsky, prevented 'Operation Ryan' from running its full course. But the attack on Grenada was just one of several acts that reinforced the Soviet image of a highly aggressive United States that was determined to use military force against its enemies. The invasion, proclaimed the Soviet vice-president Vasili Kuznetsov, proved how the Americans were guilty of 'making delirious plans for world domination...which were pushing mankind to the brink of disaster'. The Soviet press simply labelled Reagan a dangerous lunatic.[100]

The Soviets certainly had a point. Here was an American president who openly declared his ambition not just to 'contain' the Soviet Union but to 'reverse' its post-war expansion, and who was prepared to massively increase defence expenditure – the biggest increase in America's history – in order to do that. Making things worse was the president's sense of frustration with the Lebanese crisis, which had erupted just weeks before (see *Ariel Sharon*). The Israelis had invaded Lebanon but Reagan was unwilling to pick a fight with President Begin of Israel and pressure him to accept a Palestinian state. So he wanted to 'act tough' elsewhere in the world to make up for it.

If the invasion of Grenada reinforced the Kremlin's impression of a highly aggressive and untrustworthy American leader, it did nonetheless succeed in doing what President Reagan had probably always had in mind. The island had also come to symbolise the fate of the rest of central America, notably Nicaragua, where Washington's allies were coming under pressure from Soviet-leaning allies. This may have been why the president, according to one White House official, had developed 'an obsession' with Grenada and, two months before the crisis, he had talked about 'a dark future' foreshadowed by the 'tightening grip of the totalitarian left in Grenada and Nicaragua'. So by invading the island, Reagan did at least win a symbolic victory.[101]

The attack also probably helped him to vent the pent-up aggression, and the need to 'do something', that followed a devastating attack on American barracks in Beirut a few days before, when nearly 300 marines had died. And the invasion – 'a lovely little war', as one newspaper called it – not only erased something of the trauma of Beirut but also helped to restore America's military confidence, still recovering after the disasters of the Vietnam War. 'The Vietnam syndrome,' the president had declared two years before, would be 'a temporary aberration' that would be swept away by 'a new spirit'. Grenada conjured and nurtured that spirit. 'Our days of weakness are over! Our military forces are back on their feet and standing tall,' the president proclaimed at a press conference after the event. He went on to herald the invasion of Grenada as the exorcism of 'the legacies of Vietnam and Watergate (that) still haunted the conduct of our own foreign policy'. This probably also explains why the episode was followed by what one journalist called 'an orgy of self-congratulation (in which) 8,612 medals were awarded to participants – most of them to desk officers who never came within a thousand miles of island'. War, in other words, had been a way of generating a 'feel-good' factor.[102]

A revealing insight into the presidential mindset came from a speech that Reagan had given in New Hampshire during his electoral campaign. In this address he recalled an earlier age 'when Americans could be anywhere in the world ... and no one would dare lay a finger on him because they knew that the United States would go to the rescue of any of its citizens wherever they might be. How we've let that get away from us, I'll never know.' By attacking Grenada, ostensibly on the grounds of rescuing endangered American students, Ronald Reagan was perhaps able to convince himself that perhaps not of all that had indeed 'got away'.

But if the president hoped that the invasion would give him a lasting boost in the electoral polls, he was sadly mistaken. After just a few months, the outburst of national pride that followed the attack started to subside. America would have been just as safe, and his longer-term poll ratings no different, if he had kept away from Grenada and his intelligence agencies had simply monitored events there and his aid agencies had helped to develop it. And he could have found more peaceful ways of enhancing his country's greatness, perhaps spending the money he allocated to the Grenadan invasion on America's economy instead.

7

THE POST-COLD WAR ERA

President George H. Bush and the Invasion of Panama (1989)
Just six years after *Reagan's attack on Grenada,* his successor, President George Herbert Walker Bush, unleashed his own assault in America's southern hemisphere. In the early hours of 20 December 1989, thousands of American troops and hundreds of aircraft poured into Panama, overwhelming its capital, Panama City, and a number of other strategic points. There was not much fighting to do because the Panamanian army was not only tiny but also largely ineffective, particularly when it was ranged against the world's most formidable armed force. By the end of the day, most of the country lay in America's grip and 'Operation Just Cause' had brought the rule of Manuel Noriega to a swift end.

But brief though it was, the invasion took a heavy toll of local lives. American war planes and helicopters targeted a number of residential areas of both the capital and the city of El Chorrillo, which Americans and locals subsequently nicknamed 'Little Hiroshima'. Hundreds were killed, perhaps several thousand, although the true cost in human lives remains unclear and was largely hidden from the outside world because heavy restrictions were placed on the media. The invasion also inflicted considerable damage on Panama, estimated at around $2 billion.[1]

The episode had close parallels with the earlier events in Grenada because, in both cases, there was no clear reason to intervene. And in a presidential address to the nation on the day of the invasion, President Bush echoed Reagan's rhetoric of six years before, justifying the assault because it 'safeguarded American lives', although he added that it also brought freedom and democracy to people who would not otherwise have been able to enjoy such privileges. He also gave two other reasons, which were suppressing the drugs trade and protecting the Panama Canal.

But none of the cited reasons held much weight. Noriega had always been linked to the drugs trade, which was so powerful and endemic in Panama that almost everyone of importance there was linked to it too. In any case, Noriega was well known to have had a close association with the narcotics business when his relations with Washington were at their closest. Ever since he came to power in 1983, and over the following three years, Noriega had been a trusted anti-communist ally of the Americans. Before he fell out of favour in 1986, he had been on the CIA payroll, receiving sizeable payments in return for supporting Reagan's war against the Marxist 'Sandinista' rebels in neighbouring Nicaragua. In 1983 a Senate Committee had pointed out that Nicaragua was a major centre for drugs smuggling, but its findings made no difference to the strong support he received in Washington.[2]

It was true that there were 'American citizens' inside Panama on the eve of the invasion. But President Bush failed to mention that nearly all of these 12,000 Americans were soldiers who were armed and not in any way threatened by Noriega's tiny army. These soldiers were based in eighteen heavily fortified military camps that, under the terms of a 1977 treaty, the American government was entitled to operate on Panamanian soil.

Nor would Noriega have dared to obstruct the passage of maritime traffic through the Panama Canal, the crucial passageway that links the Atlantic to the Pacific Ocean. He had never threatened to do this, not least because even a mere threat would have grossly provoked the outside world, particularly the United States, which heavily depended on it. In 1989, the canal was, as it remains, one of the world's busiest waterways.

President Bush, in other words, seemed to be looking for an excuse to attack, and hours before the invasion he finally got one when an American soldier was shot dead as he went through a road block that led to a sensitive military site. Within just hours, President Bush had ordered the invasion instead of asking questions about what had happened and lodging an official protest.

The most likely explanation for the invasion is that the White House got a bit too carried away by the spirit of the times. Over the preceding few weeks, the Soviet-controlled communist regimes of Eastern Europe had crumbled before mass demonstrations. Perhaps inspired by the events in Beijing in February, when brave protestors had gathered in Tiananmen Square to protest against communist rule in China, hundreds of thousands of ordinary people came out into the streets of Poland, Hungary, East Germany, Czechoslovakia, Bulgaria and Romania. Probably the most dramatic developments, and images, of the revolutions of 1989 took place in East Berlin: on 9 November, just six weeks before the American attack on Panama, ordinary Berliners defied communist rifles and started to demolish the Berlin Wall. Ever since its construction in 1961, the Wall had been the great symbol of the 'Iron Curtain' that had divided the communist east from the democratic west.

George H. Bush and his advisers could hardly have been unmoved by such heady events. The Soviet Union had been America's enemy and counterweight ever since the end of the Second World War in 1945. But as the Soviet Empire disintegrated, America's leaders were overwhelmed by a sense of exercising unfettered power. In other words, they felt that they could do what they wanted, like a young adult who suddenly leaves home and experiences true independence for the first time. Or perhaps they just wanted to take part and contribute to the 'cause of freedom', and simply regarded Panama as an easy picking.

President Bush doubtlessly saw the electoral benefits of jumping on the freedom bandwagon. He reckoned that the invasion of Panama, dressed up in the language of 'freedom and democracy', would help to identify him with the wider spirit of liberty that seemed to be engulfing other regions of the world. Bush certainly quickly and explicitly related the assault on Panama to the wave of democracy movements that were then sweeping through Eastern Europe. 'Today we are ... living in historic times,' he announced shortly after the invasion, 'a time when a great principle is spreading across the world like wildfire. That principle, as we all know, is the revolutionary idea that people, not governments, are sovereign.'

Other Western leaders were doing the same thing, only more peacefully. Margaret Thatcher, for example, seized a good many photo-opportunities with the leaders of Eastern Europe's revolutions, twice meeting with the Czech president, Václav Havel, in the course of 1990. It was just such peaceful, simple and cost-free gestures that President Bush could have undertaken if he had wanted to boost his electoral ratings. By identifying himself with the new leaders of democratic Eastern Europe, and helping them to sort and shape their post-communist societies, he might have acquired a more enduring boost to his electoral fortunes. Instead his poll ratings shot up in the short-term – just as Reagan's did after Grenada – but he still went on to lose the 1992 presidential election.

If, on the other hand, he had genuinely wanted to oust Noriega, then there would have been simpler and easier ways of doing so than launching a full-scale invasion. Just two months before the attack, in October, some of Noriega's many enemies had plotted a coup. Major Giroldi Vega's plot failed but it would probably not have been long before others tried. Because President Bush was a former director of the CIA, he would have been well aware of how effective American money, arms and information could be at helping conspirators to find their way.

Instead, the White House undertook a course of action that was not just unnecessary but deeply damaging to its international image. Because the invasion was undertaken without the backing of the United Nations, as well as without any clear justification, it helped to foster an image of America as a lawless, reckless actor on the world stage. This became

clear on 29 December, when the UN General Assembly voted 75
to 20 with 40 abstentions in favour of a resolution calling the
intervention in Panama a 'flagrant violation of international law
and of the independence, sovereignty and territorial integrity
of the States'. Another body that condemned the attack was
the Organization of American States, which passed a similar
resolution by a margin of 20–1. But just a few weeks before,
when Washington debated intervening in Panama to support
Giroldi's coup, a White House official had stated that there
were no plans to act against the wishes of the Organization
of American States. This, he said, was because of the 'hue and
cry and the outrage that we would hear from one end of the
hemisphere to the other (that would) ... raise serious doubts
about the course of that action'.[3]

And when, just eight months later, *Saddam Hussein* invaded
Kuwait, it was not easy for President Bush or any of his supporters,
to argue why the American intervention in Panama was right but
the Iraqi intervention in the emirate was wrong.

Saddam Hussein and the First Gulf War (1990)
True to the spirit of the Arab tribal traditions in which he was
nurtured, the Iraqi leader Saddam Hussein thought nothing of
using violence and threats to get what he wanted. As a student
leader in the mid-1950s, the young Saddam had set up roving
gangs of thugs who beat up his rivals and anyone else who failed
to tow his line, such as shopkeepers who refused to protest
against government policies by shutting up their businesses. And
in 1959, when he was a twenty-two-year-old radical, he had
taken part in a daring, although botched, assassination attempt
on the Iraqi leader, General Abdul Karim Qasim, spraying his
car with automatic fire and killing the driver although only
wounding his target.

Then, as soon as he came to power, after a coup by the Ba'athist
Party in 1968, he started to acquire a reputation for brutality,
carrying out regular purges against dissidents, real and imaginary.
Suspicious of their loyalty, he showed little mercy towards Iraq's
vast population of Shia Muslims, concentrated in the south,

and to the Kurdish people who lived in the far north of Iraq, close to the Turkish border. In the mid-late 1980s, for example, Saddam ordered one of his henchmen, Ali Hassan al-Majid, to use chemical weapons against entire Kurdish villages, thereby driving their inhabitants into the waiting hands of the Iraqi army which then mowed down vast numbers of them, killing perhaps as many as 100,000. And in March 1988, as the Iranians made battlefield advances alongside some Kurdish allies, Saddam unleashed chemical weapons upon the entire city of Halabja, killing thousands but leaving his own soldiers, who had protective clothing, largely untouched.[4]

In the summer of 1990, Saddam had then turned his attention to his southern neighbour, Kuwait, and once again quickly reached for the trigger.

Tensions had been growing between the two countries ever since the end of the war between Iran and Iraq – a wholly unprovoked conflict that Saddam had unleashed against *Ayatollah Khomeini*'s regime in 1980. After eight consecutive years of war, Iraq's economy was devastated, its oil revenues squandered on sustaining a massive war effort as well as upon a highly ambitious programme of public works, such as the construction of four bridges over the Tigris and a new $7 billion 'Saddam International Airport'. Saddam was dependent upon a variety of foreign creditors, who lent him billions of dollars to keep his country afloat.

Iraq needed a high oil price to service its interest payments on these debts, as well as to stave off civil unrest at home: a year after the 1988 ceasefire, thousands of demobilised soldiers had found themselves without jobs and then gone on the rampage in protest, attacking and killing several hundred Egyptian expatriates, who they accused to taking work that rightfully belonged to them.

By the late 1980s, however, the price of oil had dropped considerably from the highs of a decade or so before, when Iraq, and Iran, had reaped huge quantities of 'petrodollars' that had allowed them to sustain their war. The price of oil is determined, quite simply, by the balance between supply and demand, and in the late 1980s there was enough oil floating around on the world's markets to satisfy demand and keep the price low.

Most oil producers belong to the Organization of the Petroleum-Exporting Countries (OPEC) and work together to calibrate their output. In early 1990, OPEC members had agreed to reduce their output in order to decrease global supply and, by doing so, then push up the price of a barrel to at least $18. In particular, the Kuwaiti government agreed to produce no more than 1.5 million barrels of oil every day, a lot lower than the levels that it was capable of sustaining. But the emirs then went back on their word, pushing out around 2.1 million barrels. At a tense OPEC conference in May 1990, Saddam lambasted the Kuwaitis and demanded an explanation. Saddam, and his foreign minister, Tariq Aziz, knew that, if the barrel price fell by just one dollar, then Iraq would lose $1 billion of income every year.[5]

It has never been entirely clear what Kuwait was trying to achieve. By pushing down the price of oil, it was hurting other oil producers, not just Iraq. Knowing how vulnerable the Iraqi leader was at his post-war hour, the emirs perhaps wanted to force him into making concessions, above all by giving ground over disputed areas of the oil-rich border region. In particular, both countries laid claim to the 'supergiant' Rumaila oil field that straddled the border. The dispute between the two countries now rumbled louder over the weeks ahead, made worse by Baghdad's accusations that the Kuwaitis were siphoning off petroleum from Rumaila using sophisticated American drilling techniques – 'slant drilling' – from an installation on their side of the border.

In other words, it seems that the Kuwaiti emirs, not Saddam, were provoking the crisis. Their refusal to respect their agreed quota limits amounted to economic warfare that was designed to make Saddam give way over border territory. Saddam cleverly tried to placate the Kuwaitis and offered them incentives – such as a right to lease two islands – to make them cooperate. But still the Kuwaitis refused to back down, prompting many commentators, not prone to conspiracy theories, to wonder why they were being so intransigent and who was encouraging them to hold out against Iraqi pressure.[6]

But on 2 August Saddam took the bait, ordering 120,000 soldiers and hundreds of tanks and warplanes to make a massive assault on the emirate. Within just four hours, Kuwait had been overrun and the capital was under occupation. His violence was probably driven by raw anger and retribution, and he saw war as a natural way of venting his fury.

But Saddam never needed to use military force. On the eve of war in August, there was probably still some scope for diplomacy because Kuwait's overproduction was hurting every oil producer, including the one with most clout: Saudi Arabia. Over the preceding few weeks the Saudis, who had previously been a close ally of Kuwait, had admitted quite openly that they wanted a higher oil price and complained about the emirs' obstinate production policies. By this time Saddam had much improved his relations with Riyadh – he had signed a non-aggression treaty with the Saudis the year before – and had some scope to use this influence to pressurise Kuwait.

Saddam also had another ally by this time whose support he could have done more to enlist: the United States. He had already raised the oil price dispute with the American ambassador to Iraq, April Glaspie, who had told him, in one of the most controversial diplomatic meetings of recent decades, that Washington had 'no opinion' on inter-Arab disputes. But less well-known is the fact that Glaspie also had 'a direct instruction from President (George H.) Bush to seek better relations with Iraq'. The president and some officials in Washington regarded Iraq as a counter-weight to America's chief regional rival and enemy, Iran. After long years of war, Iraq also offered American companies lucrative opportunities to rebuild its shattered infrastructure, particularly in its massive oil sector.[7]

Saddam had been well aware for some months that he had highly influential supporters in the American capital. On 12 April, he had interrupted his honeymoon to meet a congressional delegation led by Senator Bob Dole, who had presidential blessing to make the trip to Iraq and improve trade ties. It was symbolic, too, that talks between Kuwait and Baghdad broke down on the same day, 1 August, that a large shipment of advanced US-manufactured transmission equipment arrived in the Iraqi capital.[8]

What the Iraqi leader lacked was the political nous to exploit the divisions between his supporters and critics in Washington. He could have done this by tempting American companies, which had hugely influential supporters on Capitol Hill lobbying on their behalf, with massive contracts to work in Iraq, and by toning down his anti-Israeli rhetoric, which played into the hands of his congressional enemies.

Nor did Saddam necessarily need to target Kuwait at all if he wanted to increase his oil revenues. He could instead have stepped up pressure on the United Arab Emirates, which had also been exceeding its own daily quota. By early August, the UAE had agreed to trim its own output of 2 million barrels a day by about 400,000 barrels, and it might have kept its promises, unlike Kuwait, if it had faced extra pressure from Saudi Arabia and the United States. Had its leaders done so, then Kuwait's overproduction would not have been worth fighting over: overall, oil producers across the world pumped out around 65 million barrels every day, and Kuwait's own output, if not a mere drop in this ocean of oil, was a relatively small part of it.

If Saddam was determined to use force, then he could have taken a more flexible course than the one he did. In early 1990 Kuwait had been troubled by unrest as protestors, calling themselves 'the Constitutionalists', came into the streets to demand the restoration of parliament. On more than one occasion armed police had used batons and tear gas to break up a demonstration. It is possible that Saddam could have reached out to these agitators and found ways of fomenting their unrest, or at least publicizing the violence that the Kuwaiti security forces were using against them. Nor, if he was determined to use military force, is it clear why he needed to order an invasion of the entire emirate: if the Kuwaitis were siphoning oil from the Rumaila field, his army could have seized and sealed off a section of the border that they were allegedly using. This more limited response would not have incurred the massive American response that followed the full-scale invasion of Kuwait: advance units of the US army started to arrive in the Gulf almost at once, and within weeks General Norman Schwartzkopf had nearly 600,000 troops under his command in the region who were poised to attack.[9]

Perhaps the most mystifying question, however, is why Saddam ordered his army to stay in Kuwait, facing certain defeat, even annihilation, against a bigger and far better trained and equipped opponent. Again, his warmongering instincts seemed to have prevailed. Washington's determination to defend Kuwait became evident as soon as American forces began to arrive in neighbouring Saudi Arabia. At this stage, Saddam could have ordered his army to withdraw without much loss of face and claimed a victory: his actions, he could have argued, had shown the Kuwaitis what he was capable of doing unless they complied with their OPEC promises. Saddam could also have ordered his army to sabotage Kuwait's oil infrastructure without inflicting, as they later did, any environmental damage.

Instead, his army was routed and suffered huge losses in a devastating '72-hour war' that began at the end of January 1991. Saddam's humiliated regime also came under intense pressure from its enemies at home – the Kurds and Shia population – whose hopes of winning some freedom were raised by the scale of the Iraqi defeat. For a time it also seemed possible that the victorious allies would press their devastating advance beyond Kuwait and go all the way to Baghdad. By fighting two unnecessary wars, one against the Kuwaitis and the other against its allies, the Iraqi leader very nearly paid the same price as the soldiers who he sent to their deaths.

The most likely explanation is that Saddam was carried away by the depth of his own anger towards the Kuwaitis. Deeply frustrated and embittered by the losses of the eight-year war with Iran, he was pushed too far by Kuwait's unwillingness to reduce its oil output. But like other brutal dictators, he lacked relatively level-headed advisers were willing to speak up and criticise him, well aware of the grisly fate of anyone who displeased him.

François Mitterrand and the Genocidal Regime in Rwanda (1990)

In the early 1990s, the French government fought a covert war not against communism or militant Islam but a more surprising 'enemy': what it called 'Anglo-Saxon' influence.

Over the centuries the French had of course fought numerous wars with the British, ranging from Trafalgar and Waterloo to the epic clashes of the Hundred Years War (1337–1453). They had also fought the United States once before – a brief clash of arms during the Second World War when, in 1942, the American and British armies had invaded French North Africa and prised it from the grip of Marshal Philippe Pétain's Vichy regime. Half a century after the war, French policy makers thought they had identified a British-American, or 'Anglo-Saxon', threat to their own interests in central Africa.[10]

The chief protagonist of this 'war by proxy' was the French president, François Mitterrand. He was not a fanatical enemy of the two English-speaking countries. On the contrary, throughout his political life, Mitterrand was a mixture of all sorts of contrasting beliefs. His politics were left-leaning but he later moved to the centre and did deals with the right. During the Second World War he had supported the Vichy regime, which had struck a deal with Hitler and the German army after it overran France in 1940, but was also against it. And, on becoming president in 1981, he veered between sympathy and support of the United States as well as being critical and hostile: amongst his first actions on his election was a phone call to President Reagan, assuring him of France's contribution to the Cold War against Russia.[11]

But in October 1990, he received an urgent cable that seemed to confirm his suspicions and fears about both America and Britain. The news he received was that a rebel army had invaded Rwanda and was threatening to seize the capital, Kigali, and topple the regime led by President Juvénal Habyarimana. Immediately Mitterrand ordered the despatch of a rapid reaction force of soldiers that could defend Kigali and keep Habyarimana in power.[12]

Rwanda was thousands of miles away from France and an overpopulated, poverty-stricken land that was largely devoid of anything worth fighting for. But it mattered to Mitterrand, and a clique of hardliners in Paris, because it was a French-speaking country. The rebels who threatened it were based in neighbouring Uganda, a former British colony that was deemed to be a close ally of Washington. And Mitterrand had a 'domino theory', akin to worst-case scenarios imagined by the architects of the *Vietnam War*: if Rwanda fell under Uganda's rule, then France would lose its influence over a much wider region of French-speaking Africa, above all in the neighbouring state of Zaire.

Mitterrand judged that this was the right time and place to take a stand. Because the Soviet Union was already in the process of disintegrating, the United States seemed to possess untrammelled power. And as Kigali came under pressure, American soldiers were arriving *en masse* in Saudi Arabia, ready to recapture *Kuwait* from the Iraqi army. But while America seemed to be growing ever more powerful, France seemed to be on the defensive. In particular, it had emerged that East and West Germany, which had been divided since the end of the Second World War in 1945, were going to be united into one big state. This meant that France would be overshadowed by a much bigger neighbour, one that might even steal its place as a permanent member of the United Nations Security Council.

This prospect resonated deeply in the consciousness of a certain type of Frenchman who hated to see France overshadowed by either of the two Anglophone nations. From this viewpoint America, in particular, was an upstart nation that had no right to have any influence in a part of Africa that Paris had ruled for more than a century. Nor could Britain be allowed to humiliate France in Africa again, having done so once before, at Fashoda in Egypt in 1895, when a French expeditionary force had backed down before a British contingent that went on to fly the Union Jack over the a section of the Nile.

But the president's political judgment had often been open to question. There is compelling evidence that, during the Algerian war in the late 1950s, he had been complicit in the torture of suspected insurgents. Then, in 1959, came 'the Observatory Affair', when he faked an assassination attempt against his own self, staging a shooting from a passing car in a failed bid to seize the political limelight. Numerous other scandals rocked his fifteen-year presidency. Most notably, he was implicated in the bombing of a Greenpeace ship that caused the death of a protestor, the wiretapping of newspapers, and massive corruption scandals, the full scale of which only became apparent after his death, at the age of eighty, in 1996.[13]

Perhaps none of this was too unusual, by the standards of French politics. More important was the fact that by the early 1990s Mitterrand appears to have become obsessed with the 'threat' posed by 'Anglo-Saxons', a term that proliferated in his confidential memoranda and conferences of the time. It was this that prompted him, and his son, Jean-Christophe, to order French soldiers to fly to Kigali and buttress the Rwandan army against a rebel onslaught. By doing so, they were to begin a foreign entanglement that scandalised France and the outside world when, several years later, details about France's involvement in this remote corner of Africa, and of events on the ground, finally emerged.

The truth about Habyarimana's regime was that he, and many of his top people, harboured a fanatical hatred for the members of one of Rwanda's two main tribes. Habyarimana himself was a Hutu, and his hatred was vented towards the rival Tutsis. There had been outbursts of ferocious violence between the two ethnic groups before, and there were signs, which French representatives on the ground were aware of, that the underlying tensions could easily spill over again.[14]

Both Belgium and France, whose diplomats and agents had expert knowledge of Rwanda, were aware of what was coming. The Belgians, for example, had issued several clear warnings: as early as the spring of 1992 the Belgian Ambassador, Johan Swinnen, told his bosses that an extremist Hutu clan, was 'planning the extermination of the Tutsi of Rwanda to resolve once and for all ... the ethnic problem and to crush the internal Hutu opposition'. Both governments would have known that the 1994 genocide was being planned well in advance. Elaborate lists of potential victims were drawn up. And half a million machetes and huge numbers of axes, hammers and razors as well as guns were purchased beforehand and stockpiled, funded by international donors who were unaware of how their generosity would be abused.

Mitterrand can't be accused of warmongering just because, on that October day, he decided to intervene. The French reinforcements stopped Kigali falling to rebel forces, as Mitterrand had wanted them to, and this prevented unnecessary pillage and plunder in the capital as well as keeping 'Anglo-Saxon' influence at bay. He also protected the European nationals who were living in Kigali, as he later argued on French national television when he justified his decision to intervene.

The real criticism of President Mitterrand and his fellow hawks is that, once the rebels' advance had been checked, they deliberately failed to rein in their allies in Kigali and sue for peace. The French knew, almost as soon as their intervention began, that the rebels were too strong to be defeated – without, that is, a full-scale involvement by French troops that would have been hugely costly and unacceptable to the French public. The only realistic alternative was to strike a ceasefire, start negotiations and agree upon a power-sharing agreement between Habyarimana and his rivals and enemies. More moderate voices in Paris called for such flexibility but Mitterrand ignored and obstructed them.[15]

As the security situation deteriorated in the course of 1992, the French allowed their protégé in Kigali to attend talks, held in the Tanzanian town of Arusha, and then strike a deal. But the war hawks in Paris actively sabotaged any power-sharing agreement, regarding it as a 'sell-out' of their close ally and, by extension, of French influence in Francophone Central Africa. Mitterrand urged Habyarimana to ignore Arusha and brushed aside calls to replace him with a more moderate figure. At the same time French arms poured into Rwanda and an increasing number of military advisers, 'security experts' and shadowy intelligence officers supported Habyarimana's war effort. The war raged on.[16]

Squandering a chance for peace, and instead fighting a war that Habyarimana always looked set to lose, was bad enough. But making it worse were the clear signs of ethnic violence. As the French continued to strongly back Habyarimana's war, his security forces started to prepare for genocide against the Tutsi population, who comprised the ranks of the rebel army. In the course of 1993, roving gangs of militiamen started their grisly work. Soon the gutters of the capital and other government-controlled towns and villages were running red. Over the next year, around 500,000 Tutsis were slaughtered. Some estimates put the figure at closer to 1 million.

The complicity of the French government was well summed-up by an international human rights watchdog. In an open letter on 25 January 1994, Human Rights Watch identified France as 'the major military supporter of the government of Rwanda … providing combat assistance to a Rwandan army guilty of widespread human rights abuses, and failing to pressure the Rwandan government to curb human rights violations'.[17]

If Mitterrand had pressurised his ally to sue for peace and set up a power-sharing deal in 1992, then of course such an arrangement may not have lasted. But, at the very least, valuable time could have been bought and this delay might have saved many lives. And, from Mitterrand's own personal perspective, while multi-party government might have given 'Anglo-Saxon influence' some inroads into Rwanda, it was surely preferable to the outright defeat that the Kigali regime suffered in the summer of 1994, when the rebel forces flooded into the country and seized the capital and then the rest of the country outright. This forced vast numbers of innocent Hutus to flee. Fearing Tutsi retaliation, around 2 million fled to neighbouring countries, where many died of starvation and disease. And it also meant that an 'Anglo-Saxon' ally had won the day.

In fact, if he had wanted to keep British and American influence at bay in this region, then President Mitterrand need never have used military force at all. He could have pursued the alternative strategy that was also open to the advocates of 'the domino theory' in south-east Asia three decades before: identifying and then exploiting different ethnic and national loyalties within a region that your enemy controls. Most of Africa is rife with such ethnic conflicts, and this was one reason, amongst others, why it was misleading to ever envisage an 'Anglo-Saxon sphere of influence'. Mitterrand had at his disposal numerous Africa experts who had a close knowledge of such differences and how to 'divide and rule' by exploiting them.

Jonas Savimbi's Destruction of Angola (1992)

On 29 September 1992, the people of Angola must have wondered if they were on the verge of starting what promised to be, by their own wretched standards, a golden new age. After long decades of war, they were now voting for a new government, and all of the main parties had agreed to respect the outcome of the ballot. Hundreds of international observers were supervising the elections and there was a general consensus that they were being held freely and fairly. And the international sponsors of peace – the governments of the United States, South Africa, Portugal and the United Nations – all held high hopes that Angola was set to follow the example of Cambodia, where elections had also been undertaken with great success and a war-ravaged population was now heading for a more prosperous future.

Such hopes, however, were quickly dashed. One of the two key parties, Unita, unexpectedly lost the election, taking a much lower share of the vote than President Eduardo dos Santos' rival MPLA party. Unita's leader, Jonas Savimbi, immediately ordered his followers to resume the war against the government, and his men now withdrew from the unified national army and started to overrun whole swathes of the country. The elections would have to be held again, insisted Savimbi, and a transitional government, in which he shared power with his rival, should be established.

But Savimbi's warmongering now cost his country dear. Thousands died in the fighting and many more were forced to flee their homes. Savimbi's men pursued devastating 'scorched earth' policies, attacking and destroying the country's vital infrastructure, notably its factories, buildings, dams and power supplies, in a bid to make the government comply with his demands. A favoured Unita tactic was to force civilians to flee into areas controlled by the government and then fire artillery shells at those places of refuge: the warped, demonic logic was to put as much pressure as possible on the enemy government's resources of shelter and medical aid, and to prove that the government could not protect its citizens. At the same time, Savimbi's men scrambled to seize control of Angola's diamond mines, knowing that their vast resources were capable of financing his war effort far into the future.[18]

The civil war now raged for the next two years, shattering not just Angola but the wider region as refugees and weapons poured into neighbouring countries. In 1994 there were renewed hopes for peace when Savimbi and dos Santos signed a deal in the Zambian capital, Lusaka, but once again the agreement broke down when Savimbi ordered his men to break the ceasefire and attack government positions. Observers pointed out that he had never regarded the deal as anything other than a means of buying time, since he had signed it when his soldiers were retreating before a resurgent government army. He was indifferent, they continued, to the suffering of his own people and to the destabilisation of the wider area that the conflict was causing. Others claimed that since he himself could not govern his own country and never had any chance of winning power, he had decided to make it ungovernable for someone else. This was why he gave his soldiers a 'scorched earth' order to wreck the parts of the country that were falling out of his grip, destroying and burning buildings and infrastructure while forcing civilians to flee. He was motivated, in other words, chiefly by jealousy and spite.

The Unita leader had scotched real chances to rebuild a wrecked, traumatised country which had been at war since the late 1960s, when Angolan nationalists had started to fight the Portuguese settlers who had ruled the country ever since the sixteenth century. But Savimbi's critics pointed out that this was no surprise. For decades, they argued, peace had meant nothing to a man for whom personal power meant everything.

As a leader, Jonas Savimbi had numerous selling points. He was a hugely charismatic figure who sometimes magnetised and charmed those he met, and who was invariably surrounded by legions of loyal and adoring followers. He was also a clever man, a multi-lingual lawyer who had lived and studied in both Switzerland and Germany in the late 1950s, when he was in his mid-twenties. Travelling widely, as far afield as China, where he once went in search of arms, and the United States, he had a large array of contacts, sympathisers and admirers across the world. 'One of the most talented and charismatic of leaders in modern African history,' declared President *Ronald Reagan*, hailing him as a true champion of freedom against dos Santos' communist-backed regime in Luanda. Jeane Kirkpatrick, the Reagan administration's representative at the UN, also described him as 'one of the authentic heroes of our time'.[19]

But few outsiders knew what lurked beneath the superficial veneer of a man who told them what they wanted to hear. Savimbi smoothly assured the Chinese that he was a Maoist who shared their vision of communism. Years later, he promised the South Africans and the Americans that he was a vehement anti-communist who was desperately resisting Soviet advances in southern Africa. In London and Washington he talked about the free market, and at one meeting he was even introduced as 'the black Mrs Thatcher'. And in his distinctive red beret and combat fatigues, Savimbi had lots of appeal, striking a somewhat dashing and even romantic figure that resonated somewhere in the Western consciousness: a British parliamentarian once said that Savimbi's struggle reminded him of his own days as a Boy Scout.

As a result, few foreign leaders recognised Savimbi's glaring defect. This was his monstrous egotism, or more specifically his megalomania.[20]

Some journalists who visited his headquarters, at Jamba in the far south of Angola, saw through the carefully crafted image that Unita officials wanted them to see. For all his talk of democracy and rights, they noted, Savimbi was effectively a dictator in his own party. No one dared to question his judgement or challenge him. His own organisation, in other words, was basically a personality cult and there was a blatant contradiction between his public commitment to multi-party elections and how his own party really worked.

During the 1980s, a growing number of reports shone an unsettling light upon Savimbi's darker side. Dissenters suffered cruel deaths, sometimes condemned as witches and burnt alive or else thrown into horrifying underground prisons. And when his highly able overseas representative, Tito Chingunji, mysteriously disappeared in 1991, defectors alleged that Savimbi had murdered a man who was stealing the limelight and becoming a potential threat.[21]

By this time, it was becoming increasingly clear that Savimbi's true interest was not in brokering peace for his own country but in seizing power for himself. In 1989, he almost immediately reneged on a promise, made before a dozen African heads of state, to leave Angola for two years before competing on equal terms for political office.

Perhaps by this time he was simply addicted to war. He had participated in the nationalist struggle against the Portuguese in the early 1960s, starting off with just a handful of others and using only knives and a single pistol. After Angola won independence in 1975, he had been locked in a state of perpetual war against the Luanda regime, buttressed by a South African regime whose racialist policies he was prepared to overlook. But other lifelong warriors, of whom dos Santos was one, had laid down the gun and turned to peaceful solutions.

By 1997 the international negotiators judged that Savimbi had 'ceased to be a viable interlocutor to the solution of the Angolan conflict' and started to look to other, more moderate elements within Unita. Excluded from a new multi-party government, the Unita leader now continued his armed struggle, and it was not until his death – he was tracked down and shot, allegedly with Israeli assistance – that the firing stopped and the hush of peace finally fell over the country.

But if Jonas Savimbi was determined to pursue his megalomaniac course to seize power for himself, then he could have found and followed some peaceful strategies for doing so. If he had respected the outcome of the 1992 elections, then he would have acquired the trust and faith of his fellow Angolans. He might have forced a second ballot in the presidential elections and secured a senior ministerial role, perhaps as vice-president. He could then have reached out to his sympathisers in Washington and London, whose diplomats had worked hard on his behalf in the months before the vote.

Oil was one card he could have played with the Americans. By this time the United States was importing an increasing quantity of Angolan oil and the American economy's intake was expected to increase sharply over the years ahead. Western oil companies were also interested in exploring for petroleum across the region. As a minister in a multi-party government, Savimbi could have found important and influential supporters in Washington by offering preferential terms to explore and develop oil reserves if he came to power.

Instead he ineradicably branded Unita, as well as his own self, as a warmongering party. In 1992, it had won 34 per cent of the votes for the national parliament, while the MPLA took a 45 per cent share. A decade on, Unita's share slumped to just 10 per cent while dos Santos' party seized 81 per cent. For his warmongering, Savimbi had destroyed his country, condemned his party to near-obscurity and paid with his own life.

Madeleine's 'Humanitarian War' for Kosovo (1999)

During a crucial international conference, held at an exquisite French château outside Paris in May 1999, some Albanian delegates were hard at work when a lady visitor suddenly arrived on the scene. They were annoyed by the interruption, and one member of member of the negotiating team snapped at her arrogantly. 'Give us five minutes', he barked, 'and go away.'[22]

They did not realise, however, that their diminutive, grey-haired visitor was not a cleaning lady but the American secretary of state. Sixty-two-year-old Madeleine Albright was, in effect, the second most powerful person in the United States.

Nor did the Albanian negotiators at Rambouillet realise that their guest was also the strongest and most influential American advocate of their cause. For well over a year, she had urged her fellow members of the Clinton administration to take up the Albanian cause and to unleash the full fury of American warplanes against the Serbian leader, Slobodan Milosevic. And she had now appeared at Rambouillet believing that she could help negotiations along their way and force Serbian representatives to sign a deal that amounted, in effect, to surrender. If they failed to do so, then she knew that she would be able to finally persuade President Clinton to order an attack on Milosevic.

The crisis revolved around the Yugoslav province of Kosovo. For several years, Albanian militants belonging to the Kosovo Liberation Army (KLA) had been fighting an increasingly bitter campaign for autonomy, claiming that the rapidly increasing Albanian population deserved its own, independent state. But in the course of 1996 the militants stepped up their campaign and violence increased. Milosevic still refused to compromise, arguing passionately that the Serbian people, who made up much of the Yugoslav population, had a deep historic attachment to Kosovo. In his eyes, to grant independence to Kosovo was deeply unjust to the large number of Serbs who lived there, and who regarded it as their ancestral land.

Madeleine Albright would have known that the offer she had now put to the Serbs was not one they would sign up to. Under the proposed deal, Nato troops would arrive *en masse* in Kosovo and have a right to travel wherever and whenever they wanted, just like an army of occupation. They would then help to implement a new interim administration that would oversee a referendum, in which the Albanian-majority population would almost certainly have voted for the province's outright secession from Yugoslavia. It was no different, in other words, from the Serbs sending their own troops into a troubled British city or American state and demanding that local people could choose their own government. Even if Milosevic had accepted the deal, he had no chance of ever getting it past the Serb parliament, which was filled to the brim with nationalists far more strident than himself.

The proposed deal was effectively a pretext for war. As Henry Kissinger later wrote, it was 'a provocation, an excuse to start bombing. Rambouillet is not a document that an angelic Serb could have accepted. It was a terrible diplomatic document that should not have been presented in that form.' Lord Gilbert, the British defence minister, also admitted to parliament that 'the terms put to Milosevic at Rambouillet were absolutely intolerable ... (which) was quite deliberate'. However, for Madeleine Albright it worked its purpose. Within days of its rejection, President Bill Clinton and his close British ally, *Tony Blair*, ordered their warplanes to bomb Belgrade into submission. 'Madeleine's War', as it soon became known, had begun.[23]

But as the bombing went on, day after day, and Milosevic refused to relent, more and more people began to question her wisdom. They also wondered why, as America's ambassador to the United Nations in Bill Clinton's first administration, she had been so supportive of a disastrous intervention in Somalia, arguing in August 1993 that the United States had to 'persevere' in its efforts to turn the deeply troubled African state into 'a functioning and viable member of the community of nations'. But within weeks of making such comments, America's expeditionary force was struck by tragedy, losing eighteen men in a single incident – the downing of two helicopters – in the capital, Mogadishu. The Americans quickly pulled out, humiliated once again, and left the doctrines of 'nation-building' and 'humanitarian intervention' in tatters behind them. Madeleine's elevated rhetoric, like the two doomed helicopters, had come crashing down to earth.[24]

Albright's career, however, survived and she continued to play her ambassadorial role. Nor had she lost her appetite for war. 'What's the point of having this superb military that you're always talking about if we can't use it?' she once asked General Colin Powell. In 1998 she had also strongly advocated bombing Iraq to punish *Saddam Hussein* for his lack of cooperation with arms inspectors. Saddam had complied at the very last minute, however, and President Clinton had diverted his heavy bombers, which were already in the air and on the way, from their impending attack.

When the Kosovan crisis had begun to mount in the spring of 1998, she soon started to argue for military action against the Serbs. Promoted by this time to secretary of state, her voice carried weight. 'Madeleine's at it again,' sighed Colin Powell as he came out of one conference, noting how she persistently argued in favour of 'dropping of a soldier or two here to keep the peace, and a soldier or two there to make the world better, and sooner or later you had a policy'.[25]

Washington insiders who worked closely at her side thought they saw the reasons for her warmongering. They noticed, for a start, that she had a narrow, black-and-white view of the outside world – a characteristic that is often discernible in warmongers. 'She was convinced the villain was Slobodan Milosevic,' recalled a journalist, David Halberstam, 'and until he was dealt with, nothing good was going to happen ... saying negotiations were futile and he understood only force.'[26]

The origins of these traits probably lay in her traumatic childhood. She was old enough to remember the Second World War and in 1948, when she was just eleven years old, she had fled her native Czechoslovakia with her family just as the Iron Curtain of communist rule was fast descending. In other words, even before she arrived in the United States, as a virtually penniless refugee, she had personally experienced the rule of two highly tyrannical regimes. The forces of 'freedom' and 'oppression' had overshadowed her most formative years.[27]

This rigid mindset, which viewed the world in such dualistic terms, also seemed to engender a curious indifference towards the civilians who might be caught up in the violence or hardships that she was prepared to unleash. During a television interview on *60 Minutes* on 12 May 1996, for example, she had been asked to defend the imposition of economic sanctions against Iraq. 'We have heard that half a million children have died. I mean, that's more children than died in Hiroshima. And, you know, is the price worth it?' asked the interviewer. Albright nodded and replied unhesitatingly. 'We think the price is worth it.'

Her formative experiences in her native Czechoslovakia may also explain the curious time warp in which, as some of her contemporaries also noted, she seemed to live. Like *Anthony Eden*, *Guy Mollet* and Menachem Begin, she was obsessed with the events of the 1930s and made constant references to Munich and appeasement. 'Where do you think we are, Munich?', as she once snapped to EU foreign ministers when they suggested her approach was too harsh. Stuck in the pre-war era, her contemporaries even wondered if she had simply skipped a generation and had lived through the 1960s and early '70s wholly unaware of the *Vietnam War* and the massive student protests that had rocked America at the time.[28]

Madeleine Albright was very aware, however, of the events in the Balkans that took place just a few years before the Kosovo crisis erupted. In 1995 news had broken of a terrible massacre in the Bosnian enclave at Srebrenica. Western governments came under intense and ferocious criticism from those who argued that more could have been done to stop the war and bomb both sides into negotiations and a deal. It seems likely that Albright was suffering from a 'Srebrenica complex', which later also affected the British prime minister *David Cameron* and other architects of a later intervention in Libya. By bombing Kosovo, it seemed, she was reliving the events in the Balkans a few years before, compensating for what she felt hadn't been done then.

Blinded by the events of the 1930s and of 1995, and also by the forces of evil she seemed to see in Belgrade, Madeleine Albright failed to either recognise, or care about, the blatant illegality of the war, for the Anglo-American bombing campaign against Kosovo broke international law. Kosovo was sovereign Yugoslav territory and its troubles were therefore ultimately a domestic matter. And because the warmongers lacked a mandate from the United Nations Security Council, both countries were left open to charges of blatant, unrestrained aggression.

Equally, Mrs Albright failed to see the clear alternatives to the war that she deliberately provoked at Rambouillet. Russia had a closer relationship with Belgrade than any other foreign power and was in a position to broker an agreement or at least a ceasefire. Both the Serbs and the Russians had signalled their willingness to accept an international peacekeeping force in Kosovo but not one that was led by or comprised of Nato forces, as Madeleine Albright always insisted.

Nato troops could still have played a part in Kosovo by undertaking peacekeeping operations in certain safe havens inside the province, where civilians would have been protected from both government and KLA activity, and by sealing off the border between Kosovo and Albania. A breakdown in law and order in Albania in 1997 had led to a proliferation of arms as criminal gangs stormed army and police depots, seizing weapons that poured across the border and fuelled the KLA's insurgency.

Such options were preferable to the outcome of the seventy-eight-day 'humanitarian' bombardment of federal Yugoslavia that followed. In this time, Milosevic massively intensified the ethnic cleansing of Kosovan Albanians, and around 1,000 civilians died in the Nato bombing. When Serb resistance finally crumbled in June, Kosovo was placed under the occupation of Nato forces.

But in the months that followed, an estimated 200,000 ethnic Serbs, Roma and other minorities from south Kosovo, and almost the whole Serb population of the city of Pristina, fled their homes. In its report on Kosovo, one respected human rights watchdog, the London-based Minority Rights Group International, claimed that 'nowhere (in Europe) is there such a level of fear for so many minorities that they will be harassed or attacked, simply for who they are'. There were widespread reports of corruption and vote-rigging 'on an industrial scale' and in 2010, after a two-year investigation, a Council of Europe inquiry reported that Kosovo's leaders were really mafia bosses, murderers and drug dealers who were complicit in the shooting of prisoners and the sale of their kidneys and other organs on the black market. Albright had succeeded in ending Serb rule in Kosovo but had bequeathed a dark and unenviable legacy for the people whose interests she claimed to represent.[29]

General Musharraf Fights for Kashmir (1999)

The leader of Pakistan, General Pervez Musharraf, once told an American journalist about his favourite military training exercise, one that in his younger days he and his own soldiers had often undertaken. To complete the exercise, each soldier had to lie right next to a railway line – as close to the tracks as possible – and wait until a train came hurtling towards him. 'The train will definitely not touch you,' Musharraf always assured his stoical men, 'but you have to keep your head up and eyes open.'[30]

But the general was always a daring man, not one to walk away from danger. Within weeks of leaving cadet college, in 1965, he was engaged in a major war with India in which he was decorated for his bravery. Six years later the two countries clashed again, and this time he volunteered to undertake even more dangerous tasks, leading a unit of commandos and taking part in some very intense battles with Indian soldiers. And when, many years later, he heard that the prime minister of Pakistan, Nawaz Sharif, was going to sack him as the country's army chief, he unhesitatingly ordered his soldiers to join him and instigate an army coup. With just minutes of fuel left in its tank, his plane landed at Karachi airport and hours later he became Pakistan's new leader.

Six months before the coup, Musharraf had shown the same daring spirit when he launched a reckless mini-invasion of India and, by doing so, brought two nuclear-armed powers close to outright confrontation.

In May 1999, as soon as the snow had melted and the mountain ranges became passable, hundreds of armed militiamen had crossed the mountainous border between northern Pakistan and India. They slipped through the 'Line of Control', unnoticed by everyone other than a few shepherds, who tried to warn Indian soldiers about the worrying presence of foreigners. Then they moved onto even higher ground, crossing icy glaciers and snow-capped peaks.

Some of these insurgents were Pakistani soldiers who were wearing casual attire instead of their uniforms. Others were militants who belonged to a variety of Islamist organisations that were based in Pakistan. But all were trained and equipped for waging high-altitude warfare, and protected by Pakistani guns that were carefully positioned on the other side of the border. Soon they had established themselves at very high altitudes, above 14,000 feet, and at well-chosen places overlooking some strategically vital roads.

As they unleashed their ferocious and totally unexpected attack, which became known as 'the Kargil Offensive', Musharraf would have rubbed his hands with glee.

To those who met him, the fifty-five-year-old general did not seem like a warmonger. Invariably described as a charming and courteous host with an engaging sense of humour, he was, according to one army report, 'a capable, articulate and extremely personable officer, who made a most valuable impact here. His country is fortunate to have the services of a man of his undeniable quality.' As both an army chief, and later as Pakistan's leader, he was incorruptible, refusing to follow his predecessors by awarding lucrative government contracts to his friends and family, and instead cutting back on all manner of unnecessary expenses. He used regular commercial flights instead of specially chartered jets and continued to draw only his army pay.[31]

But Musharraf was a natural risk taker, and in the early months of 1999 he calculated that a small-scale invasion of India would push the question of Kashmir onto the international agenda.

Both India and Pakistan had hotly contested the mountainous northern state of Kashmir ever since the creation of both states in 1947. But the Indian army had seized it and subsequently kept its predominantly Muslim population under its firm control. Since the late 1980s, however, Kashmir had become even more of a burning issue. Militants based in Pakistan, often using arms left over from the *Afghan War* against the Soviet occupation, started a low-level insurgency against the Indian army. But a decade on, India's security forces still maintained their iron grip over the province and there was no sign of compromise in New Delhi. Kashmir, in other words, looked set to remain Indian. This was a matter of real importance to many Pakistanis. Some cared about the rights of local Muslims, while soldiers like Musharraf were well aware of the region's strategic importance. It offered high, mountainous ground that looked down over the Indian mainland – an indispensable asset in the event of yet another war with their much bigger neighbour.

By unleashing the Kargil offensive, Musharraf probably wanted to give new stimulus to the debate on Kashmir. If the Indians were forced to fight, then they would have to spend much more money on securing Kashmir. An attack would therefore make them question its value. Such an attack would also scupper a peace deal that both Islamabad and New Delhi had signed in Lahore in February. This was an agreement that committed both countries to nuclear cooperation but which excluded the question of who ruled Kashmir. At the same time, by mobilising Pakistan's nuclear weapons – American satellite photos clearly showed Pakistani missiles being positioned for possible deployment – Musharraf wanted to tell Washington that resolving the Kashmir dispute was a matter of vital concern for the outside world, one that it could not afford to ignore. Perhaps, too, his soldiers could seize strategic points in Indian Kashmir and then use them as bargaining-chips in the negotiations with New Delhi that he wanted to start: one such target was the 20,000-foot-high Siachen Glacier, which Indian troops had snatched from the Pakistanis in 1984.

If these were Musharraf's calculations, however, then his illusions were quickly shattered. Although the attack could hardly fail to focus an international spotlight on Kashmir, it also alienated the very people whose support Musharraf badly needed if he was to gain any ground. The Indians quickly seized their opportunity to portray Pakistan as an aggressive, dangerous, unstable and untrustworthy state that was responsible for orchestrating an unprovoked attack on their sovereign soil. Islamabad's unconvincing denials of involvement only made things even worse.

Leaders across the world, including those of the European Union, Asian countries and, above all, the United States, voiced their support for India and immediately began to blame Pakistan for its role in the attack: despite Islamabad's vehement official denials, its close links to the insurgents were never seriously in question. But at the same time New Delhi's relations with the Americans became closer, as it marketed itself as a front-line state against Islamist terrorism. And India's most intransigently nationalist political party received a big boost at the polls.

Like other warmongers, such as those who wanted to exorcise the ghosts of *Vietnam* or the Second World War, Musharraf's aim may simply have been to find catharsis. He had witnessed first-hand the severe mauling that India had inflicted on his own country in both 1965 and, above all, in 1971. He later stated that the Kargil conflict was carried out in response to the 1971 conflict because he believed in reprisal and retaliation. 'India had played a role in creating Bangladesh (at Pakistan's expense in 1971) and trying to seize Siachen', as he told a television channel in December 2014. But during the 1999 attack, he added the following year, Pakistan had 'caught India by the throat'.

On this count too, however, Musharraf's gamble also failed. During the two-month campaign, it is true that India's soldiers did struggle to oust the Pakistanis, who were highly adept at using their high ground to their own advantage. New Delhi admitted that 527 of its soldiers had died, and 1,363 were wounded, by the time the campaign was officially declared over. But the Pakistanis also lost at least as many of their own men, and in Pakistan itself the fighting was generally viewed with a sense of shock rather than jubilation.

However Musharraf could have found other ways, more subtle and effective, of striking New Delhi. He knew that India, by this time a buoyant emerging market with high ambitions as a regional superpower, was desperate to sell itself to the United States. For that reason, its leaders wanted to portray their country as a modern democratic state that cherished Western values and ideals. But India's human rights record in Kashmir was not compatible with the polished image that that New Delhi wanted to present. There were numerous well-documented atrocities, including torture, disappearances and gang rape, that the Indian security forces had perpetrated against local Muslims. This was the weak link that Musharraf could have exploited. His militants could have taken photos of the victims of Indian violence, and his public relations professionals could have exploited them. Such effective media manipulation of such actions would have badly disfigured India's image abroad.[32]

General Musharraf also knew that the Indians were notoriously sensitive, like most countries, about foreign interference within their own sovereign borders. They were never going to negotiate Kashmir's sovereignty unless they were faced with a massive, overwhelming defeat – something that was quite beyond Pakistan's military resources. It was conceivable, however, that India might have demilitarised the Siachen Glacier, which straddles the borders of both Indian and Pakistani Kashmir. There has never been any fighting between the two countries on the glacier, but around 2,000 Indian soldiers have died there as a result of accidents, mainly from avalanches and altitude sickness, since they first occupied it in 1984. There was also just a chance that New Delhi might have agreed to the demilitarisation of other areas of Kashmir if Pakistan's insurgents had done the same. And it may perhaps have granted international observers access to the region to monitor human rights abuses.

Musharraf could have enlisted American support for such moves because Pakistan was, and remains, vital in America's war against Islamic terrorism: in the late 1990s, two years before the 9/11 attacks, concern was growing fast in Western capitals about the potential threat posed by Al Qaeda and the Taliban. If Musharraf had waited just two and a half years, then he would have had enormous bargaining power over Washington and achieved these more limited ambitions without a shot even being fired.

George W. Bush: Toppling the Taliban (2001)
Almost as soon as two hijacked aircraft struck the World Trade Centre in New York on 11 September 2001, many Washington insiders felt sure they knew who the culprit was: a Saudi dissident called Osama bin Laden who was living thousands of miles away, somewhere in Afghanistan, as a guest of the ruling Taliban regime. He had already proclaimed his ambitions to strike America during a bizarre 'press conference' in a remote Afghan cave in May 1998, when he had issued a 'declaration of war' against 'the Great Satan' and its 'imperialist allies'. Two years later, in October 2000, his Al Qaeda operatives had bombed an American ship, the USS *Cole*. The attack in New York now had his fingerprints all over it.

The day after the tragedy in New York, President George W. Bush invited journalists into the Roosevelt Room at the White House and gave a press conference. The attacks on the American mainland, he decreed, were 'more than acts of terror. They were acts of war.' As a result, he continued, the United States was involved in 'a monumental struggle between good and evil' and would respond appropriately. And in the hours that followed, the president used similarly powerful words and references about what lay ahead: America had to fight a 'crusade' and 'lengthy battle', he claimed, and 'every nation in every region now has a decision to make: either you are with us or you are with the terrorists'.

In the traumatic days that followed, Bush then turned his attention to the chief suspect. On 21 September, he issued an ultimatum to the Taliban regime. Hand bin Laden over, ran the warning, or face the consequences. 'These demands are not open to negotiation or discussion', as Bush stated. 'The Taliban must act and act immediately. They will hand over the terrorists, or they will share in their fate.'

The Taliban's ruling council refused, not least because they were bound by a traditional code of honour towards their 'guest'. Some two weeks later, on 7 October, American jets started bombing Afghanistan. But their target was not bin Laden himself but rather the Taliban's entire infrastructure, civilian and military.

Unless the Taliban suddenly changed tack and surrendered their 'guest', then the Americans had now committed themselves to regime change in Kabul: to cease bombing and leave the Taliban in power with bin Laden still roaming their territory would amount to a major loss of nerve and face. But the Taliban proved unexpectedly resilient and, like the Serbs in *Kosovo*, failed to crumble as soon as American bombs started to fall. American special forces moved in, working closely with the Taliban's unsavoury domestic enemies such as General Rashid Dostum, a 'warlord' in the far north who had a reputation for practices, such as the mass suffocation of prisoners, that even Afghans, by their medieval standards, thought were barbaric.

Confronted by such overwhelming pressure, the Taliban caved in and on 13 November the militia of the enemy 'Northern Alliance' stormed into the capital, Kabul. The Taliban were now being pushed back further and further towards their ethnic heartlands around Kandahar in the south, although there was still no sign of Osama bin Laden.

But although news of the fall of Kabul caused euphoria in Western capitals, more seasoned voices had strong doubts about Bush's approach. The Senate Majority Leader Tom Daschle warned that the president's language was inappropriate, cautioning that 'war is a powerful word', while the eighty-three-year-old senator Robert Byrd emphasised that Congress would not repeat the mistake it made in the *Vietnam War* by unthinkingly signing a blank cheque. And the secretary of state, Colin Powell, also noted that Bush 'had a lot of .45 calibre instincts, cowboy instincts'.[33]

All of them thought, in other words, that Bush's words and deeds were too militaristic. America was not 'at war' just because it had suffered terrorist attacks. Although the Al Qaeda agents had inflicted terrible losses, killing 3,000 in the World Trade Centre, their attacks were no different in kind from those that London had suffered for years at the hands of Irish nationalist bombers in the 1970s and '80s. In particular, why was he trying to topple an entire regime instead of just the single ringleader of the 9/11 attacks?

Maybe George Walker Bush wanted to emulate the wartime deeds of his father, President George Herbert Bush, who had had a distinguished record in the Second World War. Bush the Younger had taken a rather different course of action at the same age, having avoided service in Vietnam after taking up a role only in the Texas Air National Guard. Or perhaps he was conscious of having been an underachiever at school, when he suffered from 'attention deficit disorder', and of being accepted into Yale University only because of his grandfather's impressive academic record. Fighting unnecessary wars helped him to redress the balance and feel better.

Bush's approach also revealed his own black-and-white outlook on the world, which he saw, like his equally blinkered political ancestors *Lyndon B. Johnson* and *Woodrow B. Wilson*, in narrow terms of 'good' and 'evil'. Perhaps this was a lifelong affair, or maybe it had been nurtured by his born-again Evangelical

Christianity: after a reckless and rebellious youth in which narcotics, heavy drinking and drink-driving all played a starring part, the younger Bush had turned to Evangelical Christianity in a desperate bid to save his marriage. 'A good and powerful day,' noted a celebrated Evangelical preacher by the appropriate name of Arthur Blessitt in 1984, 'led vice president's son to Jesus today. George Bush Jr!'[34]

Such influences help explain why 'W' had come to power in January 2001 with a strong interest in going to war as soon as he could. White House insiders were alarmed that, within days of taking office, he was showing an interest in attacking the Iraqi leader *Saddam Hussein*. And in the days that preceded the 9/11 attacks he even sidelined urgent intelligence reports about an imminent Al Qaeda attack so that he could discuss an invasion of Iraq with his senior advisers. At the same time, he shocked his State Department advisers by giving the Israeli leader *Ariel Sharon* a *carte blanche* to act as he wanted in the Middle East, shrugging aside the warnings of General Colin Powell that the Israeli leader would jump at any chance to unleash war and violence. 'A show of strength by one side can really clarify things,' sighed an indifferent president.[35]

'Bush the Younger' showed a similarly ill-judged reaction to the tragic events of 11 September. He depicted the world stage in black-and-white terminology and left no room for anything else with his 'for-or-against-us' response, even in countries where anti-American feeling was rife and where governments could therefore not easily lend Washington their wholehearted support. Other terms, like the reference to a 'crusade', were full of obvious historic resonances that were bound to anger and alienate Muslim countries, even though it was their support that President Bush needed most if he was to destroy Al Qaeda and the anti-Western values it championed. Such a term, 'crusade', was also unnecessarily militaristic. Even a mere threat of using force against Muslim countries was bound to raise fears of 'Western imperialism'. And of course war also caused deaths and casualties amongst innocent people whose suffering would be aired on television networks and on the internet, stirring up anti-American feeling just at a time when he needed popular support. Bush, in other words, needed to avoid military force unless it was really necessary.

As one of his senior security officials, Richard Clarke, pointed out, Bush could and should have done what his predecessors, such as presidents Clinton, Carter, Ford and George H. Bush, would have done by looking more closely at what lay behind the attacks of 9/11. These leaders, Clarke argued, 'might have tried to understand the phenomenon of terrorism, what led fifteen Saudis and four others to commit suicide to kill Americans. Others might have tried to build a world consensus to address the root causes ... one can imagine Clinton trying one more time to force an Israeli-Palestinian settlement, going to Saudi Arabia and addressing the Muslim people in a moving appeal for religious tolerance.'[36]

But Bush did none of these things in those tense weeks that followed the attack on the American mainland. Instead he used military force against the Taliban regime when its leaders failed to hand bin Laden over, even though there was no such compelling reason to use force on any such scale. Bush could have drastically limited the scope of his campaign, targeting and 'neutralising' only Osama bin Laden but leaving the Taliban regime untouched. Deploying special forces on the ground and unleashing cruise missiles in the air would have made a deadly combination that would have eventually struck home, or at the very least drastically curtailed Osama's contact with his sympathisers. President Clinton had nearly succeeded in killing the Al Qaeda leader in August 1998, firing a salvo of missiles that narrowly missed him. In the late 1990s Clinton had also cancelled several other assassination attempts at the last minute because the president didn't want to risk alienating various allies in the Islamic world or because he feared 'collateral damage'. Now, after 9/11, Bush had the clearest mandate possible.[37]

But toppling the Taliban meant supporting militias that were just as ruthless and often just as Islamist and as virulently anti-Western. Such an approach also risked 'mission creep' – being pulled ever deeper into a war, like Vietnam, that would be increasingly difficult to escape. And the dangers of getting involved in Afghanistan were painfully evident not just from nineteenth-century history (see *Sir William Macnaghten*) but also from the

Soviet experiences there, which had ended just over a decade before (see *Yuri Andropov*). As one former Russian soldier warned an American officer during the crisis of late 2001, 'With regret, I have to say you're really going to get the hell kicked out of you.'[38]

Instead of fighting unnecessary wars in both Afghanistan and later Iraq, the White House could have concentrated its resources on expanding and upgrading America's intelligence services, which had missed the 9/11 attacks, and the special forces which were ideally suited to confronting the semi-trained insurgents who had sworn to fight a global jihad against the United States. Such a measured response would also have helped to rally the overseas allies that America needed more than ever, particularly in the Islamic world where caution and restraint in the face of such provocation and outrage would have won admiration.

Instead, President Bush allowed his armed forces, and those of his Nato allies, to be drawn ever deeper into an Afghan quagmire. To begin with, Western soldiers formed a multinational force that was designed to help secure the peace in a post-Taliban Afghanistan. But gradually resistance increased and casualties and costs mounted. By 2015 the Allies had pulled out nearly all of their forces, leaving behind a regime that was under intense, ferocious pressure from insurgents. The British and Americans had by this stage lost 3,000 soldiers, and many more wounded, in a futile war that had cost the American taxpayer alone around $1 trillion. After the allied forces retreated, the Taliban still advanced, recapturing ground the allies claimed to have 'liberated'. It was clear that America and its allies had nothing good to show after long years of bloody effort, and had succeeded only in haemorrhaging blood and dollars into the sand.

Tony Blair, Saddam Hussein and Iraq (2003)

At a dinner in Washington that was held just days after the 11 September attacks on the US mainland, the American president *George W. Bush* asked the British prime minister, Tony Blair, to help him remove the Iraqi leader, *Saddam Hussein*, from power. Bush had long held this ambition, and appears to have been obsessed with regime change in Baghdad before he even became president in January 2001. But this was the first time that he is known to have put forward his idea to his British counterpart, or indeed to any foreign leader.

Blair's initial reaction, according to the British ambassador in Washington, was reserved and cautious. It was important, counselled the prime minister, that the two allies weren't distracted from what really mattered, which was countering the terrorist threat from Osama bin Laden and his Al Qaeda network in Afghanistan and elsewhere. Bush was undeterred by the cool response. 'I agree with you, Tony. We must deal with this first. But when we have dealt with Afghanistan, we must come back to Iraq.'[39]

But whatever reservations he may initially have held, Tony Blair soon became an accomplice in President Bush's wholly unnecessary war against Saddam, which began eighteen months later, on 20 March 2003. Although Blair always publicly claimed that 'no decision had been taken' about Iraq until just before the invasion got underway, both Western leaders had in fact resolved to attack Saddam a long time before. A White House official who read the transcript of a telephone call, held between the two men at the end of July 2002, had no doubts that 'Blair did not need any convincing' about the planned invasion. 'There was no, "Come on, Tony, we've got to get you on board."' As General Colin Powell told Bush, 'on Iraq, Blair will be with us should military operations be necessary'. By the autumn, as the countdown to the invasion began, Blair publicly committed his troops to the attack, and five months later 45,000 British soldiers were despatched to the Middle East and played a central part in the American-led war.[40]

Had the invasion of Iraq been unavoidable, then of course the British prime minister's actions may have been commendable. But although apologists for the war worked hard to draw parallels with the Second World War – the media was saturated with the predictable but unconvincing parallels with Hitler, appeasement and Munich – they could not disguise the truth. The attack on Iraq was illegal in international law, carried out without a clear United Nations mandate and not undertaken in response to an armed attack: this was particularly ironic because, just two years before, Blair had proclaimed that he wanted 'a world ruled by law and by international cooperation' and that 'we have to support the UN as its central pillar'. And it was wholly unnecessary.

On close inspection, all of the arguments for war against Saddam were hollow. The main justification for the attack was Saddam's supposed possession of 'Weapons of Mass Destruction' (nuclear, biological, and chemical weapons or 'WMD') that posed a dire threat to the outside world. The British government's official case for war, which later became known as 'the dodgy dossier', even claimed that the Iraqis could deploy such weapons within just forty-five minutes of being given the order. But no one seemed quite sure exactly what weapons these were, or why this was more true in September 2002 than at any previous time.

These claims were subsequently exposed as entirely fallacious, based on a myriad of very dubious or even non-existent sources, such as a mendacious asylum seeker, codenamed 'Curveball', who later admitted his own fabrications. And another source of the 'intelligence' may even have been an émigré taxi driver who claimed to have overheard a conversation between two passengers, both of whom were Iraqi army officers. Instead, as Sir John Chilcott's official enquiry into the disaster later put it with a style of classic understatement and 'officialese', 'the judgments about Iraq's capabilities ... were presented with a certainty that was not justified'.[41]

But even if Bush and Blair had a good excuse for misapprehending the 'intelligence' about Saddam, then there was no reason why they needed to use military force to attack and topple him. The obvious response to an Iraqi WMD programme was a regime of international inspections, which Saddam had agreed to comply with soon after his defeat in *Kuwait* in 1991. It was at this time that the United Nations had created a new weapons inspection body to find and dismantle the stockpile of deadly weapons that Saddam had built up during the *Iran–Iraq War*. After four years of non-compliance, Saddam had then bowed to international pressure and allowed independent weapons inspectors, led by Hans Blix, back into his country in November 2002 under a new UN resolution. Yet Blair and Bush looked away from this before they needed to: in the words of the Chilcott Report, 'the UK chose to join the invasion of Iraq before the peaceful options for disarmament had been exhausted. Military action at that time was not a last resort.'

On 14 February 2003, Blix reported to the UN Security Council that Saddam was cooperating with the inspectors. His report should have stopped the drive to war in its tracks, and Blair and Bush could and should have allowed the inspectors to continue their work. Blix later added that Saddam would have become much more cooperative if the Bush administration had halted its military build-up in the region. Instead, the influx of thousands of American soldiers into the Middle East, as Bush prepared for war, simply convinced Saddam that the United States and its allies were determined to attack, no matter what he did, and that the UN inspectors were just working on their behalf. Meanwhile, Blair continued to misrepresent military intelligence in order to secure parliamentary and public approval to invade Iraq, and ordered the British spy service to 'sex up' intelligence about Saddam's non-existent weapons programme.

Bush and Blair also claimed that the invasion would 'democratise' Iraq and the wider Middle East. But by doing so they associated 'democracy' with 'Western imperialism' in the minds of the very people they said they wanted to liberate. Their approach was also an invitation to international anarchy: it gave every country a right to invade others and impose its own vision of 'right' and 'wrong'. And in the Middle East, a region that has had a very limited experience of 'democracy', such grandiose ideas were also particularly hubristic.

Had they been really determined to sponsor democracy there, then the two Western leaders could have found ways of supporting democracy in particular areas of the Middle East that already had some semblance of it, and where America already had some real influence: this was true, for example, of Jordan, Kuwait and the Kurdish areas of northern Iraq. Britain and America could also have undertaken initiatives to eliminate or reduce corruption in the region, or to supervise the holding of local elections. Otherwise there was little they could do to so profoundly alter the innate character of an entire region.

But even if Bush was determined to invade Iraq, Tony Blair could have done all sorts of things differently in the course of 2002 and early 2003. He could have simply refused to commit British troops to support America's illegal and unnecessary war, following the example that his predecessor, prime minister Harold Wilson, had set in the 1960s, when he resisted *President Johnson*'s determined efforts to recruit Britain into the Vietnam conflict.

At the very least, he could struck a harder bargain, making British involvement conditional upon giving Saddam and inspections more time. Although British diplomats worked hard to persuade Bush to win United Nations backing for the invasion, Blair could equally have insisted that the Americans should have a clear administrative and governmental plan for a post-Saddam Iraq. This, as events turned out, was painfully lacking: Bush had clearly given much consideration about how to remove Iraq's existing leader but none to what might follow. The British prime minister was, after all, well aware of this huge gap in the American plan. At a meeting in London on 23 July 2002, the head of British intelligence had given Blair a report on a trip that he had just made to Washington. Military action was now 'inevitable', he reported, adding that 'the intelligence and fact were being fixed around the policy'. But he cautioned that 'there was little discussion in Washington of the aftermath after military action'.[42]

If Blair had made his own support for the invasion conditional upon proper post-war planning, then there was a chance that Bush may have postponed the invasion until after the 2004 presidential election. In this scenario, Bush could have used a prospective war in Iraq as a central plank of his campaign for re-election against a Democratic candidate who he could have portrayed as 'untrustworthy' on national security. But by that time the security situation in Afghanistan had started to deteriorate considerably, and this would probably have forced President Bush to admit, as his more level-headed advisers had always warned him, that his army would be too overstretched to embark on an unnecessary war in Iraq.

One reason why Tony Blair had become an unadulterated warmonger was the strong personal bond, a true 'special relationship', that he had established with the American leader. One journalist compared him with a child in a playground who was drawn inexorably to the biggest, most powerful gang and who desperately wanted to join it. After Blair's election as prime minister in 1997, the most powerful 'gang' initially seemed to be not the United States, where Bill Clinton's presidency was on the wane, but the European Union, whose praises he sang and whose leaders he desperately wanted to impress. But after the election of George W. Bush as president, Blair was magnetised by events across the Atlantic. He now wanted to be a fully paid-up and respected member of 'George's gang'. Before long, the British leader was mocked as 'Bush's poodle' and his rhetoric, particularly about events and developments in the Middle East, started to closely echo the vocabulary and tone of the White House. 'I will be with you, whatever,' vowed an enraptured British leader, eight months before the invasion.[43]

Blair's admiration for President Bush merged with another trait: the ease with which he reached for the trigger. In early 1998 he had been poised to retaliate against Saddam for his lack of cooperation with international arms inspectors. The UN chief, Kofi Annan, ironically congratulated Blair as a 'perfect peacemaker' for his willingness to use force to bring about peace, but the British leader's hawkish position contrasted strongly with that of his French counterpart, Jacques Chirac, who argued that Western countries had much to lose by bombing Iraq. The following year the prime minister had been one of the loudest advocates of military action against Slobodan Milosevic in *Kosovo*, strongly supporting *Madeleine Albright*'s drive for war and arguing in favour of deploying ground troops, as well as air strikes, to force Milosevic into surrender. In 2000, Blair also undertook a brief intervention in Sierra Leone.[44]

The Iraq war also revealed a third trait in Tony Blair's mindset. This was the rigid, black-and-white 'Manichaean' way in which he appears to have viewed the outside world, a characteristic that was just as true of other warmongers such as *Madeleine Albright, Anthony Eden, George W. Bush* and Menachem Begin. He saw the war against Milosevic as 'a battle between good and evil; between civilisation and barbarity; between democracy and dictatorship'. And in a newspaper interview just weeks before the attack on Saddam, he conjured the same familiar parallels and allusions: 'A majority of decent and well-meaning people said there was no need to confront Hitler and that those who did were warmongers,' he said. 'When people decided not to confront fascism, they were doing the popular thing, they were doing it for good reasons and they were good people ... but they made the wrong decision.'[45]

The invasion of Iraq also manifested one further aspect of the Blairite mindset. This was his desire to change things when there was no obvious reason to do so. As a prefect at his Scottish public school, the young Tony Blair had raised the eyebrows of his headmaster by asking why long-established rules were in place and suggesting that they should be abolished. As prime minister, he tinkered with aspects of the unwritten constitution that, however imperfect, were nonetheless functioning perfectly adequately, scrapping the right of hereditary peers to sit in the House of Lords and holding referenda in Scotland and Wales for the introduction of home rule. Most drastically, he allowed massive immigration into Britain, perhaps because he thought it would change what was left of his country's traditional character. It was just the same desire to meddle with the 'working imperfections' of the Middle East that led him to intervene in Iraq. By Western standards, it was true that Saddam Hussein was a brutal tyrant. But by the standards of the Middle East, and particularly of the barbaric Islamic State movement that followed in his wake more than a decade on, he was nothing out of the ordinary.

The price of the Blair-Bush warmongery proved to be very high, despite efforts to hide it with catchy and media-friendly slogans about 'bringing democracy' to the people of Iraq. Thousands of servicemen and women, and hundreds of thousands of Iraqi civilians, died during the initial campaign and in the vicious insurgent war that followed. Had Saddam remained in power, it seems most unlikely that the Islamic State movement would have emerged, or at least won any real influence within his borders. Not surprisingly, Blair's name became ineradicably stained by both the build-up to and the execution of the Iraq war. The Middle East had long been a graveyard of reputations, and it had now claimed another victim.

'Dave's War' in the Middle East (2011)

In early 2011, Libya suddenly began to feel the rising temperatures of 'the Arab Spring' – the outbreak of popular protests that had started to gather pace in North Africa and the Middle East over the preceding few weeks. In Libya the trouble had flared on 15 February, when a human rights activist called Fathi Terbil was arrested in the city of Benghazi and crowds came out into the streets to protest. Fights broke out, shots were fired, demonstrators appeared and events started to spiral out of control, in Benghazi and beyond. A few days later there were reports that the Libyan leader, 'Colonel' Muammar Gaddafi, had started to use warplanes to bomb protestors. Then two Libyan pilots landed their jets in Malta, stating that they had preferred to defect rather than to perpetrate such a heinous act.

As the country seemed to slide ever deeper into a state of chaos and violence, there were increasing calls for the outside world 'do something'. Chief among them was Libya's representative to the United Nations. He suddenly spoke up against the Tripoli regime, claiming that Gaddafi was already unleashing 'genocide' against his own people and calling for the outside world to militarily intervene.

In London, as well as Washington and Paris, there was frantic talk of enforcing a 'no-fly zone' over Libya that would prevent Gaddafi's jets from striking the protestors, perhaps killing huge numbers by doing so. A United Nations resolution that imposed economic sanctions was deemed to be insufficient and diplomats soon started to draft a more drastic response. Less than a month later, on 17 March, the UN Security Council adopted Resolution 1973, which imposed a no-fly zone and allowed the outside world to use 'all necessary measures' – short of occupying the country – to protect the Libyan people from the wrath of its leader. The reference to 'all necessary measures' meant that foreign counties could, if they chose, effectively declare war, although without actually invading the country.

One of the chief protagonists of war was the British prime minister, David Cameron. His advisers had wanted him to support the first, more limited UN resolution but he had pressed for a more hard-hitting response and demanded a military option. Britain, he insisted, would 'play its part' in the fight against a regime that was carrying out 'brutal attacks' on civilians. In a letter to the president of the European Council, Herman Van Rompuy, he accused Gaddafi of 'crimes against humanity' and called on him and his 'clique' to stand down. At the same time he endorsed the rebels, represented by 'the Libyan Transitional National Council', as 'an important voice for the Libyan people'.

But forty-five-year-old 'Dave' was not an old foreign policy hand. After winning power, less than a year before, he had been preoccupied with more urgent matters at home – reducing a mammoth budget deficit and shoring up his uneasy coalition government – than sorting out the world's affairs. When events in Libya did turn nasty and evolved into his first foreign crisis, then he was not well qualified to handle them, since he had never previously shown any real interest in foreign policy or defence matters. His chief of defence staff even told him that 'being in the Combined Cadet Force at Eton' did not give him the expertise required to fight his own battles. 'Cameron's military and strategic inexperience is the risk that democracy takes in its choice of leaders,' added General Sir David Richards. Nor was Cameron helped much by a cash-starved Whitehall apparatus that lacked the expertise and information that it should have had.[46]

But on that March day, when the United Nations had approved the resolution for a no-fly zone over Libya, Cameron proudly justified his militaristic course. Gaddafi, he pointed out, had already killed 'more than 1,000' of his own. people, and had 'begun airstrikes in anticipation of what we expect to be a brutal attack using air, land and sea forces' that would show 'no mercy and no pity'. There was a 'responsibility', chimed Cameron and the French president *Nicolas Sarkozy*, 'to protect'. As the American leader, Barack Obama, later added, 'We knew that if we waited one more day, Benghazi – a city nearly the size of Charlotte – could suffer a massacre that would have reverberated across the region and stained the conscience of the world.'[47]

Within hours, British jets were roaring out of their bases and heading for Libyan airspace. It was too late to question a great many of the claims that the British prime minister, and other Western warmongers, were making. But some independent human rights watchdogs viewed reports with a much more sceptical eye. One reckoned that by 20 February, a crucial time at the United Nations, Gaddafi's men had in fact killed far fewer than 1,000 protestors. The real figure was around one-third of that number, and most of these had been killed in street battles between government troops and armed militia. 'There are grounds for questioning the more sensational reports that the regime was using its air force to slaughter demonstrators, let alone engaging in anything remotely warranting use of the term "genocide",' as the International Crisis Group concluded later in the year.[48]

But even if Gaddafi's army had stormed Benghazi, there was no reason to suppose that they would carry out the ferocious, almost genocidal violence that Western audiences were led to believe had taken place. Tripoli had faced other uprisings before and it had always been the ringleaders, not innocent civilians, who were executed. In fact, Gaddafi had never shown the same ruthlessness as other Arab leaders, whose bloodthirst had often been ignored by Western leaders: on 10 March, just as Western leaders worked themselves into a frenzy about Libya, Saudi security forces were opening fire on unarmed protesters who had been staging a peaceful pro-democracy demonstration in the eastern city of Qatif. And the story about Libyan warplanes striking protestors seemed on close inspection to have been fabricated, spun by Gaddafi's rebels and then aired by an Arab news network but never seriously questioned. Claims of such atrocities are usually backed up by footage and photographs which go viral on the web, but they were conspicuously absent on this occasion.

A parliamentary enquiry into the Libyan intervention later concluded that 'despite his rhetoric, the proposition that Muammar Gaddafi would have ordered the massacre of civilians in Benghazi was not supported by the available evidence'. Instead, Cameron 'selectively took elements of Muammar Gaddafi's rhetoric at face value', just as he failed to question the assurances of Libyan exiles that the country would not disintegrate into warring tribal factions if Gaddafi was removed from power. Instead he looked away from all the obstacles that the use of force posed: 'There were some very real difficulties that Number 10 didn't really want to hear,' noted Richards.[49]

In fact, by using force Cameron violated the terms of the UN resolution that he himself had sponsored. This resolution called for 'the immediate establishment of a ceasefire and a complete end to violence ... with the aim of facilitating dialogue ...(to) find a peaceful and sustainable solution'. In other words, the use of force was merely a final option that could be used only in a worst-case scenario where dialogue had failed. And he could have pursued this peaceful alternative without even resorting to the United Nations: by early March several governments, notably those of the African Union, Turkey and Germany, were supporting a detailed proposal drawn up by a non-governmental organisation. This called for an immediate ceasefire followed by negotiations 'aimed at replacing the current regime with a more accountable, representative and law-abiding government'.

In other words, the British leader was trying to find an excuse to go to war. Gaddafi immediately complied with the United Nations resolution by calling for a 'ceasefire' and offering to open negotiations, but his offer was quickly rejected by the Libyan rebels while a scathing British foreign secretary, William Hague, commented only that 'we will judge him by his actions not his words'.[50]

Instead, British and French jets continued to pound Libyan positions. Gaddafi repeated his offer of a ceasefire but was once again ignored. Efforts by both Turkey and the African Union to mediate were brushed aside, even though General Richards urged Cameron to negotiate. Gaddafi had to resign, the Libyan rebels now insisted, as they raised the bar even higher, before there was any ceasefire. Still Tripoli offered more ceasefires, on 30 April, 26 May and 9 June, but still such offers were rejected, by the rebels and by the British, American and French governments.[51]

By the third week of March, British and French warplanes had struck Libya hard, having flown thousands of missions that had helped clear the way for rebel forces as they marched from their strongholds towards the capital. By the end of August they had Tripoli in their grip, and on 20 October Colonel Gaddafi was savagely beaten and then shot by a mob in the city of Sirte, reputedly at the instigation of the French intelligence services.

Gaddafi had gone and the architects of war could not contain their glee. In September, Cameron and Sarkozy triumphantly visited Tripoli and Benghazi, where they were greeted by large, cheering crowds and championed by a beaming representative of the 'transitional government' who thanked them for the 'brave positions' they had taken. 'Your city was an example to the world as you threw off a dictator and chose freedom,' proclaimed a jubilant British prime minister. 'Your friends in Britain and France will stand with you as you build your democracy!'

They made the most of their photo opportunities but their moments of triumph did not last long. Within just months, Libya started to disintegrate into a collection of warring tribes and militias, as the critics of intervention always warned it would. One by one, Western embassies and then foreign journalists made their exodus as the security situation deteriorated and entire regions became a haven for insurgents. Soon the northern coast had become a hub of migrant trafficking used by huge numbers of refugees who made their way across the Mediterranean to Western shores on a scale that no one had previously imagined. Egypt, Algeria and Tunisia all tried to seal their borders to curb the influx of guns, drugs, criminals and refugees, while the Libyans themselves suffered from endemic killings, rape and torture. In London and elsewhere, searching questions about the entire episode were increasingly being asked. 'There seems to have been very little detailed, intelligent analysis of what might follow' the toppling of Gaddafi, as one scathing former ambassador to the Middle East wrote.[52]

It is not clear exactly why 'Dave' wanted to topple the Tripoli regime rather than just strike a deal, as Gaddafi had offered this option. Maybe he saw it as an opportunity to prove that, despite the onset of economic recession, his country was still great, even though British and French forces exhausted their supplies of ammunition during the conflict and had to ask the Americans to bail them out. Perhaps he simply wanted to impress domestic audiences, knowing that he was considered by many to be lightweight on foreign and defence affairs. 'This was David Cameron's big war,' noted Richards afterwards. 'Understandably, he enjoyed the influence that came with it.' In other words, the war provided a kind of 'feel-good' factor after long years of economic recession and even longer decades of post-imperial decline.[53]

Or maybe the British prime minister lived under the shadow of one of his predecessors, *Tony Blair*. Although politically discredited by the time of his resignation as prime minister in 2007, and responsible for the disastrous Iraq intervention, 'Teflon Tony' Blair had nonetheless been a politically invincible politician during his decade-long tenure of power. Insiders revealed the strong grip that Blair exerted over the prime minister's imagination, and because his predecessor had always been a proponent of 'humanitarian intervention' in the world, Dave may well have wanted to follow the example that 'The Master', as he reputedly called him, had set. And since he expected his own involvement in Libya to go better than the disastrous interventions in Iraq and Afghanistan, Cameron probably hoped to beat his predecessor at this own game.[54]

There were other events from the past that haunted Cameron's present. One was an outbreak of genocidal slaughter in Rwanda in 1993 and 1994, when hundreds of thousands of innocent men, women and children were butchered by machete-wielding gangs who were members of a rival tribe (see *François Mitterrand*). Much closer to home, however, was a tragedy in the Balkans. In the summer of 1995, thousands of innocent Muslim civilians had died brutal deaths at the hands of Serb paramilitaries in the enclave of Srebrenica in Bosnia. As the full scale of the tragedy became apparent, searching questions were asked about what the outside world could have done differently to prevent it. Some fingers were pointed at the British government and allegations made that it could have done much more not just to have saved the victims of Srebrenica but to have ended the civil war. 'Given the lack of reliable intelligence on which to build policy,' the government enquiry later noted, 'British politicians and policymakers may have attached undue weight to their individual and collective memories of the appalling events at Srebrenica.'[55]

At the time, David Cameron was a high-ranking governmental adviser and he had close working relationships with some of the individuals who were deemed guilty of not doing enough. So like *Madeleine Albright* he would have shared something of a 'Srebrenica complex' – the feelings of guilt about the tragedy that subsequently took hold among some of those who were in power at the time, and among some members of the general public. He would have been more receptive than most to what Kofi Annan called 'the cardinal lesson of Srebrenica: that a deliberate and systematic attempt to terrorise, expel or murder an entire people must be met decisively with all necessary means'. Such sentiments were shared more widely. At a press conference in March 2011, Dennis Ross, a White House adviser, expressed his fear of Benghazi becoming like 'Srebrenica on steroids' if Gaddafi was allowed a free hand to retaliate against the rebels there. And a Whitehall insider later revealed that 'there was a very strong feeling at the top of this government that Benghazi could very easily become the Srebrenica of our watch. The generation that has lived through Bosnia is not going to be the pull-up-the-drawbridge generation.'[56]

David Cameron's intervention in Libya, in other words, may well have been the outcome of a 'Srebrenica complex' that was just as powerful as the complexes, born of earlier traumas, that haunted other leaders, notably *Anthony Eden* and Menachem Begin, both of whom seemed to be reliving the events of the 1930s. Perhaps such a complex enabled him to develop a curious blind spot towards the more recent developments in Afghanistan and Iraq: both interventions had been fiascos yet Cameron, and Sarkozy, were able to overlook them, just as contemporaries wondered if *Madeleine Albright* had somehow forgotten about, or never witnessed, the 1960s.

Equally curious is that David Cameron did not lose his taste for unnecessary wars after the failings of his disastrous Libyan venture became obvious to see. On the contrary, two years later he was still willing to resort to military action in Syria, which was by this stage embroiled in a bitter and protracted civil war, far more quickly than he should have done and needed to.

In August 2013, he went to parliament to win its approval for using military force against the Syrian regime of Bashar al-Assad. Cameron's wife, ran the rumour in London, had just returned from a trip to the Middle East and persuaded her husband that something had to be done to stop the war and to prevent Bashar from using ruthless and bloody tactics against civilian targets, such as the alleged use of 'barrel bombs' and chemical weapons.

But there were some obvious and uneasy parallels with *the invasion of Iraq* a decade before. That invasion was undertaken on the false premise that Saddam had weapons of mass destruction that posed a serious threat to Western security. Now David Cameron, and the American president Barack Obama, claimed that Assad had used chemical weapons against his enemies. But when he was challenged on the point, he had no evidence to back up his claims. Bashar's 'chemical weapons' seemed to be just as much of a Middle Eastern chimera as Saddam's WMD. Instead British experts reputedly obtained a sample of the sarin poison and concluded that it didn't match anything in the Syrian army's arsenal. Just hours before Obama was ready to strike Damascus, the attack was called off.[57]

Instead of reaching for the trigger so fast, David Cameron could have offered a compromise solution along the same lines as a Russian proposal that resolved the crisis. Under a framework deal signed on 14 September, Bashar agreed to destroy his stock of chemical weapons, and allowed an international watchdog to enforce his promise.

There was another reason why David Cameron, and indeed his French and American opposite numbers, did not need to take such a belligerent line. Western governments could have insisted, for example, on allowing Bashar to stay in power as Syria's ruler but severely curtailed his powers, and perhaps even allowed him to assume a role of only nominal importance. But although such a flexible approach would have increased the scope for finding a settlement, or even just a lasting ceasefire, the three Western governments nonetheless took an uncompromising position on the issue almost as soon as the Syrian civil war erupted, in the spring of 2011.

Perhaps it was no coincidence that their belligerence pleased Bashar's main opponents – the Saudis and other Gulf states, whose vast wealth offered foreign countries so many commercial opportunities.

Nicolas Sarkozy's Libyan Crusade (2011)

When he came to power in 2007, the French president, Nicolas Sarkozy, inherited a strong national tradition of *activisme* that emphasises the use of military force, rather than dialogue and diplomacy, to resolve a crisis. Unlike Britain, which has centuries of parliamentary rule, France has evolved without a strong legislative power that allows for negotiations, discussion and compromise. So the French have been more inclined to resolve disputes not by peaceful means but by protests and demonstrations, of which the revolution of 1789 and the disturbances of 1968 are the most obvious examples. In the same spirit, French presidents are expected to take a stand against any foreign threat and put up a fight: President Giscard d'Éstaing did this to great effect in 1978, parachuting foreign legionnaires into Zaire to protect Western expatriates and then, the following year, executing a well-organised and effective coup that toppled the deranged leader of the Central African Republic, Jean-Bédel Bokhassa.

Nicolas Sarkozy's activist, warmongering spirit quickly became apparent as tension mounted in Libya in the opening weeks of 2011. He was the first leader to propose a no-fly zone, putting forward the idea five days before David Cameron. Then, at the end of February, before the United Nations had even authorised the use of force against Tripoli, the president ordered his spy service to establish links with the Libyan rebels, led by Mustafa Abdul

Jalil, and to offer them 'money and guidance' as well as diplomatic support and recognition if they seized power. And at a dinner on 11 March, he became so infuriated by the negative attitude of other world leaders that he dramatically stormed out. David Cameron followed and tried to placate him but Sarkozy just snapped back. 'Forget it – I've had enough of these people. It is better to tell the media they are complete weaklings who are happy to see Gaddafi massacre innocent people!"[58]

If any of his allies had doubts about what might lie ahead if France intervened in Libya, then Sarkozy was quick to dispel them, inviting Hillary Clinton, the American secretary of state, over to Paris on 18 March and assuring her that he and David Cameron were not repeating the mistakes made in Iraq a few years before. But Sarkozy was going too fast, too soon even for his fellow warmonger. 'What about air defences?' Cameron had asked the French president. Sarkozy looked baffled by the question and quickly turned round to his generals. 'What about air defences?' he reiterated before parroting the general's response. Everyone seemed satisfied with the general's answer and they then headed off to lunch.

Hours later, French planes struck Libyan targets, initially in the no-fly zone and then beyond, before Britain and America had even been consulted. 'David, we are not schoolboys in short trousers, we are men,' he reputedly told Cameron afterwards, as he constantly pushed his British counterpart to take more drastic measures.[59]

'Sarko' probably didn't want to be reminded that, less than four years before, he had seen the Libyan leader in rather different terms. In July 2007, just weeks after coming to office, he had visited Libya, greeting Colonel Gaddafi warmly before signing major deals for the sale of French arms and to provide technical know-how on nuclear energy. In December the following year, the colonel then made his own return visit to the French capital, his first such trip since 1973. Gaddafi's lavish five-day visitation infuriated human rights protestors but amused onlookers who watched his large entourage of 400 servants and 40 female bodyguards follow him around and pitch an enormous tent outside his official guesthouse. French businesses had by this time acquired a sizeable stake in his oil-rich economy, and there were rumours, later to emerge as a major political scandal, that Gaddafi was also secretly funding Sarkozy's political campaigning.

One explanation for the *volte-face* from conciliation to warmongery is that Sarkozy wanted to win public adulation by appealing to the spirit of *activisme*. He had already done this once, sending troops into Mali in 2008 in order to bolster the embattled regime of President Idriss Déby and to evacuate Western expatriates. As a result, his popularity ratings had soared. But three years on, his poll ratings were once again going into freefall. Sarko judged that a successful intervention would distract the nation from its woes and bring it back onto his side, just as *Margaret Thatcher* had benefited from the Falklands War. Little more than a year before the next presidential election, he badly needed a boost. He knew that he could win huge plaudits by restoring something of France's long-lost greatness: his country, he tellingly claimed, had a 'role before history' in stopping Gaddafi's 'killing spree' against people whose only crime was to seek to 'liberate themselves from servitude'.

Perhaps Sarkozy was also afraid that Tripoli would allow migrants to cross from the Libyan coast into Western Europe, further fuelling the political rise of the far right in France and stealing even more votes from him: on 8 March, just as Sarkozy was leading the charge against Libya, a new opinion poll gave Marine Le Pen's National Front enough votes to win the presidential election. Gaddafi had previously threatened to 'turn Europe black' unless he was given what he wanted. As the crisis in Benghazi mounted, or maybe before, he would have tried to pull the same strings, warning of retaliation against any European leaders who tried to meddle in his own affairs. Perhaps Nicolas Sarkozy calculated that a new, more compliant regime in Tripoli would not dare to turn against the Western powers that had backed it.

For the same reason, Sarko may have thought that a new regime in Tripoli would help French companies win new contracts. 'In return for their assistance,' wrote one Washington official in an email that was later leaked, 'the DGSE (French intelligence) officers indicated that they expected the new government of Libya to favour French firms and national interests, particularly regarding the oil industry in Libya.' Another leaked American government memorandum also disclosed that representatives of leading French companies, notably in the oil and defence sectors, regularly boarded humanitarian flights from Paris to Tripoli, where they were met and escorted to meetings by armed French undercover officers.[60]

For a time, the Elysée basked in the adulation of victory. French newspapers were even more reverential and deferential than usual and even blacked out awkward news reports, such as a tragic incident on 19 June when a French missile smashed into a block of flats in Tripoli, killing nine and injuring many more. But gradually the truth about Sarkozy's warmongering emerged: although around 1,000 people were killed in the air onslaught that he unleashed, within less than a year that number had increased nearly eightfold, as the country disintegrated into chaos. At the same time, French oil companies lost out to Italian rivals and the president's popularity ratings dipped to a new low. The following year he lost the presidential election to his socialist rival, François Hollande. In a bid to stir up popular enthusiasm for a foreign war, Nicolas Sarkozy had warmongered and paid a heavy price for doing so.

He would have done better to have pursued some more peaceful strategies. As the Tripoli regime came under pressure in early 2011, Sarkozy could have reached out to Gaddafi and offered him diplomatic support if, in return, the Libyan leader promised to curtail migration. And the French president could have found much simpler ways of building up his prestige before a doubting electorate, not least by spearheading international efforts to tackle ongoing issues such as the financial crisis, climate change and a resurgent Russia. If he had been determined to intervene in Libya, he could have confined his efforts to establishing a no-fly zone while allowing a less recalcitrant Gaddafi to remain in power.

King Salman's War for Yemen (2015)

In the course of 2016, the outside world became increasingly aware of a brutal war in one of the poorest countries in the Arab world, Yemen. Even to foreign audiences that had grown used to images of suffering in Syria and Iraq, the plight of the Yemeni people was disturbing. Civilian casualties were high, amounting to perhaps 10,000 dead by the year's end but maybe much higher. Around three-quarters of the population was in urgent need of food, water and other basic assistance. And perhaps as many as 3 million civilians were trying to flee the fighting. Yemen, as a senior spokesman for a relief organisation put it, was a 'humanitarian disaster'.

Much of the suffering was inflicted by Saudi artillery and warplanes, which fired randomly and indiscriminately into civilian areas. Other countries were also to blame since they were members of the Saudi-led coalition of Gulf States: Qatar, Kuwait and United Arab Emirates, for example, were also strongly supporting the military offensive in Yemen.

Trouble had flared up in Yemen towards the end of 2014, when an insurgent group, the Houthis, had seized control over swathes of the country's northern regions and then swept into the capital, Sana'a. These developments were watched with deep alarm in Saudi Arabia, which shares a long, porous border with its southern neighbour. In particular, King Salman of Saudi Arabia suspected the Houthis of having close ties with his regional rival Iran, with which they share the Shi'ite Islamic faith in contrast to the Sunni faith of Saudi and other Gulf kingdoms. Within weeks of the fall of Sana'a, in March 2015, King Salman had forged an alliance with the other Gulf States and started to bomb Houthi targets inside Yemen.

It was unclear if the Houthis really did have any links with Iran, as the Saudis always alleged. On one occasion, in October 2016, the American government backed up the Saudis by claiming to have intercepted Iranian weapons that were being smuggled into Yemen through Oman. But no evidence was ever put forward to support either this claim or allegations that the Iranians had any presence inside Yemen, or indeed any influence there at all.

What was not in doubt, however, was the mistrust and suspicion between Riyadh and Tehran, which have been at loggerheads ever since the Islamic Revolution of 1979, when *Ayatollah Khomeini* swept away Iran's traditional form of government, which was based on hereditary monarchy. 'We will not accept any interference in the internal affairs of Yemen,' warned King Salman in a thinly veiled threat against the Tehran regime, even if his comment was a curious one when he himself was doing just that.

Soon, horrifying atrocity stories emerged of Saudi tactics. While the Western world sold voluminous quantities of arms to Riyadh, there were unconfirmed reports that the Saudis were deliberately targeting Yemen's farms, fields and crops in a bid to starve the Houthis into surrender. Numerous other disturbing reports emerged, such as the targeting of a crowded funeral procession in Sana'a on 8 October 2016, in which around 150 civilians died and 600 were wounded, while a coalition airstrike on Souq al-Hinood, a densely populated neighbourhood in Hodeida, on September 21 killed at least twenty-eight civilians, including 8 children, and wounded thirty-two others.[61]

Saudi's involvement in Yemen from 2015 was ultimately the decision of its leader, King Salman bin Abdul Aziz Al Saud, even if it was implemented by one of his nine sons, thirty-year-old Mohammad bin Salman Al Saud, the deputy prime minister and minister of defence. Not many people doubted the king's ruthlessness. He had come to the Saudi throne in January 2015, at the age of seventy-nine, and within weeks of his accession his security forces had started to crack down on domestic dissent, real or imaginary. International watchdogs noted that in the course of the first year of King Salman's reign, Saudi executioners were busier than at any time over the previous two decades, executing forty-seven people in a single day on 2 January 2016. Many of these individuals were victims of vaguely worded 'anti-terrorist' laws that were also routinely abused.[62]

But if King Salman, and the 4,000 princes who comprised his royal family, wanted to keep Yemen out of Iran's hands or influence, then it was difficult to see why they needed to unleash a war, particularly a war against its civilian population. A much less drastic solution, but one that was much more closely targeted, was to impose a naval blockade.

The Saudi Navy had started to impose just such a blockade in early 2015. This, unfortunately, was a blanket ban on all incoming ships, not just on those that were carrying arms, or military advisers, from abroad. As a result, Yemen's food imports soon slumped to only a fraction, about 15 per cent, of its pre-war levels, even though it is hugely reliant upon them to meet the needs of its growing population. And the Saudis were also stopping or turning back tankers that were carrying petrol, diesel and fuel oil, crippling the country's electricity supply and forcing the mass closure of hospitals and schools. 'There are less and less of the basic necessities. People are queuing all day long,' as an aid worker told one British newspaper. 'The blockade means it's impossible to bring anything into the country. There are lots of ships, with basic things like flour, that are not allowed to approach. The situation is deteriorating, hospitals are now shutting down, without diesel. People are dying of simple diseases. It is becoming almost impossible to survive.'[63]

But Riyadh would have found foreign backers, notably Britain, France and America, to help it enforce a more targeted approach. The Saudis could have tempted these and other foreign powers with offers of massive arms deals in a bid to win not just their diplomatic support for such an embargo but for their intelligence information. The three Western countries had at their disposal first-class satellite and electronic eavesdropping intelligence that vastly surpassed what the Saudis had access to, and this would have allowed Saudi to undertake an 'intelligence-led interdiction', stopping and searching only those individual ships that they had good reason to suspect were carrying arms.

In this scenario, the Houthi regime in Yemen would not have presented any possible threat to the Saudis, who could have struck up a peace deal with their new neighbours. At the same time, they would have moved closer to their Western allies while sparing so many civilians from so much suffering.

CONCLUSION

This is not meant as an anti-war book, for there are occasions when war should and must be used, most obviously in self-defence. Instead, this book's purpose is to act only as a reminder that war should *as a rule* only be a last resort, and when violence does have to be used then it should be proportionate. Each and every case in this book shows that there have been times and places when politicians have reached too quickly for the trigger, or when their advisers have either urged them to do that or else failed to try and stop them. This may happen after a long period of peace, when the realities of war have been forgotten. This was probably true of Britain on the eve of the First World War, when memories of the Crimean War – the last time British troops had seen active service on the continent – had long faded. And it helps explain, too, America's involvement in Iraq in 2003, which took place a whole generation after Vietnam.

However, there may well be occasions when it is quite reasonable or even desirable to use force before other, less drastic options have been pursued. Europe in the 1930s presents the most obvious example: as Winston Churchill argued in his book *The Gathering Storm*, pre-emptive war against Nazi Germany at the time of the occupation of the Rhineland in 1936 would have spared the world a great deal more bloodshed at a later stage. However, such examples are rare: there have been very few political leaders who have been prepared to go to war with the same fanatical determination as Hitler, rendering futile any efforts to strike a peaceful deal. Instead, unnecessarily unleashing force guarantees death and destruction that might well otherwise be avoided.

Perhaps this message – that war should generally be a last resort – will become more important in the future. For in the years ahead, the temptation to unleash 'wars of first resort' will grow if the technological gap between more advanced states and the rest of the world becomes wider still: if the United States or Russia develop 'killer robots' for example, as the media has speculated, then they will be less inhibited about using them against a less sophisticated foe, knowing that they will not be confronted by the spectre of mass casualties that made so many other conflicts politically, as well as militarily, untenable.

It is against just such scenarios that this book seeks to guard. Anyone who calls for, or authorises, the use of force against an opponent should be challenged to answer what might be called 'the proportionality test': are all political avenues exhausted, and if force really is necessary are there more limited options available?

At another level, the book is a call not just for vigilance against disproportionate actions and responses but against the underlying causes of warmongering that underwrite the specific examples in this book. These have been outlined in the Introduction as the 'five deadly sins' – hubris, obsession, raw emotion, the holding of assumptions and a lack of advisers. Unfortunately recognising all of these traits, other than the last, is a very demanding task because it requires a degree of detachment that is very difficult to acquire in the circumstances of the moment: after the Argentine invasion of the Falklands in 1982, for example, it was very problematic for anyone to stand back and see some of the policy options that Margaret Thatcher had before her. As a wave of anger swept over Britain in the wake of the attack, only very few of the prime minister's more level-headed advisers, notably the minister John Biffen, argued for a more restrained and cautious approach than the one championed by his more gung-ho leader. However, political leaders are able to surround themselves with a wide range of advisers who are able to give them balanced advice if they are confronted by a situation in which force has to be used. Equally, their electorates, or elected representatives, are often in a position to notice whether or not their leaders have this wide counsel of opinion.

But perhaps it is expecting too much to suppose that any amount of vigilance will make any difference to the advent of 'unnecessary wars' in the future. As long as wars can be fought, mistakes made, opportunities squandered and alternatives overlooked, many of them will always be to some degree 'unnecessary'.

BIBLIOGRAPHY

Abdurish, Said *Saddam Hussein: The Politics of Revenge* Bloomsbury (2000)

Adams, Henry *History of the United States of America Volume 3* Cambridge University Press (2011)

Adams, John Quincy *Writings of John Quincy Adams Volume 4* Macmillan (1913)

Albright, Madeleine *Madam Secretary: A Memoir* Harper (2003)

Andrew, Jason *The Origins of Canadian and American Political Differences* Harvard University Press (2009)

Applebaum, Anne *Gulag: A History* Doubleday (2003)

Axworthy, Michael *Revolutionary Iran: A History of the Islamic Republic* Allen Lane (2013)

Bailey, T. A. *Woodrow Wilson and the Lost Peace* Franklin Watts (1978)

Ball, George *The Past Has Another Pattern* WW Norton (1982)

Barzini, L. *The Italians* Touchstone (1976)

Basler, Roy P. *Collected Works of Abraham Lincoln* Rutgers (1953)

Benn, Carl *The War of 1812* Osprey Books (2003)

Beschloss, Michael R *The Johnson White House Tapes 1963-4* Simon & Schuster (1998)

Beschloss, Michael R (ed.) *Taking Charge: The Johnson White House Tapes 1963-4* (1998)

Blanning, Tim *The Origins of the French Revolutionary Wars* Longman (1986)

Bourne, Peter G. *Jimmy Carter: A Comprehensive Biography from Plains to Post-Presidency* Scribner (1997)

Braithwaite, Rodric *Afgantsy: The Russians in Afghanistan 1979-89* Profile (2012)

Bridgland, Fred *Jonas Savimbi: A Key to Africa* Paragon House (1987)

Brissaud, A. *Mussolini* Volume I, Perrin (1983)

Brittain, Vera *Diary of the Thirties 1932-9* Orion (2000)

Brogan, Hugh *The Pelican History of the United States of America* Penguin (1985)

Brands, H. W. *Woodrow Wilson: The American Presidents Series: The 28th President, 1913-21* Macmillan (2003)

Brendon, Piers *The Dark Valley* Jonathan Cape (2000)

Bulloch, John and Morris, Harvey *The Gulf War: Its Origins, History and Consequences* Methuen (1989)

Cannon, Lou *President Reagan: The Role of a Lifetime* Public Affairs (2000)

Caputi, Robert J. *Neville Chamberlain and Appeasement* Susquehanna University Press (2000)

Caute, D. *Communism and the French Intellectuals* André Deutsch (1964)

Chambers, James *Palmerston : 'The People's Darling'* John Murray (2005)

Chappell, John D. *Before the Bomb: How America Approached the End of the Pacific War* University Press of Kentucky (2006)

Cheney, Lynne *James Madison: A Life Reconsidered* Penguin (2014)

Ciano, Galeazzo *Ciano's Diary 1937-8* Phoenix (2002)

Clark, Christopher *The Sleepwalkers* Allen Lane (2012)

Clarke, Richard A. *Against all Enemies: Inside America's War on Terror* Simon & Schuster (2004)

Connaughton, Richard *Rising Sun and Tumbling Bear* Cassell (2003)

Crile, George *Charlie Wilson's War* Grove Press (2007)

Dallek, Robert *Nixon and Kissinger: Partners in Power* Harper (2007)

Dallek, Robert *John F. Kennedy : An Unfinished Life 1917–1963* Penguin (2013)

Dalrymple, William *The Return of a King: The Battle for Afghanistan* Bloomsbury (2012)

David, Saul *Victoria's Wars: The Rise of Empire* Penguin (2006)

Dobbs, Michael *Six Months in 1945: FDR, Stalin, Churchill and Truman* Vintage (2013)

Donald, David Herbert *Lincoln* Simon & Schuster (1995)

Draper, Theodore *A Struggle for Power: The American Revolution* Random House (1996)

Dwyer, Philip *Citizen Emperor: Napoleon in Power* Bloomsbury (2014)

Eisenhower, Dwight D. *Waging Peace 1956-61* Doubleday (2000)

Fenby, Jonathan *The History of Modern France: From the Revolution to the War on Terror* Simon & Schuster (2015)

Ferguson, Niall *The Pity of War* Penguin (1998)

Ferro, Merro *Nicholas II: The Last of the Tsars* Oxford University Press (1990)

Figes, Orlando *Crimea: The Last Crusade* Penguin (2010)

Fisher, B. J. *King Zog and the Struggle for Stability in Albania* East European Monographs (1984)

Fleury, Comte Maurice *Memoirs of the Empress Eugénie* Hardpress Publishing (2012)

Freedman, Lawrence *Kennedy's Wars: Berlin, Cuba, Laos, and Vietnam* OUP (2000)

Freedman, Lawrence and Gamba-Stonehouse, Virginia *Signals of War: The Falklands Conflict of 1982* Princeton University Press (1990)

Freedman, Lawrence *The Official History of the Falklands Campaign Volume I* Routledge (2005)

Gandin, Greg *Kissinger's Shadow: The Long Reach of America's Most Controversial Statesman* Macmillan (2015)

Geyer, Georgie Anne *Guerrilla Prince: The Untold Story of Fidel Castro* Little, Brown (1991)

Goldfield, David *America Aflame: How the Civil War Created a Nation* Bloomsbury (2013)

Grenade, Wendy C. (ed.) *The Grenada Revolution: Reflections and Lesson* University of Mississippi Press (2015)

Hamby, Alonzo L. *Man of the People: A Life of Harry S. Truman* OUP (1995)

Hamilton, Nigel *American Caesars: Lives of the US Presidents* Bodley Head (2010)

Hamilton, Richard F. *President McKinley, War and Empire: President McKinley and America's New Empire* Transaction (2007)

Hamilton, Richard F. and Herwig, Holger H. *The Origins of World War I* Cambridge University Press (2003)

Harris, Robin *Not For Turning: The Life of Margaret Thatcher* Bantam Press (2013)

Hart, Alan *Arafat, Terrorist or Peacemaker?* Sidgwick and Jackson (1984)

Hastings, Max *The Korean War* Macmillan (1987)

Heidler, David Stephen and Heidler, Jeanne T. *The War of 1812* Greenwood Publishing (2002)

Herring, George C. *The Pentagon Papers* McGraw-Hill (1993)

Herzog, Chaim *The Arab-Israeli Wars: War and Peace in the Middle East* Vintage (2005)

Hiro, Dilip *Neighbours Not Friends: Iraq and Iraq after the Gulf Wars* Routledge (2001)

Holland, Neil *Elusive Dove: The Search for Peace During World War I* McFarland (2013)

Horne, Alistair *Seven Ages of Paris* Pan Macmillan (2002)

Howard, Michael *The Franco-Prussian War: The German Invasion of France 1870–1871* Routledge (1961)

Hunt, Gaillard *The Writings of James Madison Volume 6: 1808–1819 by James Madison* Kessinger (2010)

Hutchison, E. H. *Violent Truce: A Military Observer Looks at the Arab-Israeli Conflict 1951-55* Devin-Adair Co. (1956)

Jennings, Christian *Across the Red River* Phoenix (2001)

Jones, Howard *Crucible of Power: A History of U.S. Foreign Relations Since 1897* Rowman & Littlefield (2001)

Jones, Thai *More Powerful Than Dynamite: Radicals, Plutocrats, Progressives, and New York's Year of Anarchy* Bloomsbury (2012)

Kalb, Marvin and Kalb, Bernard *Kissinger* Little, Brown & Co (1979)

Kampfner, John *Blair's Wars* Simon and Schuster (2004)

Kekewich, Margaret Lucille *Princes and Peoples: France and the British Isles, 1620–1714: An Anthology* Manchester University Press (1994)

Ketcham, Ralph *Selected Writings of James Madison* Hackett (2006)

Keynes J. M. *The Economic Consequences of Peace* Createspace Independent Publishing Platform (2010)

Kolkey, Jonathan Martin *Germany on the March: A Reinterpretation of War and Domestic Politics Over the Past Two Centuries* University Press of America (1995)

Kilroy, David P. and Nojeim, Michael J. *Days of Decision: Turning Points in U.S. Foreign Policy* Potomac Books (2011)

Kissinger, Henry *Ending the Vietnam War: A History of America's Involvement in and Extrication from the Vietnam War* Simon & Schuster (2003)

Kyle, Keith *Suez 1956* IB Tauris (1991)

Laurens, F. D. *France and the Italo-Ethiopian Crisis 1935-6* Mouton (1967)

Link, Arthur S. *Wilson, Volume II: The New Freedom* Princeton University Press (1947)

Lynn, John A. *The Wars of Louis XIV 1667–1714* Routledge (1999)

McMeekin, Sean *Countdown to War* Icon Books (2014)

McNamara, Robert *In Retrospect: The Tragedy and Lessons of Vietnam* Times Books (1995)

Martel, Gordon *The Month that Changed the World: July 1914* OUP (2014)

Manchester, William *American Caesar: Douglas MacArthur 1880–1964* Back Bay Books (2008)

Marx, Karl *The Eastern Question* Routledge (1994)

Matthews, Chris *Kennedy & Nixon: The Rivalry that Shaped Post-War America* Simon & Schuster (1997)

Mearsheimer, John and Walt, Stephen *The Israel Lobby and US Foreign Policy* Penguin (2007)

Miller, Merle *Plain Speaking: An Oral Biography of Harry S. Truman* Black Dog & Leventhal (2005)

Miller, Randall and Stout, Harry *Religion and the American Civil War* Oxford University Press (1998)

Moin, Baqer *Khomeini: Life of the Ayatollah* IB Tauris (1999)

Mombauer, Annika *Helmuth von Moltke and the Origins of the First World War* Cambridge University Press (2008)

Mosley, L. *Haile Selassie: The Conquering Lion* Prentice-Hall (1964)

Mueller, John *The Remnants of War* Cornell University Press (2004)

Murphy, Orville T. *Charles Gravier, Comte de Vergennes: French Diplomacy in the Age of Revolution 1719-77* State University of New York Press (1982)

Nutting, Anthony *No End of a Lesson: The Story of Suez* Constable (1967)

Oborne, Peter *Not the Chilcott Report* Head of Zeus (2016)

Ogg, David *Louis XIV* Oxford University Press (1963)

Orwell, George *George Orwell The Collected Essays Vol. 4* Secker & Warburg (1968)

O'Shaughnessy, Andrew *The Men Who Lost America* Oneworld (2013)

Otte, T. G. *July Crisis: The World's Descent into War, Summer 1914* Cambridge University Press (2014)

Padover, S. K. *The Life and Death of Louis XVI* D. Appleton-Century (1939)

Paléologue, Maurice *The Tragic Empress: Intimate Conversations With the Empress Eugénie, 1901 to 1911* Thornton Butterworth (1928)

Parmet, Herbert S. *George Bush: The Life of a Lone Star Yankee* Transaction (2000)

Payne, Stanley *Franco and Hitler: Spain, Germany, and World War II* Yale University Press (2009)

Pearson, Michael *Those Damned Rebels: The American Revolution As Seen Through British Eyes* Da Capo (2000)

Pederson D, John R. Vile and Williams Frank J. *James Madison: Philosopher, Founder and Statesman* Ohio University Press (2008)

Phillips, Kevin *William McKinley: The 25th President, 1897–1901* Times Books (2003)

Pinkney, William and Wheaton, Henry *Some Account of the Life, Writings, and Speeches of William Pinkney* University of Michigan Libraries (1826)

Prunier, Gérard *The Rwanda Crisis: History of a Genocide 1959-94* Hurst & Co (1995)

Puryear, Vernon John *International Economics and Diplomacy in the Near East: A Study of British Commercial Policy in the Levant 1834-53* Shoe String Press (1969)

Razoux, Pierre *The Iran-Iraq War* Harvard University Press (2015)

Reeves, Richard *President Reagan: The Triumph of Imagination* Simon & Schuster (2005)

Reeves, Richard *President Nixon: Alone in the White House* Simon & Schuster (2002)

Reynolds, David *Britannia Overruled: British Policy and World Power in the Twentieth Century* Routledge (2013)

Richards, David *Taking Command: The Autobiography* Headline (2014)

Riddell, George *Intimate Diary of the Peace Conference and After 1918-23* Victor Gollancz (1933)

Ridley, Jasper *Napoleon III and Eugénie* Constable (1979)

Robb, David *The Gumshoe and the Shrink* Santa Monica Press (2012)

Roberts, Andrew *Napoleon the Great* Penguin (2015)

Rose, Gideon *How Wars End: Why We Always Fight the Last Battle* Simon & Schuster (2012)

Sabato, Larry J. *The Kennedy Half-Century: The Presidency, Assassination and Lasting Legacy* Bloomsbury (2013)

Schiff, Ze'ev and Yari, Ehud *Israel's Lebanon War* Touchstone (1985)

Secunda, Eugene and Moran, Terence *Selling War to America: From the Spanish American War to the Global War on Terror* Praeger Security (2007)

Sharon, Ariel *Warrior* Macdonald (1989)

Shawcross, William *Deliver Us From Evil* Bloomsbury (2001)

Shlaim, Avi *The Iron Wall: Israel and the Arab World* Penguin (2000)

Short, Philip *Mitterrand : A Study in Ambiguity* Bodley Head (2013)

Smith, David *Louis XIV* Cambridge University Press (2010)

Smith, Joseph *The Spanish-American War 1895–1902: Conflict in the Caribbean and the Pacific* Routledge (2015)

Sonnino, Paul *Louis XIV and the Origins of the Dutch War* Cambridge University Press (1988)

Street, G. L. *A Date in the Desert* Hodder and Stoughton (1939)

Stewart, Desmond *Eugénie: The Empress and Her Empire* The History Press (2004)

Stockley, Andrew *Britain and France at the Birth of America: The European Powers and the Peace Negotiations of 1782-83* Liverpool University Press (2001)

Suskind, Ron *The Price of Loyalty: George W. Bush, The White House and the Education of Paul O'Neill* Simon and Schuster (2004)

Szulc, Tad *The Illusion of Peace: Foreign Policy in the Nixon Years* Viking Press (1978)

Taylor, Alan & Taylor Irene *Those Who Marched Away: An Anthology of the World's Greatest War Diaries* Canongate (2009)

Teveth, Shabtai *Moshe Dayan* Weidenfeld and Nicholson (1972)

Thomas, Evan *The Very Best Men: Four Who Dared: The Early Years of the CIA* Pocket Books (1997)

Thomas, Evan *Being Nixon: A Man Divided* Random House (2015)

Tombs, Robert *France 1814–1914* Routledge (1996)

Troubetzkoy, Alexis *The Crimean War* Robinson (2006)

Unger, Harlow *John Hancock: Merchant King and American Patriot* Wiley (2000)

Unger, Irwin *LBJ: A Life* Wiley (1999)

Van Evera, Stephen *Causes of War: Power and the Roots of Conflict* Cornell University Press (2001)

Waite, James *The End of the First Indochina War: A Global History* Routledge (2012)

Wallis, Andrew *Silent Accomplice* IB Tauris (2006)

Weintraub, Stanley *MacArthur's War: Korea and the Undoing of an American Hero* Free Press (2008)

Wittner, Lawrence *The Struggle Against the Bomb Volume 3* Stanford University Press (1995)

Worth, Richard and Kras, Sara Louise *Pervez Musharraf* Chelsea House (2003)

Zamoyski, Adam *Moscow 1812: Napoleon's Fatal March* Harper (2005)

NOTES

Introduction & 1 The Post-Westphalian Era

1. On the questionable importance of the 1648 treaty, see for example 'A Westphalian Peace for the Middle East: Why an Old Framework Could Work' by Michael Axworthy and Patrick Milton, *Foreign Affairs* 10 October 2016

2. *The Wars of Louis XIV 1667–1714* by John A. Lynn, Routledge (1999), Chapter 4

3. *Louis XIV and the Origins of the Dutch War* by Paul Sonnino, Cambridge University Press (1988)

4. Deferential courtiers – *Louis XIV* by David Smith, Cambridge University Press (2010)

5. Vauban – *Louis XIV* by David Ogg, Oxford University Press (1963) pp.29, 36

6. *Princes and Peoples: France and the British Isles, 1620–1714: An Anthology* by Margaret Lucille Kekewich, Manchester University Press (1994) pp.225–7

2 The Age of Revolutions

1. *John Hancock: Merchant King and American Patriot* by Harlow Unger, Wiley (2000) pp.162–7

2. *The Men Who Lost America* by Andrew O'Shaughnessy, Oneworld (2013)

3. Dickinson – *A Struggle for Power: The American Revolution* by Theodore Draper, Random House (1996) p.446. Draper op. cit. p.433

4. Draper op. cit. p.473

5. Lord North – Draper op. cit. p.491

6. Hugh Brogan, *The Pelican History of the United States of America*, Penguin (1985) pp.194–201

7. See 'The Strange Case of the Chevalier d'Eon' by Jonathan Conlin, *History Today* April 2010

8. Point of despair – *Charles Gravier, Comte de Vergennes: French Diplomacy in the Age of Revolution 1719–77* by Orville T. Murphy, State University of New York Press (1982) p.233

9. *Those Damned Rebels: The American Revolution As Seen Through British Eyes* by Michael Pearson, Da Capo (2000) p.299

10. Vergennes – *Britain and France at the Birth of America: The European Powers and the Peace Negotiations of 1782–83* by Andrew Stockley, Liverpool University Press (2001) p.18

11. Tim Blanning, *The Origins of the French Revolutionary Wars*, Longman (1986) pp.48–9

12. SK Padover *The Life and Death of Louis XVI* D. Appleton-Century (1939) 116

13. Adam Zamoyski *Moscow 1812: Napoleon's Fatal March* Harper (2005)

14. *Citizen Emperor: Napoleon in Power* by Philip Dwyer, Bloomsbury (2014) p.356

15. Zamoyski op. cit. p.76

16. Dwyer op. cit. p.357

17. Zamoyski op. cit. p.131

18. Andrew Roberts *Napoleon the Great,* Penguin (2015) p.628

19. *James Madison: A Life Reconsidered* by Lynne Cheney, Penguin (2014)

20. *Selected Writings of James Madison* by James Madison edited by Ralph Ketcham, Hackett (2006) p.287

21. *The War of 1812* by David Stephen Heidler, Jeanne T. Heidler, Greenwood Publishing (2002) p.166

22. *The Writings of James Madison Volume 6: 1808–1819* by James Madison edited by Gaillard Hunt, Kessinger (2010) p.44; *Some Account of the Life, Writings, and Speeches of William Pinkney* By William Pinkney, Henry Wheaton, University of Michigan Libraries (1826) p.428

23. *The Origins of Canadian and American Political Differences* by Jason Andrew, Harvard University Press (2009) p.151

24. *The War of 1812* by Carl Benn, Osprey Books (2003) p.26

25. Adams – *Writings of John Quincy Adams Volume 4* by John Quincy Adams, Macmillan (1913) p.388. *James Madison: Philosopher, Founder and Statesman* edited by John R. Vile, William D. Pederson, Frank J. Williams, Ohio University Press (2008), p.241

26. Madison op.cit. p.208

27. *History of the United States of America Volume 3* by Henry Adams, Cambridge University Press (2011), p.85

3 The Post-Napoleonic Era

1. Ulsterman – *The Return of a King: The Battle for Afghanistan* By William Dalrymple, Bloomsbury xxii (2012) Burnes – Dalrymple op. cit. p.155

2. Orlando Figes *Crimea: The Last Crusade* Penguin (2010) p.48

3. Historian – *International Economics and Diplomacy in the Near East: A Study of British Commercial Policy in the Levant 1834–53* by Vernon John Puryear, Shoe String Press (1969) p.61

4. Russian theologian – Figes op. cit. p.4

5. To Queen Victoria – Figes op.cit.66

6. Massacres – Figes op. cit. p.59

7. Missionary – Figes op. cit. p.25

8. Russell – *The Eastern Question* by Karl Marx, Routledge (1994) p.300

9. Figes op. cit. p156

10. Quoted in Alexis Troubetzkoy *The Crimean War*, Robinson (2006) p.50

11. Hostile act – Figes op. cit. p.122

12. As foreign secretary – *Victoria's Wars: The Rise of Empire* by Saul David, Penguin (2006); Prince Albert – see *Palmerston : 'The People's Darling'* by James Chambers, John Murray (2005)

13. See in general *Napoleon III and Eugénie* by Jasper Ridley, Constable (1979); *Eugénie : The Empress and Her Empire* by Desmond Stewart, The History Press (2004)

14. 'Sacred bayonets' – the phrase was used in 1841 by the French newspaper *L'Atelier*. See Robert Tombs *France 1814–1914* Routledge (1996) p.84

15. *The Tragic Empress: Intimate Conversations With the Empress Eugénie, 1901 to 1911*, London, Thornton Butterworth (1928) pp.100–1

16. *Those Who Marched Away: An Anthology of the World's Greatest War Diaries* by Alan & Irene Taylor, Canongate (2009) p.360

17. Figes op. cit. p.102

18. *The History of Modern France: From the Revolution to the War on Terror* by Jonathan Fenby, Simon & Schuster (2015) p.128

19. *The Franco-Prussian War: The German Invasion of France 1870–1871* by Michael Howard, Routledge (1961)

20. Napoleon quoted in *Germany on the March: A Reinterpretation of War and Domestic Politics Over the Past Two Centuries* by Jonathan Martin Kolkey, University Press of America (1995) p.135

21. *Seven Ages of Paris* by Alistair Horne, Pan Macmillan (2002) p.285

22. *Memoirs of the Empress Eugénie* by Comte Maurice Fleury, Hardpress Publishing (2012)

23. 'Napoleonic ideal – *Europe in the 19th & 20th Centuries* by Ephraim Lipson, Black, London (1957) p.34

24. *Selling War to America: From the Spanish American War to the Global War on Terror* by Eugene Secunda and Terence P. Moran, Praeger Security (2007) p.15

25. See in general *William McKinley: The 25th President, 1897–1901* by Kevin Phillips, Times Books (2003)

26. *Days of Decision: Turning Points in U.S. Foreign Policy* by Michael J. Nojeim and David P. Kilroy, Potomac Books (2011) p.13

27. *The Spanish-American War 1895–1902: Conflict in the Caribbean and the Pacific* by Joseph Smith, Routledge (2015) p.26

28. *President McKinley, War and Empire: President McKinley and America's New Empire* by Richard F. Hamilton, Transaction (2007) p.81

29. Critic – Smith op. cit. p.209

30. Richard Connaughton *Rising Sun and Tumbling Bear* Cassell (2003)

31. *Nicholas II : The Last of the Tsars* by Marc Ferro, Oxford University Press (1990) p.68

4 The Run-up to the First World War

1. *Wilson, Volume II: The New Freedom* by Arthur S. Link, Princeton University Press (1947) p.396

2. *Woodrow Wilson: The American Presidents Series: The 28th President, 1913–21* by H. W. Brands, Macmillan (2003) p.47; 'Wilson the Just', TA Bailey *Woodrow Wilson and the Lost Peace*, Franklin Watts (1978) p.111; Nonconformist – *The Economic Consequences of Peace* by JM Keynes, Createspace Independent Publishing Platform (2010) Chapter 3; Jesus Christ – this was the remark of Georges Clemenceau, quoted in Lord Riddell *Intimate Diary of the Peace Conference and After 1918–23* Victor Gollancz (1933) p.78

3. Maynard op. cit. p.253

4. *Crucible of Power: A History of U.S. Foreign Relations Since 1897* by Howard Jones, Rowman & Littlefield (2001) p.63

5. *More Powerful Than Dynamite: Radicals, Plutocrats, Progressives, and New York's Year of Anarchy* by Thai Jones, Bloomsbury (2012) p.196

6. Christopher Clark *The Sleepwalkers*, Allen Lane (2012) pp.266–70

7. Clark op. cit. pp.513–4

8. Clark p.461

9. *Countdown to War* by Sean McMeekin, Icon Books (2014) Chapter 14

10. Clark op. cit. pp.457–69

11. Clark op. cit. pp.278–9

12. *Helmuth von Moltke and the Origins of the First World War* by Annika Mombauer, Cambridge University Press (2008) p.52

13. *The Origins of World War I* edited by Richard F. Hamilton and Holger H. Herwig, Cambridge University Press (2003) p.166

14. *Causes of War: Power and the Roots of Conflict* by Stephen van Evera, Cornell University Press (2001) p.214

15. *Elusive Dove: The Search for Peace During World* War I by Neil Holland, McFarland (2013) p.76

16. Clark op. cit. pp.539–40

17. *July Crisis: The World's Descent into War, Summer 1914* By T. G. Otte, Cambridge University Press (2014) p.473

18. Lloyd George: *The Remnants of War* by John Mueller, Cornell University Press (2004) p.46. Royal Navy – *The Pity of War* by Niall Ferguson, Penguin (1998) pp.162–3

19. *The Month that Changed the World: July 1914* by Gordon Martel, OUP (2014) p.305

20. Clark op. cit. p.202

21. Crowe – Clark op. cit. p.540

22. *Britannia Overruled: British Policy and World Power in the Twentieth Century* by D. Reynolds, Routledge (2013) p.75

23. Moltke – Ferguson op. cit. p.169

24. 'British commanders' – Ferguson op. cit. p.86. Churchill – Clark op. cit. p.210

5 The Age of Dictators

1. Age limit – *Ciano's Diary 1937–8* by Galeazzo Ciano, Phoenix (2002) p.8

2. Free hand – FD Laurens *France and the Italo-Ethiopian Crisis 1935–6* Mouton (1967) pp.23–30. See Piers Brendon *The Dark Valley*, Jonathan Cape (2000) p.261

3. Feudal Lords – *Spectator* 19 July 1935; Brendon op. cit. p.265

4. Like a god – L. Barzini *The Italians*, Touchstone (1976), 146; Ambassador – A.Brissaud *Mussolini* Volume I, Perrin (1983) p.406

5. L. Mosley *Haile Selassie: The Conquering Lion* Prentice-Hall (1964) p.216

6. Fascist triumph – GL Street *A Date in the Desert* Hodder and Stoughton (1939) p.132

7. Irrigation – Italo Balbo and the Colonization of Libya, Claudio G. Segre, *Journal of Contemporary History*, Vol. 7, No. 3/4 (Jul. – Oct. 1972) pp.141–155

8. BJ Fisher *King Zog and the Struggle for Stability in Albania*, East European Monographs (1984) p.279

9. Churchill – see David Carlton 'Churchill and the Soviet Union', Manchester 2000 pp.15, 18, 20, 32, 37; See in general *Neville Chamberlain and Appeasement* by Robert J. Caputi, Susquehanna University Press (2000)

10. Vera Brittain – *Diary of the Thirties 1932–9* Orion (2000) p.256; Chamberlain – Speech at a National Government rally, Kettering, Northants, 2 July 1938; Bonnet – S. Butterworth 'Daladier and the Munich Crisis: A Reappraisal', *Journal of Contemporary History*, July 1974, p.207

11. *Franco and Hitler: Spain, Germany, and World War II* by Stanley Payne, Yale University Press (2009)

12. Quoted in D. Caute *Communism and the French Intellectuals* Andre Deutsch (1964) p.117

13. *Before the Bomb: How America Approached the End of the Pacific War* by John D. Chappell, University Press of Kentucky (2006) pp.140–1

14. 'The Decision to use the Bomb', by Henry Lewis Stimson, *Harpers Magazine* February 1947

15. Quoted in *Six Months in 1945: FDR, Stalin, Churchill and Truman* by Michael Dobbs, Vintage (2013) p.240

16. Quoted in *Man of the People: A Life of Harry S. Truman* by Alonzo L. Hamby OUP (1995)

17. David Holloway on: Soviet Reactions to Hiroshima, 'Race for the Superbomb', American Experience Television, January 1999

6 The Cold War Era

1. McCloy – Memorandum of 7 November 1945, Foreign Relations of the United States 1945, Volume 6 pp.1122–24

2. Officer – quoted in Max Hastings *The Korean War* Macmillan (1987) p.52

3. *American Caesar: Douglas MacArthur 1880–1964* by William Manchester, Back Bay Books (2008)

4. See in general *MacArthur's War: Korea and the Undoing of an American Hero* by Stanley Weintraub, Free Press (2008)

5. See the cabinet discussions of the British government, 13 November 1950, CM 73, National Archives, Kew

6. Hastings op. cit. p.40

7. Curtis Lemay quoted in Richard Rhodes, "The General and World War III," *The New Yorker*, June 19, 1995, p.53

8. *Plain Speaking: An Oral Biography of Harry S. Truman* by Merle Miller, Black Dog & Leventhal (2005) p.291

9. Alan Hart, *Arafat, Terrorist or Peacemaker?* Sidgwick and Jackson (1984) pp.107–10; Ariel Sharon, *Warrior*, Macdonald (1989) p.102

10. Avi Shlaim, *The Iron Wall: Israel and the Arab World* Penguin Books (2000) p.127

11. Sharett – Keith Kyle *Suez 1956* IB Tauris (1991) p.66; Diplomatic Despatch from British ambassador to London, 10 May 1954, FO 371/111071, National Archives, Kew

12. Anthony Nutting, *No End of a Lesson: The Story of Suez* Constable (1967) p.92

13. See in general Kyle *Suez* pp.388–9

14. Kyle op. cit. pp.201–4

15. Dwight D. Eisenhower *Waging Peace 1956–61* Doubleday (2000) pp.669–71

16. PREM 11/1103; CM 74 (56), 25 October 1956, National Archives, Kew; Kyle op.cit.334; see also the personal archive of Sir Walter Monckton, Bodleian Library, Oxford Walter: Monckton minute, Sept. 1956.

17. Quoted in Kyle op. cit. p.137

18. Strauss – *Natural Right and History*, University of Chicago (2008); Nutting interviewed in 'Suez – The Missing Dimension' BBC Radio 4, 28 October 2006.

19. Kyle op. cit. p.160

20. FO 80/734, 'Record of a Meeting Held at Chequers', 11 March 1956, National Archives, Kew

21. 'General Paul Aussaresses – Obituary', *Daily Telegraph*, 4 December 2013

22. Kyle op. cit. p.116

23. See Alistair Horne *A Savage War of Peace*, NYRB Books (2006) p.129. Abdul Qadir Chanderli, one of the FLN's leaders who had been head of its arms procurement in Yugoslavia, later said that Nasser's involvement with Algeria had been 'negligible (but) because of the need for solidarity we could not say so'.

24. *John F. Kennedy : An Unfinished Life 1917–1963* by Robert Dallek, Penguin (2013)

25. *The Eisenhower Years* by Michael S. Mayer, Introduction p.1, Facts on File (2009)

26. Arthur Schlesinger to JFL, 11 February 1961. See *The Kennedy Half-Century: The Presidency, Assassination and Lasting Legacy* by Larry J. Sabato, Bloomsbury (2013) p.82

27. Dallek op. cit. p.359

28. Dallek op. cit. p.359

29. Dallek op. cit. p.370

30. *The Very Best Men: Four Who Dared: The Early Years of the CIA* by Evan Thomas, Pocket Books (1997) p.245

31. Dallek op. cit. p.

32. *Kennedy's Wars: Berlin, Cuba, Laos, and Vietnam* by Lawrence Freedman, OUP (2000) p.123

33. *Guerrilla Prince: The Untold Story of Fidel Castro* by Georgie Anne Geyer, Little, Brown (1991) p.275

34. May 1964 conversation – for example, in his conversation with Senator Richard Russell, 27 May 1964: conversation number WH6405.10 #3519,

#3520, #3521, http://millercenter.org; *The Johnson White House Tapes 1963–4* by Michael R. Beschloss, Simon & Schuster (1998) Saturday 7 March 1964 p.271

35. McNamara later admitted his errors. See in general *In Retrospect: The Tragedy and Lessons of Vietnam*, Times Books (1995)

36. George Ball *The Past Has Another Pattern*, WW Norton (1982) p.365; Tad Szulc *The Illusion of Peace: Foreign Policy in the Nixon Years* Viking Press (1978) p.150

37. *LBJ : A Life* by Irwin Unger, Wiley (1999)

38. Unger op. cit. pp.88–9

39. Michael Beschloss (ed.) *Taking Charge: The Johnson White House Tapes 1963–4*, Saturday 8 February 1964 p.231; 4 June 1964, p.382

40. G. Herring *The Pentagon Papers*, McGraw-Hill (1993) p.129

41. Ball op. cit. pp.377–79

42. *The End of the First Indochina War: A Global History* by James Waite, Routledge (2012) p.69; *Kennedy & Nixon: The Rivalry that Shaped Postwar America* by Chris Matthews, Simon & Schuster (1997); Hamilton op. cit. p.139

43. Hamilton op. cit. p.227

44. *Being Nixon: A Man Divided* by Evan Thomas, Random House (2015); *President Nixon: Alone in the White House*, Richard Reeves, Simon & Schuster (2002); Reeves op.cit. p.13; Nixon's relations with his personal psychologist are detailed in *The Gumshoe and the Shrink* by David L. Robb, Santa Monica Press (2012)

45. Thomas op. cit. p.68

46. President Nixon, Address to the Nation on the War in Vietnam, November 3, 1969; Marvin and Bernard Kalb, *Kissinger*, Little, Brown & Co (1979) p.279; Robert Dallek, *Nixon and Kissinger* Harper (2007) p.107

47. *Life* magazine quoted in Reeves op. cit. p.564

48. Ball op. cit. pp.413–4

49. Genocidal – Hamilton op. cit. pp.232–3. Reeves op. cit. pp.58–59

50. To Thieu – *How Wars End: Why We Always Fight the Last Battle* by Gideon Rose, Simon & Schuster (2012) p.190; Henry Kissinger, *Ending the Vietnam War: A History of America's Involvement in and Extrication from the Vietnam War*, Simon & Schuster (2003) p.402

51. National Security Archives interview with Zbigniew Brzezinski www.gwu.edu/~nsarchiv/coldwar/intreviews/episode-17/brzezinski.html; Interview with Brzezinksi, *Le Nouvel Observateur* 15 January 1998

52. Nigel Hamilton, *American Caesars: Lives of the US Presidents*, Bodley Head (2010) p.329

53. Interview with Brzezinksi, *Le Nouvel Observateur* 15 January 1998

54. On Kissinger's role in orchestrating the shah's medical treatment in the US, see 'Why Carter Admitted the Shah', *New York Times* 19 May 1981

55. Peter G. Bourne, *Jimmy Carter: A Comprehensive Biography from Plains to Post-Presidency* Scribner (1997) p.460

56. See in general Rodric Braithwaite *Afgantsy : The Russians in Afghanistan, 1979–89* Profile (2012)

57. Anne Applebaum *Gulag: A History*, Doubleday (2003)

58. 'Andropov's Hungarian Complex: Andropov and the Lessons of History' by Timothy Andrews Sayle, *Cold War History* Vol. 9, Issue 3, 2009

59. Braithwaite op.cit

60. 'Former Rep. Charlie Wilson Dies' *Washington Post* 11 February 2010; see in general *Charlie Wilson's War* by George Crile, Grove Press (2007) chs. 1, 4 and 5 *passim*

61. Crile op. cit. p.262

62. 'Such, Such Were the Joys' published in *George Orwell The Collected Essays Vol. 4* Secker & Warburg (1968)

63. See in general *The Gulf War: Its Origins, History and Consequences* by John Bulloch and Harvey Morris, Methuen (1989)

64. Government statements – Michael Axworthy, *Revolutionary Iran: A History of the Islamic Republic*, Allen Lane (2013) pp.226–232

65. Baqer Moin *Khomeini: Life of the Ayatollah*, IB Tauris (1999) pp.207–8

66. Moin op. cit. chapters 1–4 passim

67. Moin op. cit.

68. Moin op. cit. p.17

69. Axworthy op. cit. p.228

70. Iran's Involvement in Iraq, Council on Foreign Relations, 3 March 2008

71. Lawrence Freedman and Virginia Gamba-Stonehouse, *Signals of War: The Falklands Conflict of 1982*, Princeton University Press (1990) pp.14–5

72. Lawrence Freedman *The Official History of the Falklands Campaign Volume I*, Routledge (2005) p.132

73. 'Falklands: Transfer of Falklands sovereignty proposed', *The Times*, 26 November 1980

74. Freedman *Signals* op. cit. p.81

75. Freedman *Signals* op. cit. p.35

76. 'With Friends Like These' *New York Times* 27 February 2012

77. Freedman *Signals* op. cit. p.28

78. Jane Barder interviewing Sir Anthony Parsons on 22nd March 1996 at home in Devon. Parsons archive, Churchill College, Cambridge

79. Lawrence Freedman *The Official History of the Falklands Campaign* Volume II p.360

80. Lawrence Freedman *The Official History of the Falklands Campaign* Volume II p.362

81. *The UK Defence Programme: The Way Forward* Cm 8288

82. Robin Harris *Not For Turning: The Life of Margaret Thatcher*, Bantam Press (2013) pp.28–9, 34, 133, 191, 204, 365, 372–3, 433

83. Avi Shlaim, *The Iron Wall: Israel and the Arab World*, Penguin (2000) pp.400–4

84. 'Feel for battle': Chaim Herzog *The Arab-Israeli Wars: War and Peace in the Middle East*, Vintage (2005) p.120. Qibya attack: Shabtai Teveth, *Moshe Dayan*, Weidenfeld and Nicholson (1972) pp.211–4; the violence of the raid was described by Cdr E.H. Hutchison, *Violent Truce: A Military Observer Looks at the Arab-Israeli Conflict 1951–55*, Devin-Adair Co. (1956) p.44

85. Shlaim op. cit. p.397

86. Ze'ev Schiff and Ehud Ya'ari *Israel's Lebanon War*, Touchstone (1985) pp.65–6

87. Shlaim op. cit. p.404; on Sharon and Iran see *The Israel Lobby and US Foreign Policy* by John Mearsheimer and Stephen Walt, Penguin (2007) pp.232-8

88. *President Reagan : The Triumph of Imagination* by Richard Reeves p.123, Simon & Schuster (2005)

89. Shlaim op. cit. p.411

90. Ze'ev Schiff and Ehud Yari, *Israel's Lebanon War* Touchstone (1985) p.301

91. See for example 'Israel's Right Needs Perpetual War' by Zeev Sternhell, *Haaretz*, 15 October 2010

92. 'Swaggering Goering' – see 'Ariel the Unlucky' by David Gilmour *LRB* 5 April 1990; Sharon is praised as 'a man of peace': 'Middle East Turmoil', *New York Times* 19 April 2002; Blair and Annan – William Shawcross *Deliver us From Evil*, Bloomsbury (2001) pp.246, 331

93. This Israeli policy has only once been condemned by the UN Security Council. On 23 December 2016, the US abstained from voting for UNSC Resolution 2334.

94. Lou Cannon, *President Reagan: The Role of a Lifetime* Public Affairs (2000) p.430

95. Cannon op.cit.p.386

96. 'School's chancellor says invasion was not necessary to save lives', *New York Times* 26 October 1983

97. Reeves, *Ronald Reagan* p.183

98. *The Grenada Revolution: Reflections and Lesson* edited by Wendy C. Grenade, University of Mississippi Press (2015)

99. Reagan Library Archive, Record of telephone conversation 26 October 1983

100. Quoted in *The Struggle Against the Bomb Volume 3* by Lawrence Wittner, Stanford University Press (1995) p.306

101. Cannon op. cit. p.391

102. Stephen Kinzer '30 Years On: The Legacy of Reagan's Invasion of Grenada', *Al Jazeera*, 25 October 2013

7 The Post-Cold War Era

1. 'The 25th Anniversary of the U.S. Invasion of Panama', *Huffington Post* 19 December 2014

2. 'Who's Who on the CIA Payroll', *Time* 28 October 2009

3. Quoted in *Kissinger's Shadow: The Long Reach of America's Most Controversial Statesman* by Greg Gandin, Macmillan (2015) p.198

4. *The Iran-Iraq War* by Pierre Razoux, Harvard University Press (2015)

5. Dilip Hiro, *Neighbours Not Friends: Iraq and Iraq After the Gulf Wars*, Routledge (2001) p.28

6. Said Abdurish *Saddam Hussein: The Politics of Revenge*, Bloomsbury (2000) p.278

7. Glaspie – cited in Hiro op. cit. p.29

8. Abdurish op .cit. p.276

9. Demonstrators – Hiro op. cit. pp.27–8

10. In 1940, a WW1 hero, Marshal Philippe Pétain, signed an armistice with Germany and set up a new authoritarian French state in the town of Vichy in central France.

11. See in general Philip Short's biography *Mitterrand : A Study in Ambiguity*, Bodley Head (2013)

12. Gérard Prunier, *The Rwanda Crisis: History of a Genocide 1959–94*, Hurst & Co (1995) pp.100–101

13. Algeria – Mitterrand 'knew of torture in Algeria', *Daily Telegraph* 3 May 2001

14. See Dr Andrew Wallis, *Silent Accomplice*, IB Tauris (London) 2006, Chapter 4. See also the author's book *Power and Glory: France's Secret Wars with Britain and America* (2016) Chapter 13.

15. Wallis op. cit. p.40

16. Christian Jennings, *Across the Red River* Phoenix (2001)

17. Wallis op. cit. p.75

18. See Human Rights Watch, 'Angola: Human Rights Development' available at https://www.hrw.org/legacy/wr2k2/africa1.html accessed on 31 December 2016

19. Fred Bridgland, *Jonas Savimbi: A Key to Africa*, Paragon House (1987)

20. Richard Dowden, 'Not as nice as he looked' *The Independent* 15 October 1992

21. 'Ex-Allies Say Angola Rebels Torture and Slay Dissenters', *New York Times* 10 March 1989

22. 'Albright Wiped Floor with Men', *The Guardian* 28 January 2000

23. Kissinger – *Daily Telegraph* 28 June 1999

24. 'Yes, There Is a Reason to Be in Somalia', *New York Times* 10 August 1993

25. *War in a Time of Peace* by David Halberstam, Simon & Schuster (2001) p.378

26. Halberstam op. cit. p.376

27. See in general Albright's autobiography *Madam Secretary: A Memoir* Harper (2003)

28. 'Madeleine's War', *Time* 9 May 1999

29. 'Inhuman treatment of people and illicit trafficking in human organs in Kosovo', Committee on Legal Affairs and Human Rights 12 December 2010

30. 'Dangerous Ground', *Time* 22 July 2002

31. *Pervez Musharraf* by Richard Worth and Sara Louise Kras, Infobase Publishing (2015) p.50

32. Atrocities – see for example, 'India: Jammu/Kashmir government should implement human rights program' Amnesty International report 27 October 2002; and the US State Department report '2010 Human Rights Reports: India'.

33. *Farewell to All That: An Oral History of the Bush White House*, Cullen Murphy and Todd S. Purdum, *Vanity Fair* 28 December 2008

34. Herbert S. Parmet *George Bush: The Life of a Lone Star Yankee*, Transaction (2000) p.132

35. 9/11 – See in general *Against all Enemies: Inside America's War on Terror* by Richard A. Clarke, Simon & Schuster (2004). Ron Suskind *The Price of Loyalty: George W. Bush, The White House and the Education of Paul O'Neill*, Simon and Schuster (2004) p.72

36. *Against all Enemies: Inside America's War on Terror* by Richard A. Clarke, Simon & Schuster, 2004, p.244

37. 'Bill Clinton: 'I could have killed' Osama bin Laden in 1998', *Los Angeles Times* 1 August 2014

38. Quoted in Hamilton op. cit. p.498

39. 'Bush and Blair made secret pact for Iraq war', *The Guardian* 4 April 2004

40. 'Blair and Bush went to war in Iraq despite South Africa's WMD assurances', *The Guardian* 30 November 2015; 'Bush and Blair made secret pact for Iraq war', *The Guardian* 4 April 2004

41. Curveball – 'Defector admits to WMD lies that triggered Iraq war' *The Guardian* 15 February 2011. Taxi driver – '45-minute WMD claim 'may have come from an Iraqi taxi driver' *The Guardian* 8 December 2009

42. 'British Intelligence Warned of Iraq War', *Washington Post* 13 May 2005

43. 'The Iraq Inquiry' ('The Chilcott Report'), 6 July 2016, available at http://www.iraqinquiry.org.uk/the-report/ accessed on 31 December 2016. See also Peter Oborne's book *Not the Chilcott Report*, Head of Zeus (2016)

44. John Kampfner *Blair's Wars* Simon and Schuster (2004)

45. *Sunday Telegraph* 4 April 1999. 'No moving a prime minister whose mind is made up' *The Guardian* 1 March 2003

46. Richards – *Taking Command: The Autobiography* by General David Richards, Headline (2014) p.318. 'Libya: Examination of intervention and collapse and the UK's future policy options', House of Commons Select Committee (HCSC) 9 September 2016, Section I, paras 25–27 'The evidence base: intelligence'

47. 'Prime Minister statement on the UN Security Council Resolution on Libya', FCO Announcement 18 March 2011

48. Real figure – 'Libya: Governments Should Demand End to Unlawful Killings', HRW News 20 February 2011. 'Popular Protest in North Africa and the Middle East: Making Sense of Libya', ICG Middle East/North Africa Report 107, 6 June 2011

49. See in general Hugh Roberts' article 'Who Said Gaddafi had to go? *London Review of Books*, Volume 33 Number 22, 17 November 2011. HCSC op. cit. I, paras 32–38.

50. 'Foreign Secretary on Qadhafi: "We will judge him by his actions, not his words", FCO Announcement 21 March 2011

51. 'Turkey offers to broker Libya ceasefire as rebels advance on Sirte' *The Guardian* 27 March 2011

52. 'Cameron 'bears some responsibility' for crisis in Libya, says Miliband', *The Guardian* 24 April 2015

53. Richards op. cit. p.318

54. 'This infatuation with Blair will damage Cameron's reputation', *Daily Telegraph* 18 December 2014

55. HCSC op. cit. I, paras 39–40

56. 'David Cameron's Libyan war: why the PM felt Gaddafi had to be stopped', *The Guardian* 2 October 2011

57. 'The Red Line and the Rat Line' by Seymour Hersh, *LRB* 17 April 2014

58. This is based on leaked emails from Sidney Blumenthal to Secretary of State Hillary Clinton. See 'Emails to Hillary contradict French tale on Libya war', *Al Monitor* 23 June 2015

59. 'Ex-Army head: PM is to blame for rise of ISIS', *Daily Mail* 29 August 2015

60. *Al Monitor* op. cit.

61. Saudi Arabia 'deliberately targeting impoverished Yemen's farms and agricultural industry', *Independent* 23 October 2016; Yemen: US-Made Bombs Used in Unlawful Airstrikes, Human Rights Watch, 8 December 2016.

62. 'King Salman's first year in power in Saudi Arabia has been a dark year for human rights', Amnesty International 25 January 2016

63. 'Saudi-led naval blockade leaves 20m Yemenis facing humanitarian disaster', *The Guardian* 5 June 2015